IMAGES
of America

WEED

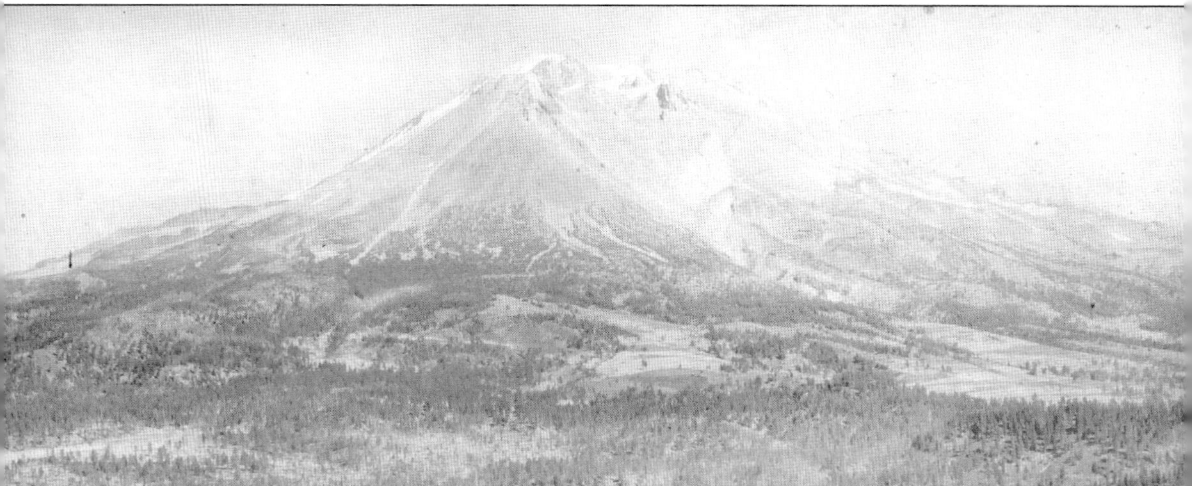

Taken in 1901, this is the first known photograph that shows both Mount Shasta and the sawmill at Weed, California. Mill No. 1 is the large building on the left. Adjacent to it is the powerhouse, with three stacks. Hidden in the trees, to the left, is the general manager's house, first occupied by Charles E. Evans. Beyond the mill is the machine shop, the first building constructed in Weed, in 1900, which is still standing. Behind the mill and to the left is the log pond. The train is beside the log dump where the logs from the train are dumped into the pond. The original bunkhouses are on the right with Rooming House No. 1 to the left and Rooming House No. 2 to the right. Visitors and lower management slept on the second floor of Rooming House No. 1; the cookhouse was on the lower floor. The trees around the mill were logged first. (Courtesy Weed Historic Lumber Town Museum.)

On the Cover: Attached to a four-horse team are slip-tongue big wheels, which are standing in front of the log pond at Abner Weed's first sawmill in 1901. Beyond them is the log dump and A-frame where the logging locomotives dumped their loads. Mount Shasta is in the distance. (Courtesy Weed Historic Lumber Town Museum.)

IMAGES
of America

WEED

Weed Historic Lumber Town Museum

ARCADIA
PUBLISHING

ISBN 978-0-7385-6932-1

Published by Arcadia Publishing
Charleston, South Carolina

Printed in the United States of America

Library of Congress Control Number: 2008940095

For all general information contact Arcadia Publishing at:
Telephone 843-853-2070
Fax 843-853-0044
E-mail sales@arcadiapublishing.com
For customer service and orders:
Toll-Free 1-888-313-2665

Visit us on the Internet at www.arcadiapublishing.com

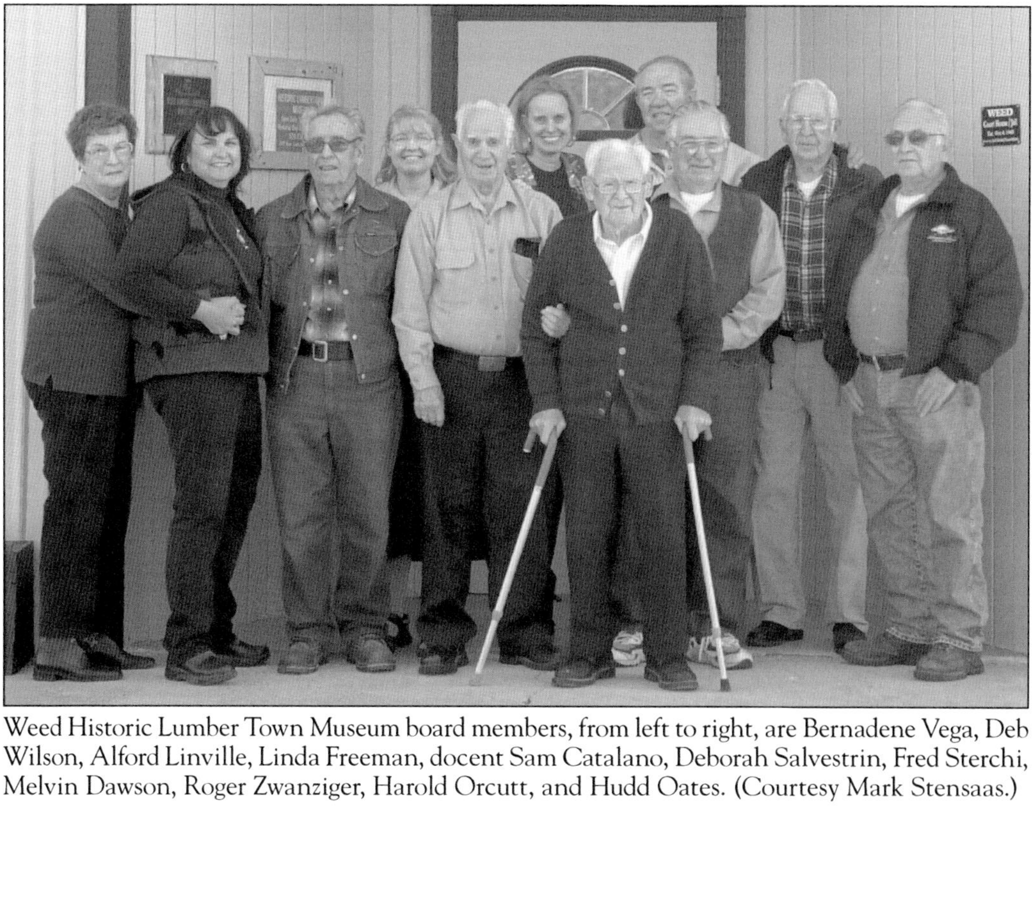

Weed Historic Lumber Town Museum board members, from left to right, are Bernadene Vega, Deb Wilson, Alford Linville, Linda Freeman, docent Sam Catalano, Deborah Salvestrin, Fred Sterchi, Melvin Dawson, Roger Zwanziger, Harold Orcutt, and Hudd Oates. (Courtesy Mark Stensaas.)

CONTENTS

Acknowledgments		6
Introduction		7
1.	Abner Weed	9
2.	Early Mills	15
3.	Logging in the Field	23
4.	Work in the Mill	39
5.	Tennant	67
6.	Weed	73
7.	Shastina	107
Bibliography		127

ACKNOWLEDGMENTS

This book was written and edited by Linda Freeman with assistant editors Deb Wilson and Deborah Salvestrin under the auspices of the Weed Historic Lumber Town Museum.

Many thanks go to Dennis Freeman, director of the College of the Siskiyous Library and founder of the Mount Shasta Collection. Other library staff members who provided us with their enthusiastic support include Marcia Eblen and Cheryl Rosen. We would also like to thank Ernie Miller and the College of the Siskiyous Writing Lab staff for providing us with comments and suggestions on the manuscript.

Numerous people have graciously donated photographs and artifacts to the Weed Historic Lumber Town Museum over the years. If we know the names of the donors or photographers of the images in our collection we acknowledge them in the credits. Photographs that are not credited are part of the Weed Historic Lumber Town Museum's general collection. Several people permitted us to scan their photographs and provided us with information. In particular, we would like to thank Harold Barnum, Donna Kohn Brooks, Terry and Larry Dalin, Dr. Scott Durbin, Madelon Gilman, Jim Gubetta, Robert C. Lemon, Alford Linville, Vivian Welborn Mauden, Glenna Pittock, Donna Steffenson Sartor, Carol Steele, and Roger Zwanziger. Thanks also to Mark Stensaas for taking our photograph.

The museum board would also like to thank Kelly Reed, acquisitions editor, for answering our questions and keeping us on track; Ryan Easterling for copy editing; Weed Historic Lumber Town Museum board members Alford Linville for proposing to write a book about Weed, taking photographs over the years, answering our questions about logging in the field and mill work, singing Siskiyou songs, and reciting poetry to us; Harold Orcutt, museum curator, for helping find (and refind) historic photographs and documents and answering questions; Roger Zwanziger, president of the board, for providing us with information about Abner Weed, the Weed Lumber Company, ranching, and mill work; Sam Catalano, museum docent, for providing information about the mill, great stories about Weed, and overall moral support; and Melvin Dawson, Bernadine Vega, Hudd Oates, and Fred Sterchi for the work they do to support the museum.

Introduction

The city of Weed is located in Siskiyou County at the southern end of Shasta Valley surrounded by Mount Shasta on the east, Black Butte to the south, and Mount Eddy to the west. Black Butte Summit forms a natural and cultural boundary between the Shasta Valley and the Shasta Indians to the north and Strawberry Valley and the Achumawi Indians to the south. There has been a major route through this site since humans arrived in California. Explorers, gold miners, and settlers traversed this route in the 19th century. After Southern Pacific took over the railroad from Central Pacific, which was stalled at Delta, the railroad quickly reached Berryvale and Igerna, both in 1887. Mills sprang up along the railroad to supply it with railroad ties, fuel, and lumber. Several mills were located on either side of Black Butte Summit. Abner Weed noticed the prevailing winds south of Igerna, which would give him an edge in the lumber market by drying the wood faster, so he relocated his mill to Weed. He purchased land from George Decker in 1900 and built the machine shop that year. By 1905, the company town of Weed offered almost all the needs of the growing community with a mill, housing, mercantile system, bank, hospital, post office, and courthouse.

Before Abner and Rachel (Cunningham) Weed moved from Igerna to Weed, Thomas and Georgeanna "Anna" (Sullaway) Sullivan bought some land in 1898 from James and Eva (Decker) Preston, who had squatted the land in 1893. The Sullivans had a ranch and sold food products to the residents of Igerna. In 1905, they subdivided a portion of their land and began selling lots in Shastina. By 1910, there were at least 10 saloons in the town of Shastina. A business district also grew along Main Street, south of Division Street, to serve the needs of millworkers and their families.

This Weed book in the Images of America series from Arcadia Publishing will guide you through the history of Weed, introducing you to Abner Weed, early mills, logging in the field, and work in the mill, Weed, Tennant, and Shastina.

TIMELINE

1842 Abner Edward Weed born in Dixmont, Maine
1858 James A. Maxwell and sons establish sawmill near headwaters of Shasta River
1860 Mr. Hedge and Mr. Tibbs build first sawmill in Igerna
1863 Abner Weed enlists to fight in Civil War
1878 Milton P. Maxwell, son of James A. Maxwell, purchases Summit Mill in Igerna
1881 James A. Maxwell sells lumber mill to James Dobkins
1883 J. H. Maxwell buys into brother's sawmill in Igerna, renamed Maxwell Brothers Mill
1884 Summit School established
1887 Railroad reaches Sisson and Igerna
1888 James A. Maxwell sells mill to James Dobkins; James N. Durney moves to Sisson
1889 Abner Weed runs Durney's Mill
1890 Lowell, Clifford, and C. S. Coggins buy 160 acres in Igerna
1893 James Preston homesteads 200 acres
1894 Coggins Brothers Company builds mill and box factory in Igerna; James A. Maxwell dies
1897 Abner Weed purchases Maxwell Brothers Mill
1898 Thomas and Anna Sullivan buy property from James and Eva Preston
1900 Abner Weed purchases land from George Decker; Weed builds machine shop for new mill; Weed elected Siskiyou County supervisor
1901 Abner Weed builds circular sawmill; Weed receives contract to supply railroad ties to Southern Pacific; Weed buys Nelson Harvey Eddy Ranch; Weed forms the Northeastern Railway Company
1902 Abner Weed installs band saw at mill No. 2
1903 Weed Lumber Company goes public
1905 Abner Weed sells interest in Weed Lumber Company to Long-Bell Lumber Company; Weed sells interest in railroad to a subsidiary of the Southern Pacific; Weed Hospital is built
1906 Abner Weed elected to state senate
1907 Summit School moved to Angel Valley
1911 First plywood plant in California built in Weed
1913 Igerna burns down
1917 Long-Bell Lumber Company builds new mill; Abner Weed dies during 1917 influenza epidemic; Weed High School established; fire destroys most of Shastina
1921 Tennant founded
1937 John Steinbeck writes *Of Mice and Men*, which puts the town of Weed's name "fleetingly on the lips of thousands across the nation." (Abner Weed Jr., 1974)
1956 Long-Bell Lumber Company sells out to International Paper
1961 City of Weed incorporated
2001 Weed celebrates centennial

One

Abner Weed

Weed acquired its unusual name from Abner Weed, who started a lumber mill here in 1900. Abner Edward Weed was born on September 18, 1842, in Dixmont, Maine, to Abner and Sarah (Ryan) Weed. From 1863 to 1866, he served in the Civil War and was with Grant when Lee surrendered. He married Rachael Cobb Cunningham in Searsmont, Maine, where Rachael was born. Their first two children were born in Maine: Abbie in 1868 and Edward in 1874. In 1869, Weed moved to Iowa and tried his hand at farming, but this venture did not work out so he moved back to Maine. The Weed family eventually moved to Truckee, California, where their other two children were born: Eleanor in 1878 and Horace in 1880. Eleanor died young; her remains were moved to the family plot in Dunsmuir.

After logging for several years in the Truckee area, Abner and his family moved to Sisson in 1889, where he operated what was later known as Durney's Mill. He bought the Maxwell Brothers Mill in 1896. Weed purchased land from George Decker at Milepost 348 on the Southern Pacific's Shasta Route, where the winds dried the lumber more quickly, giving him an edge on the market. He used lumber from the former Maxwell Brothers Mill to build his new one in Weed.

Abner Weed obtained a contract from Southern Pacific to supply them with railroad ties, which was the beginning of a successful venture. Weed Lumber Company went public in April 1903, and, within two years, Weed had sold most of his shares to Long-Bell Lumber Company. Weed was a county supervisor from 1900 to 1908 and served as a state senator from 1906 to 1910. In July 1901, Weed bought the Nelson Harvey Eddy Ranch. He raised "milking shorthorns" to feed the mill workers. In 1904, he built Hotel Weed in Dunsmuir on the corner of Dunsmuir and Sacramento Avenues. When Abner Weed died during the 1917 influenza epidemic, his daughter Abbie and her husband, Alex, later inherited what became known as the Albee Ranch. In 1950, Roger Zwanziger, great-grandson of Abner, purchased the ranch from his uncle Ralph Albee. Roger and his son Martin continue to run the Zwanziger Ranch.

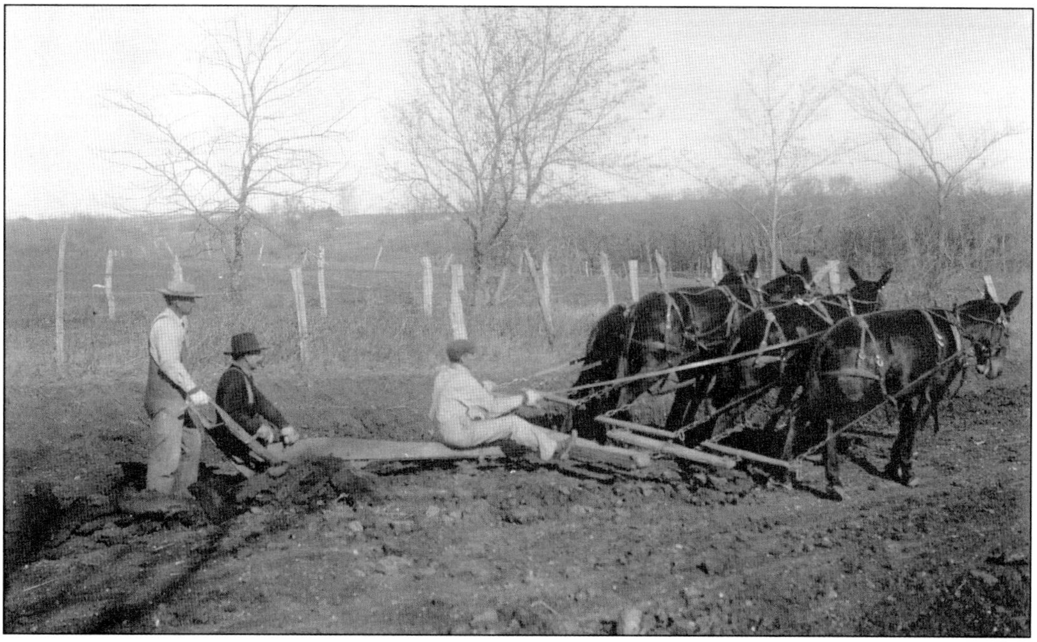

Abner Weed worked on his parents' farm in Maine and also farmed in Iowa for a short time (above). After he moved to California in 1869, he focused on the lumber industry, establishing the highly successful Weed Lumber Company. After he sold out to Long-Bell Lumber Company, he returned to farming and ranching. Below, Abner and Rachael Weed's daughter Abbie married Alexander "Alex" Albee (below). Alex worked for his father-in-law in the mill and on the farm. Abbie and Alex had three children: Ralph, Camille, and Cecil. Abbie and Alex Albee were set up on the ranch Weed bought from Nelson Harvey Eddy, which became known as the Albee Ranch. (Courtesy Roger Zwanziger.)

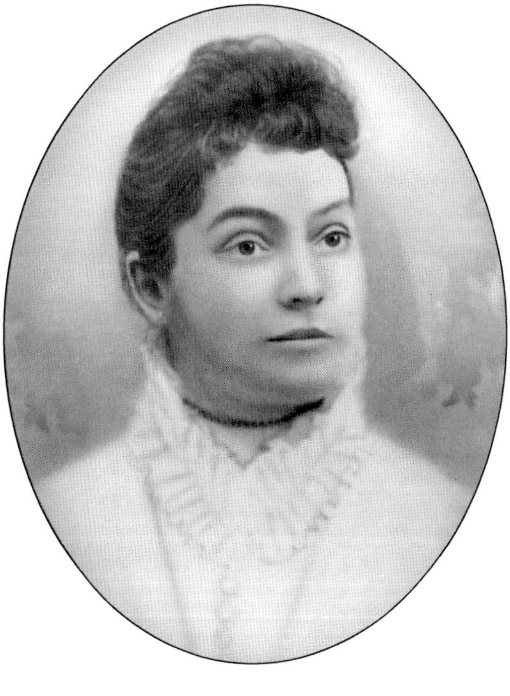

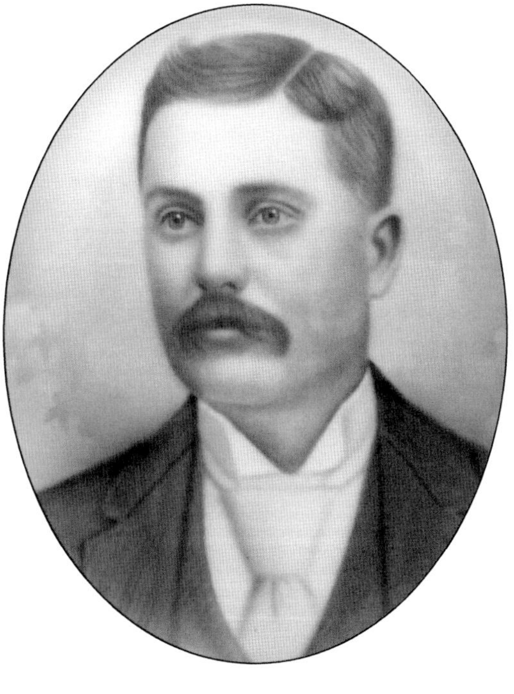

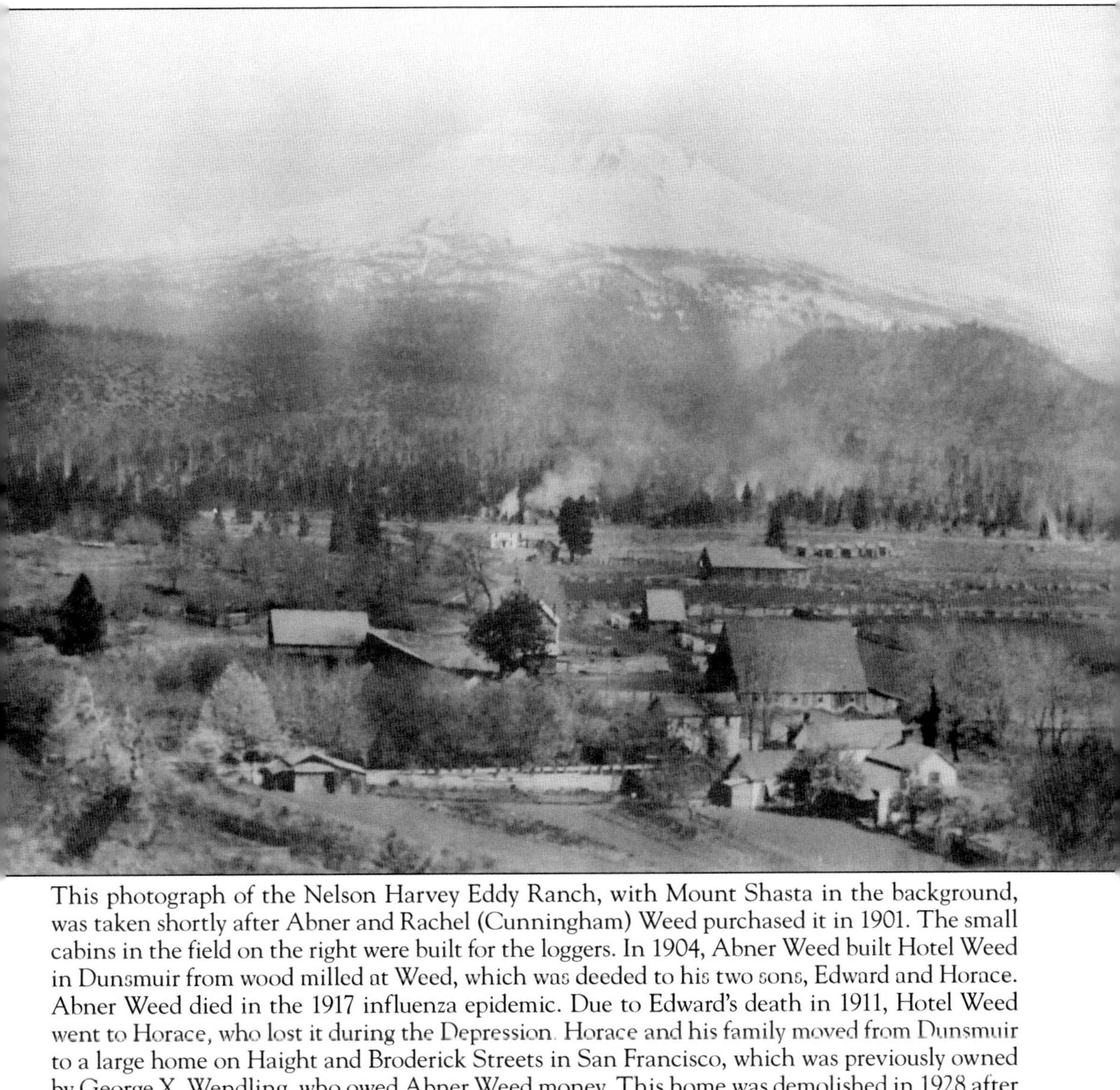

This photograph of the Nelson Harvey Eddy Ranch, with Mount Shasta in the background, was taken shortly after Abner and Rachel (Cunningham) Weed purchased it in 1901. The small cabins in the field on the right were built for the loggers. In 1904, Abner Weed built Hotel Weed in Dunsmuir from wood milled at Weed, which was deeded to his two sons, Edward and Horace. Abner Weed died in the 1917 influenza epidemic. Due to Edward's death in 1911, Hotel Weed went to Horace, who lost it during the Depression. Horace and his family moved from Dunsmuir to a large home on Haight and Broderick Streets in San Francisco, which was previously owned by George X. Wendling, who owed Abner Weed money. This home was demolished in 1928 after Horace sold it to a real estate developer. Rachael remained living on the ranch shown above, known as the Albee Ranch at the time, until her death at age 97. Rachael belonged to the Methodist church, Eastern Star, and the Rebekah Lodge. Upton Mortuary handled the arrangements, and she was buried in the family plot in Dunsmuir Cemetery, along with Abner, Edward, Horace, and Eleanor May, who died at age two in Truckee, California, and was reburied in the family plot in Dunsmuir. (Courtesy Roger Zwanziger.)

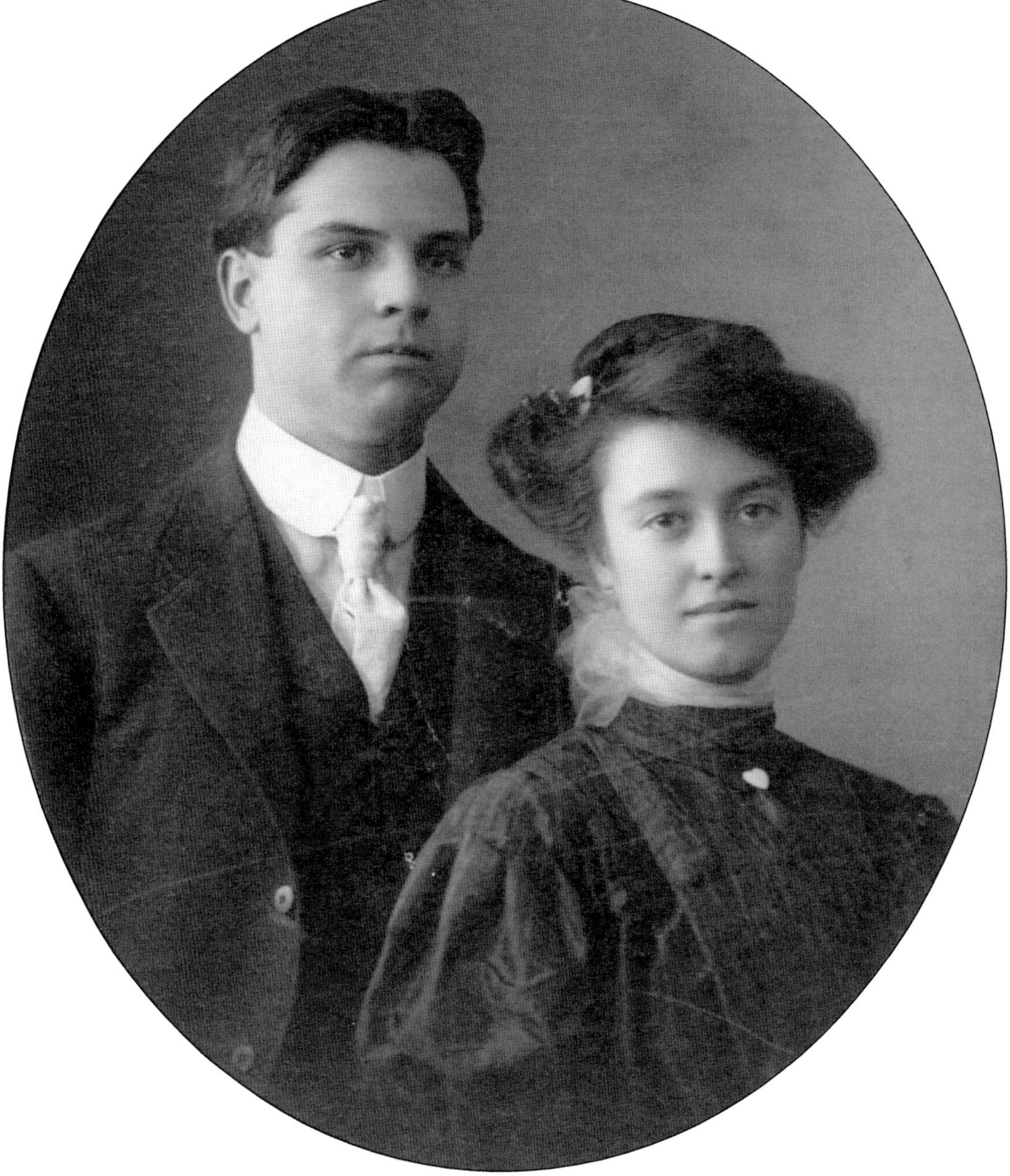

This is the 1905 wedding photograph of Abner and Rachael Weed's son Horace and his wife, Pearl (Payne) Weed. A *Sacramento Bee* article published on January 7, 1905, states: "A double wedding that had been planned to take place in this city [Redding] yesterday afternoon miscarried because one of the couples took a sudden notion to have the ceremony performed in the morning . . . The second couple got wind of what was up . . . but they didn't have time to get the license before the train left . . . The couple who got married ahead of schedule time were Clarence COOPER, of Weed, Siskiyou County, and Miss Clara COULTER, the youngest daughter of Mr. and Mrs. James Coulter, of this city. The couple who acted as witnesses at the wedding of Mr. Cooper and Miss Coulter, but who had to wait til they reached San Francisco to have their own wedding solemnized, are H. A. WEED, son of the founder of the town of Weed, Siskiyou County, and Miss Pearl PAYNE, of this city." (Courtesy Heidi Jonathan and Robert C. Lemon.)

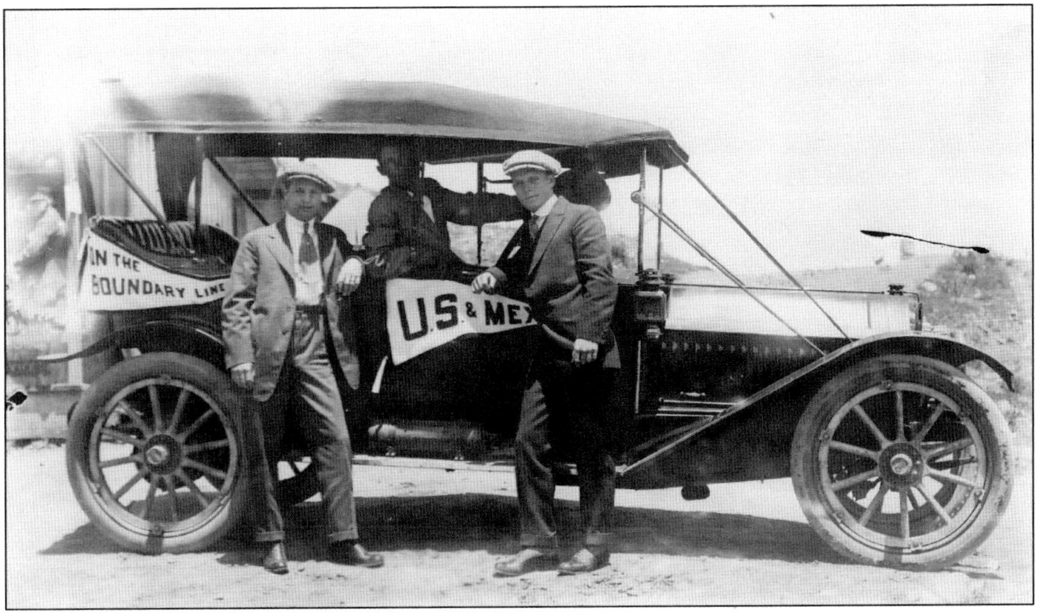

Abner Weed served as a county supervisor from 1900 to 1908. During this time, Clifford Coggins was the representative for California's 2nd State Senate District. Weed successfully ran for state senator (replacing Coggins) and served from 1906 to 1910. Some suggest Weed's pro-railroad stance helped him get elected. At the Weed Historic Lumber Town Museum there is a photograph of Abner Weed in session in Sacramento. Randolph Collier served this position from 1938 to 1966. Collier's Rest Stop north of Yreka is named after him. The slogan "On the Boundary Line" (above) refers to the water dispute between the United States and Mexico regarding the distribution of the waters of the Rio Grande, which was resolved in May 1906. (Both courtesy Roger Zwanziger.)

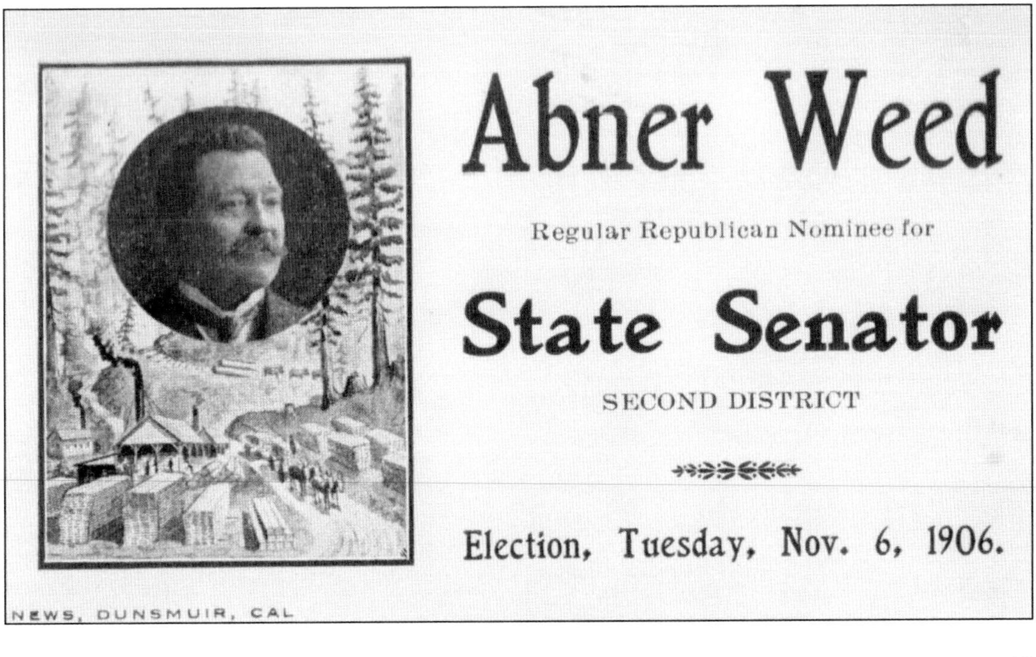

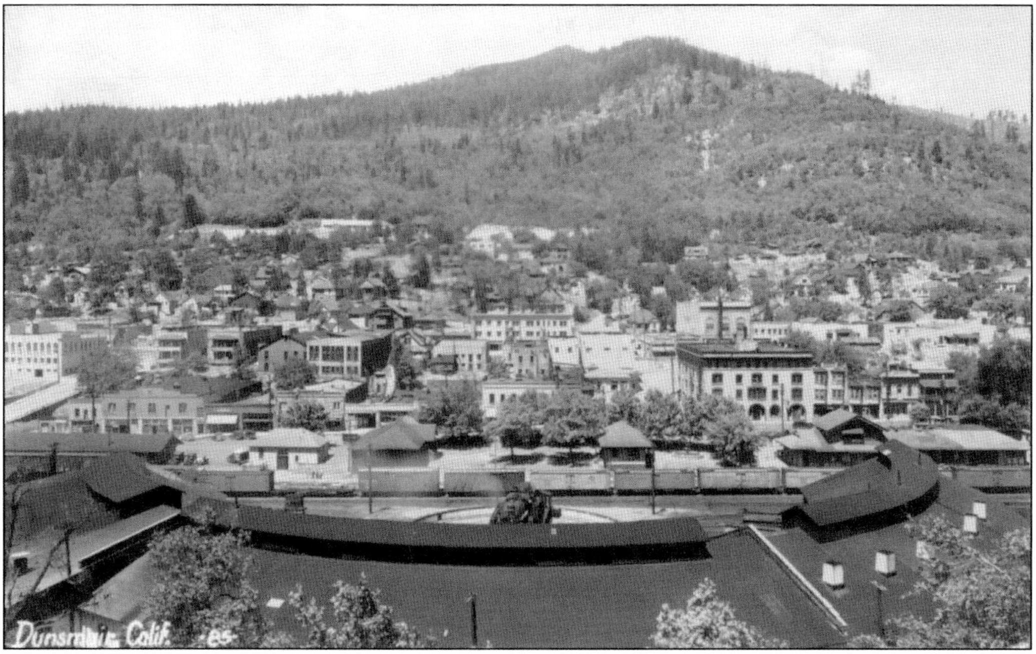

The roof of the Southern Pacific roundhouse at Dunsmuir can be seen in the foreground (above). The largest building, with the arched doorways, is Hotel Weed (below), built by Abner Weed in 1904. Hotel Weed, now on the National Register of Historic Places, was built in the Richardson Romanesque–style, which was in vogue during the late 1800s and early 1900s. The style was developed by the architect Henry Hobson Richardson in the 1870s and is characterized by massive walls, rows of windows (some of them arched), and recessed doorways. An art moderne addition was added in 1945, a year after this photograph was taken. (Below image photographed by J. H. Eastman; both courtesy College of the Siskiyous Library Mount Shasta Collection.)

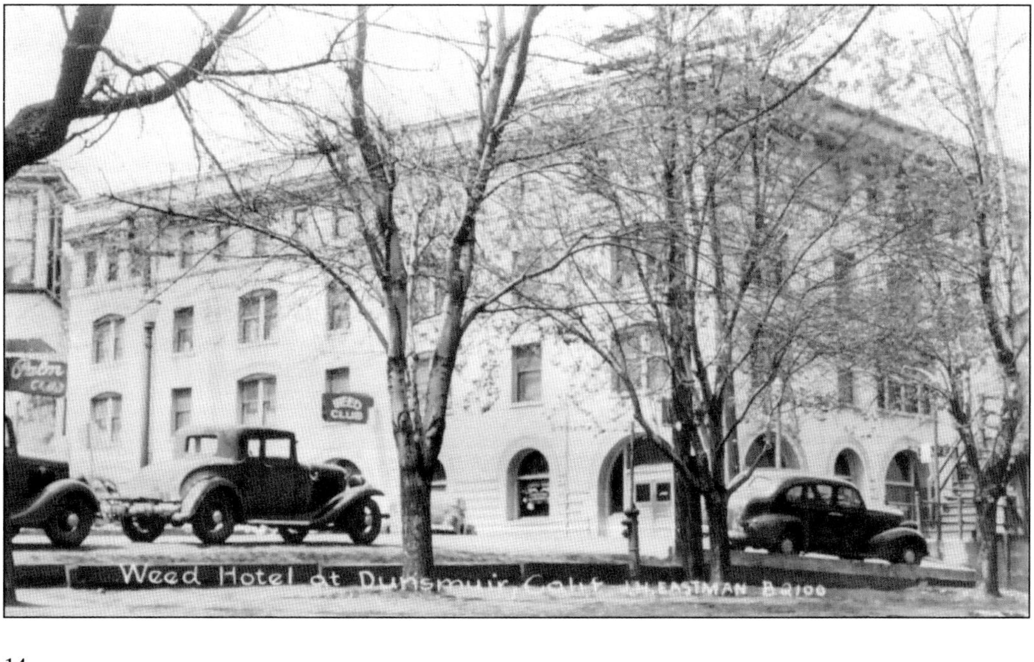

Two

Early Mills

Mills sprang up in Siskiyou County during the 1850s, serving the Gold Rush communities. According to Harry L. Wells, who wrote *The History of Siskiyou County* in 1881, Maxwell Mill and Dobkin's Mill were located on the "headwaters of the Sacramento." Logs were hauled to the steam- or water-powered mills by horse and oxen. A few, such as the Coggins' mill in Lamoine, had flumes to help transport the logs. Early California sawmills produced 200,000–90 million feet of lumber each year.

Mills changed hands several times or were moved to new locations. Cy Rippon, local writer and publisher of *Weed Press*, informs everyone that "some early day sawmills on the Old Stage Road Westerly of what is now Weed, were the Durney Sawmill, the Deetz Sawmill, the Dobkins Sawmill, the Maxwell Sawmill, the Hearst Sawmill, the Bummerville Sawmill, the McKenzie & Nelson Sawmill, the Burns & Mayhew Sawmill, the Dale Sawmill, the Coggins Brothers Igerna Sawmill, and a number of others." The March 24, 1875, issue of the *Yreka Journal* states: "Dobkins, of the old Maxwell mill, expects to get out about a million feet this summer . . . Maxwell & Son are putting up a new mill at their place of residence . . . Hearst, of the Summit Mill, is already at work with his mill." Milton P. Maxwell, who had been working for his father, James A. Maxwell, purchased Summit Mill in 1878. Milton's brother J. H. Maxwell joined him in 1883, and thereafter it was called the Maxwell Brothers Mill. James A. Maxwell sold his mill to James Dobkins and then ran a lumberyard in Yreka until 1884. Dobkins ran this mill until 1888. Some outfits stayed just ahead of the railroad, supplying it with ties and fuel wood. After the railroad reached Igerna in 1887, several mills shipped from there. A 1902 *Sacramento Bee* reported both Coggins Brothers and J. N. Durney as having 175 employees each. Durney's Mill burned down in 1905.

Abner Weed operated Durney's Mill then purchased the Maxwell Brothers Mill in 1897. He built Weed Lumber Company on land purchased along the railroad 3 miles north of Igerna in 1900. Igerna burned down in 1913. Long-Bell Lumber Company gained complete ownership of Weed Lumber Company between 1916–1922, beginning a new era of logging.

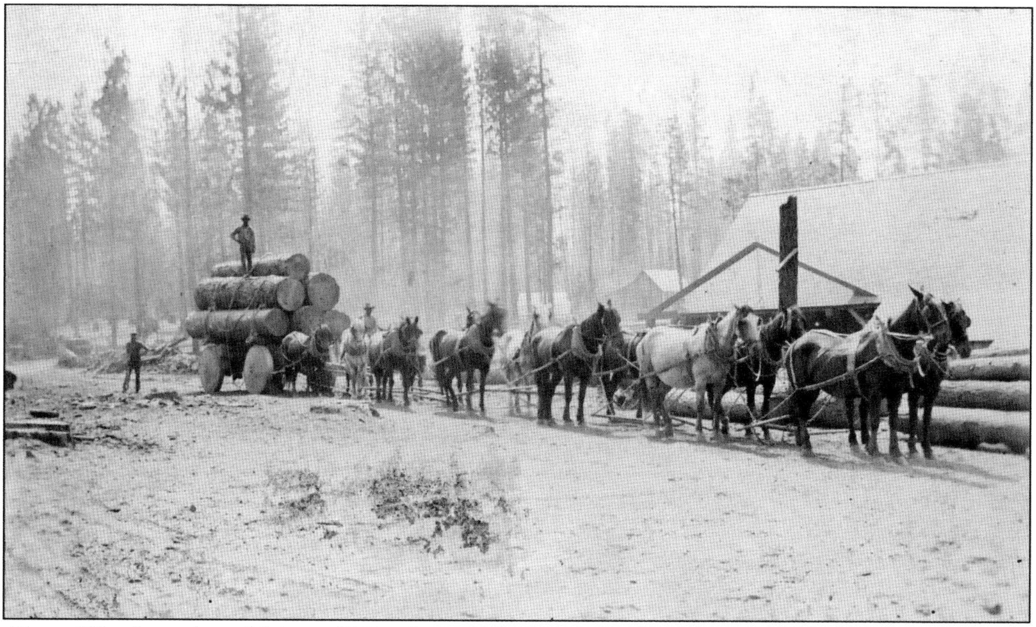

Abner Weed purchased Maxwell Brothers Mill in 1896 and used it to build his mill in Weed in 1900. These 1898 photographs show Abner Weed's team at his mill in Igerna. The team above has two mules up front followed by 10 horses. The team below includes 10 horses and two oxen in the rear. Note the view of Diller Canyon on Mount Shasta. (Above courtesy Eldon Hoy; below courtesy Roger Zwanziger.)

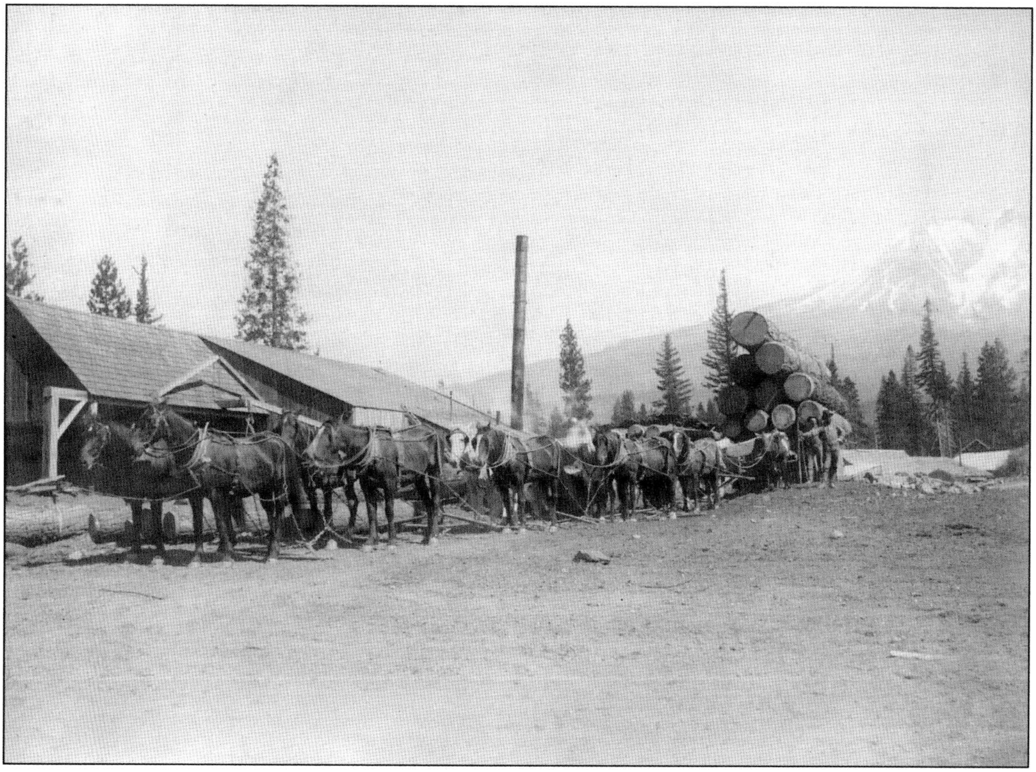

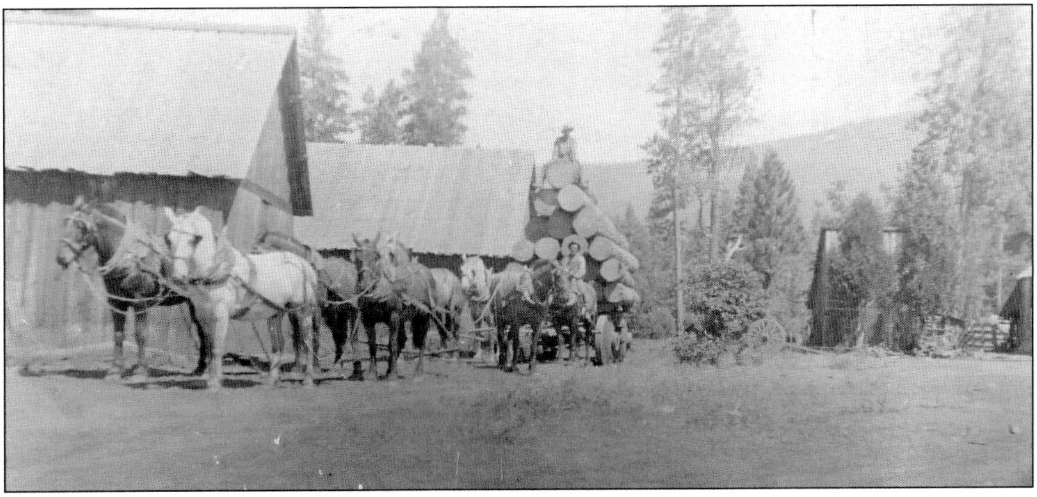

Abner's team (above) has 12 horses. The man standing on the logs is Charles "Chub" Ferguson. He named his daughter Igerna, after the town she was born in, on July 2, 1900. Igerna (Ferguson) Hefner (below, left) stands next to her parents, Clara and Chub Ferguson, and sisters Beulah (Ferguson) King and Thelma (Ferguson) Black, on her parents' 50th anniversary. When Igerna was 99, she wrote, "My Mother and Father, Charles and Clara Ferguson came to California by train from Indiana in 1896 when my one and only brother, Forest, was four years old." Igerna turned 100 years old in the year 2000. Her sister Beulah was born in 1904 in Callahan, and Thelma, weighing only 2.5 pounds, was born in 1911, along with a twin brother who died at birth. (Above courtesy Roger Zwanziger; below courtesy Bernita Sutcliffe.)

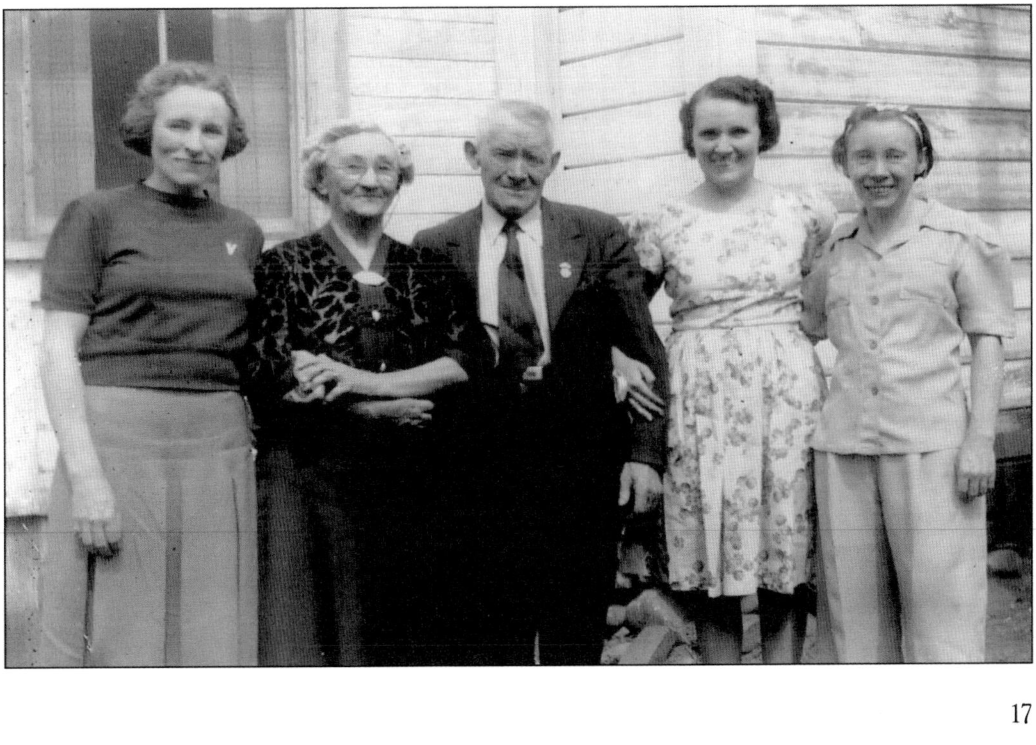

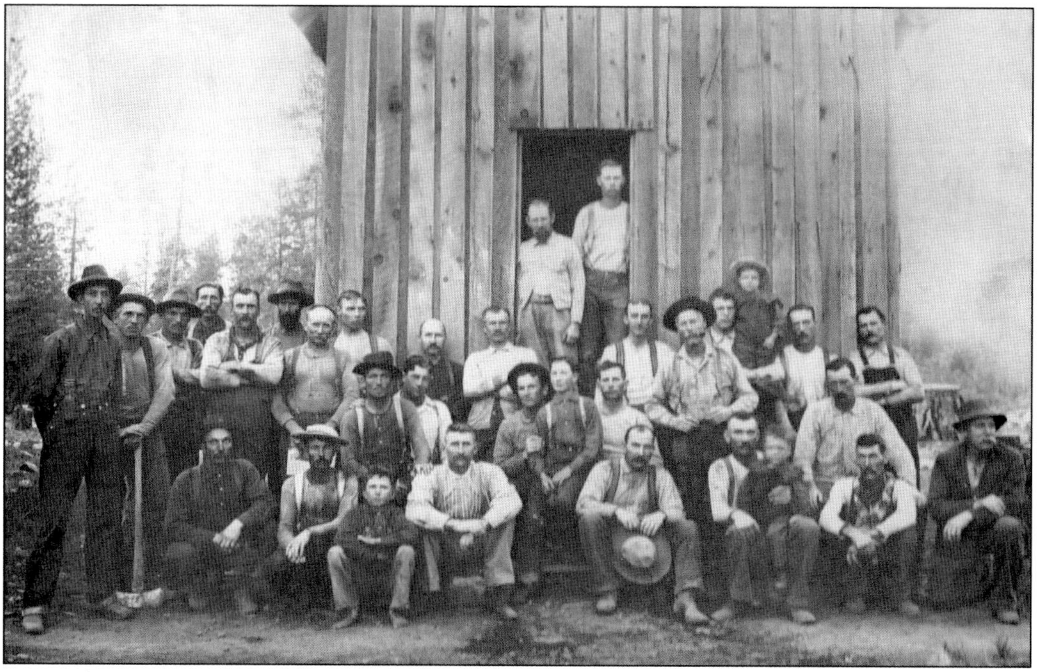

Pictured are men at work in the 1890s at the Maxwell Brothers Mill. The photograph below shows workers at a mill near the summit of Black Butte. Alex Albee is the fourth man from the left in the back row. He married Abner Weed's daughter Abbie in May 1891. In 1901, Weed purchased the Nelson Harvey Eddy Ranch, after which Mount Eddy is named. Alex, at age 48, is listed as a farmer among 1910 voters. Abbie and Alex Albee inherited the ranch, and it was known as the Albee Ranch until Roger Zwanziger purchased it from his uncle Ralph Albee in 1954. (Both courtesy Roger Zwanziger.)

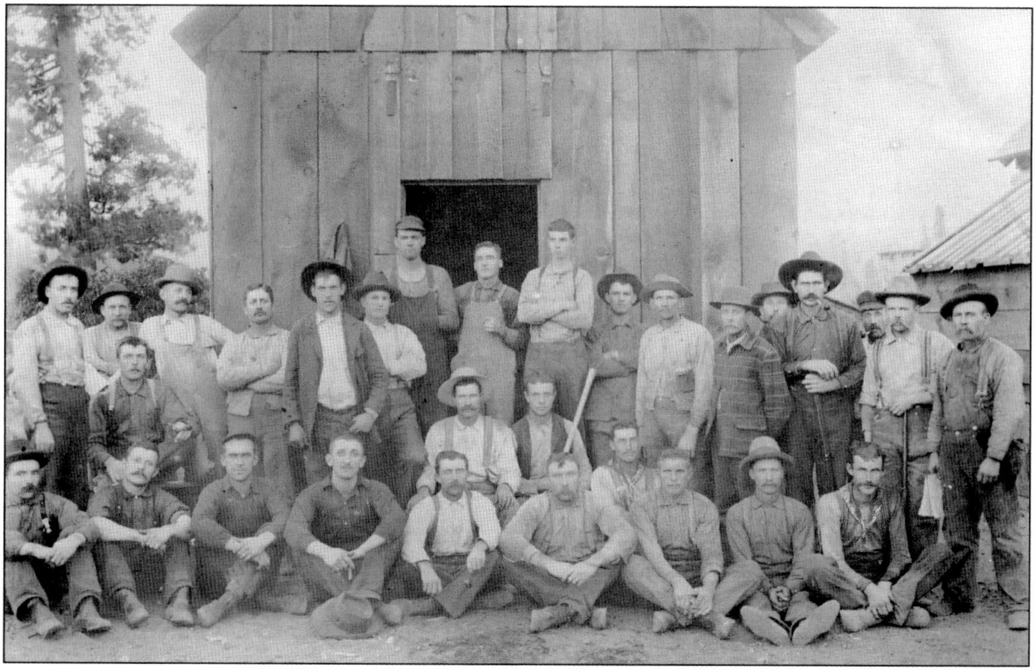

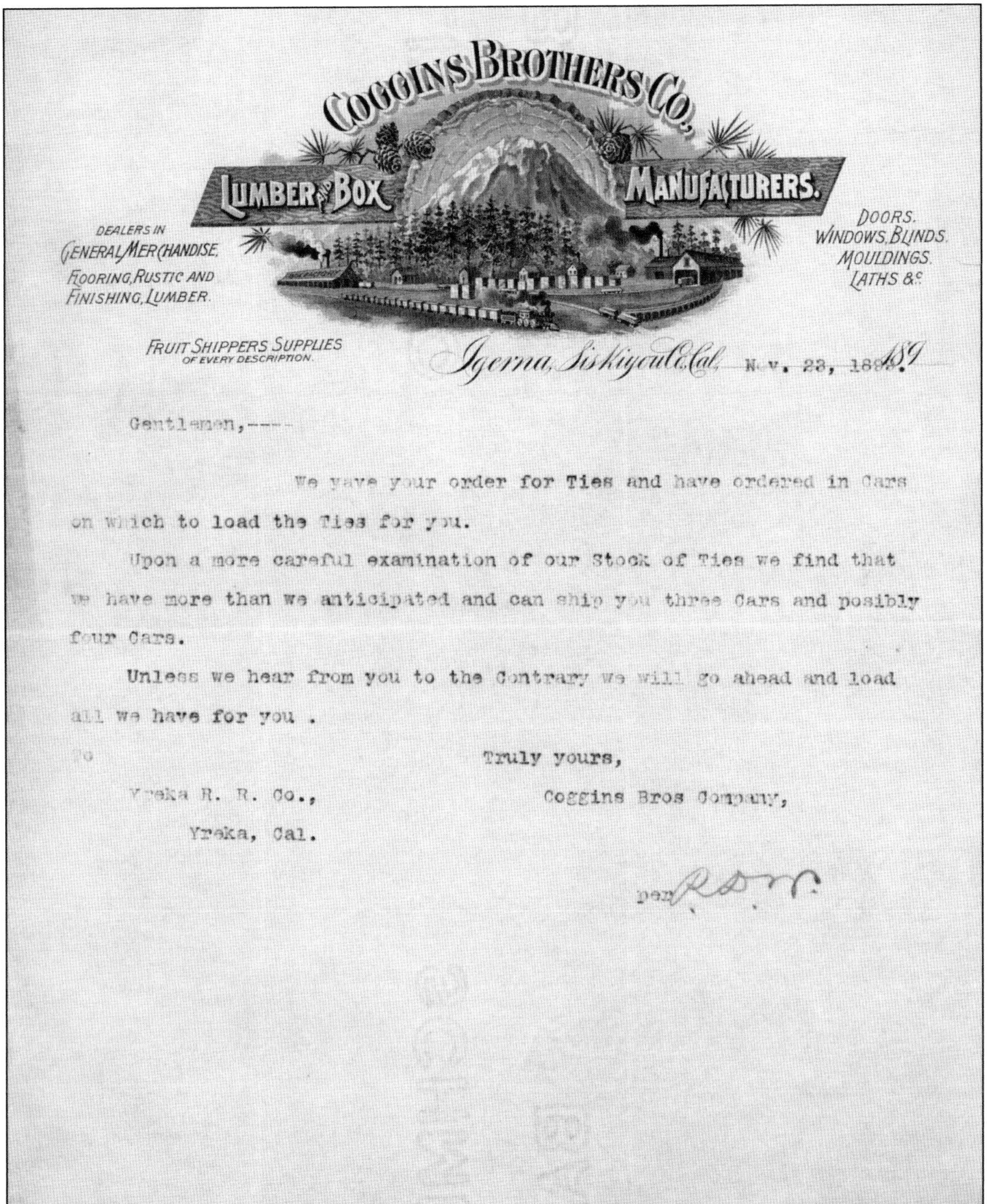

COGGINS BROTHERS CO.

LUMBER AND BOX MANUFACTURERS.

DEALERS IN GENERAL MERCHANDISE, FLOORING, RUSTIC AND FINISHING LUMBER.

DOORS. WINDOWS, BLINDS, MOULDINGS, LATHS &c.

FRUIT SHIPPERS SUPPLIES OF EVERY DESCRIPTION.

Igerna, Siskiyou Co, Cal. Nov. 23, 189

Gentlemen,----

We have your order for Ties and have ordered in Cars on which to load the Ties for you.

Upon a more careful examination of our Stock of Ties we find that we have more than we anticipated and can ship you three Cars and posibly four Cars.

Unless we hear from you to the Contrary we will go ahead and load all we have for you .

Truly yours,

Coggins Bros Company,

per [illegible]

To

Yreka R. R. Co.,

Yreka, Cal.

Charles Sanford, Clifford, and Lowell are three of eight children born to Wallace and Eunice (Young) Coggins of Lamoine, Maine, in the 1850s. Charles and Lowell were living in Chico according to the 1880 census. Lowell married Alice Mary Hodgkins of Lamoine, Maine, in 1885, and then they moved to Upton, near Black Butte, in 1888 and operated a mill there. In 1890, the Southern Pacific installed Coggins Spur. In 1897, Coggins Spur No. 2 was added. The following year, they started the Lamoine Lumber and Trading Company in Lamoine, south of Dunsmuir. In 1900, they built a 6-mile railroad. In 1902, they are listed as employing 175 men in Igerna. Charles died that year and, in 1906, Lowell and Clifford sold out to Abner Weed.

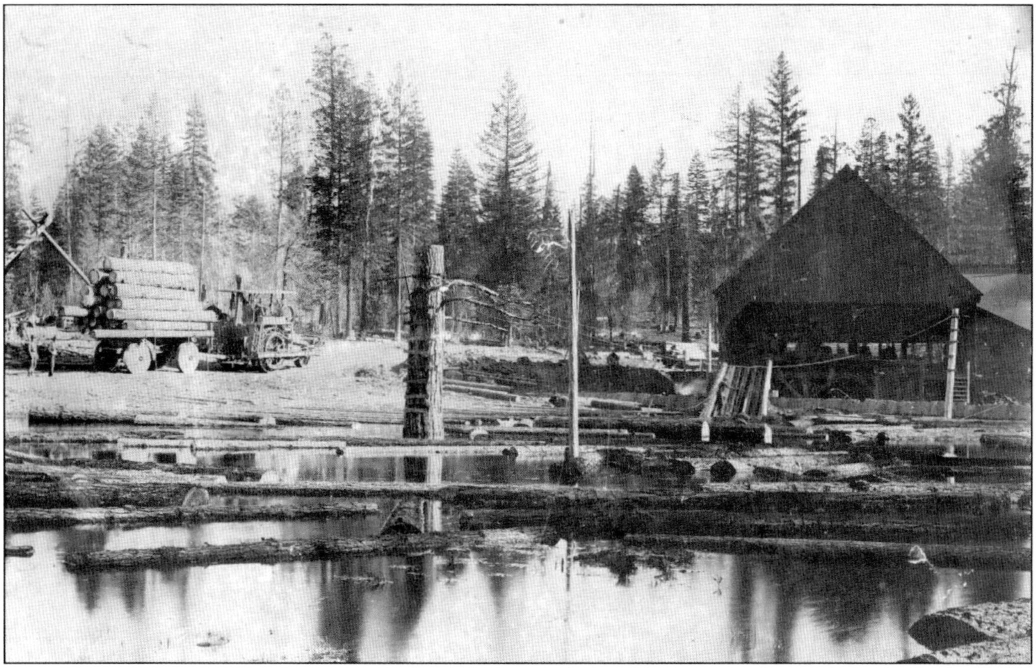

James N. Durney set up a mill in Delta, 40 miles north of Redding, in 1877. The railroad reached Delta in 1884 and remained there until Southern Pacific took over. The railroad made it to Dunsmuir in 1886 and Sisson in 1887. Durney moved his mill to Sisson in 1888. Abner Weed briefly operated this mill and then bought one in Igerna. Abner Weed sold this mill to Durney in 1897. Durney closed his Sisson mill in 1899 and moved it to the site where Hammond's Pond is now located. Both photographs of Durney's Mill were taken in the early 1900s. (Both courtesy Eugene Durney.)

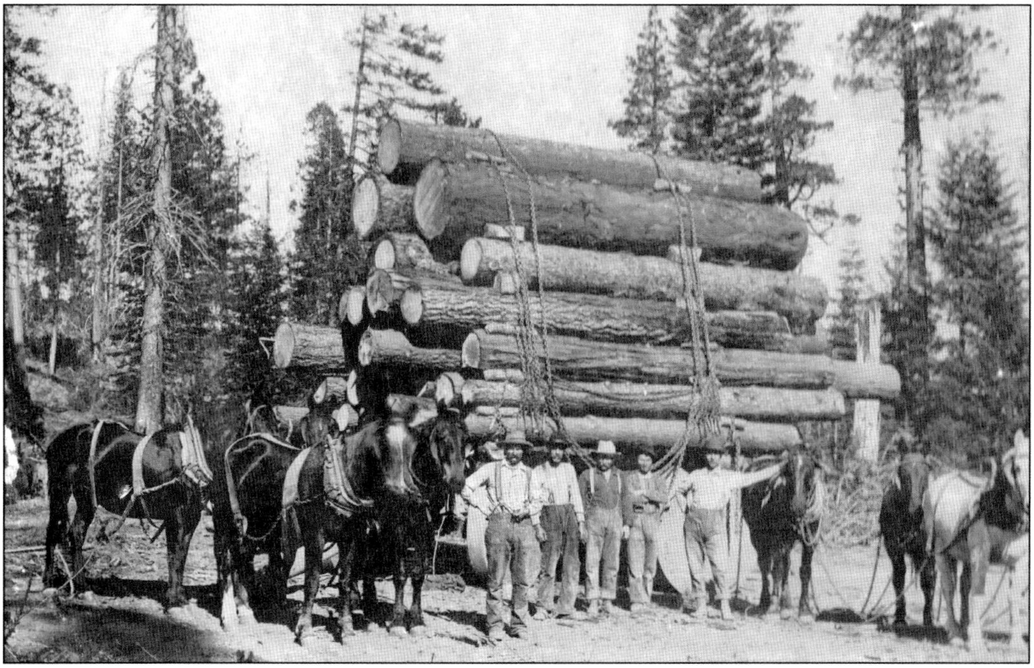

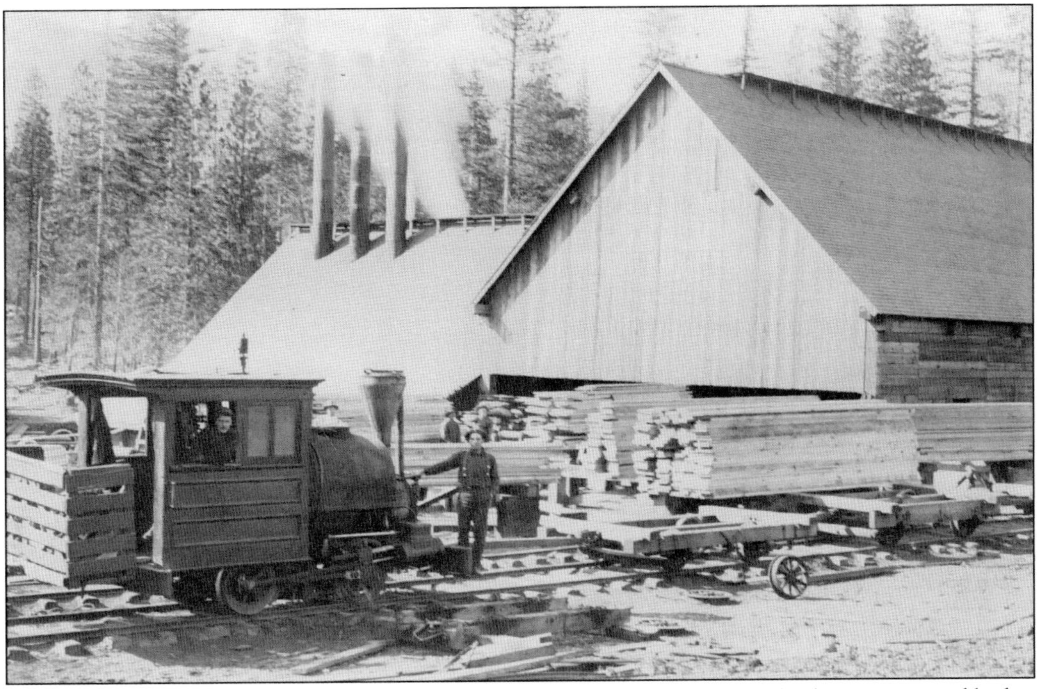

In 1901, Durney purchased a little locomotive named "Annie" (above), which was operated by his son Eugene. A December 28, 1901, *Sisson Mirror* article reports: "Durney says that his little engine has enough power to pull over sixty tons of lumber . . . and will make good time up the grade and over the hills to Igerna." A May 20, 1909, *Sisson Headlight* article stated, "The big traction engine recently purchased by J. N. Durney from the Algomah Lumber Company at Algomah, was driven through town Monday en route to his mill at Igerna, where the machine will be used in logging this summer. Gene Durney and George Hill were in charge of the machine" (pictured below). Algomah is an old sawmill north of Klamath Falls, Oregon. The old millpond and part of the dry kilns are still there. (Both courtesy Eugene Durney.)

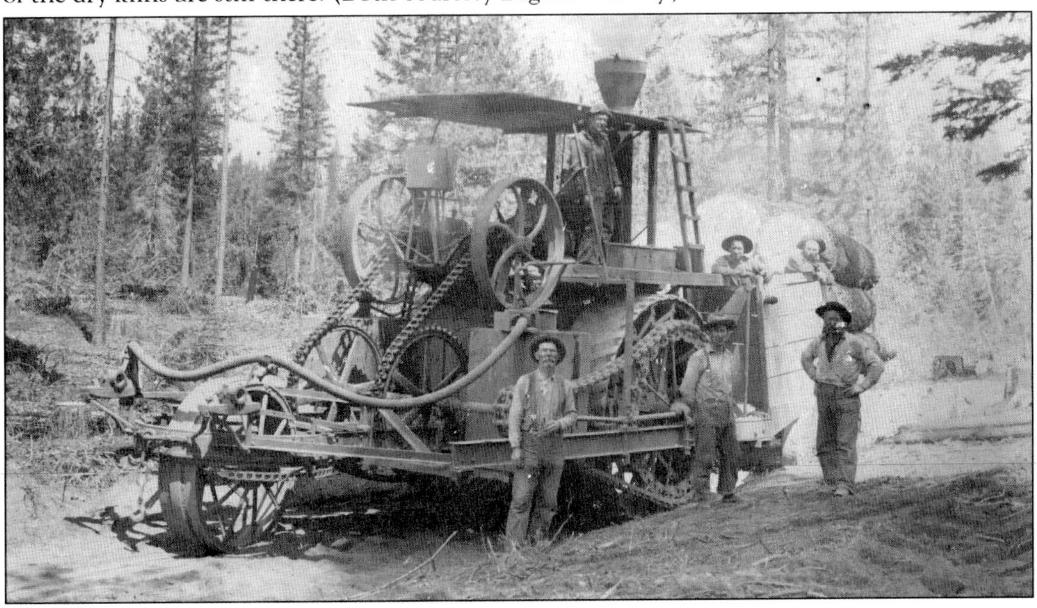

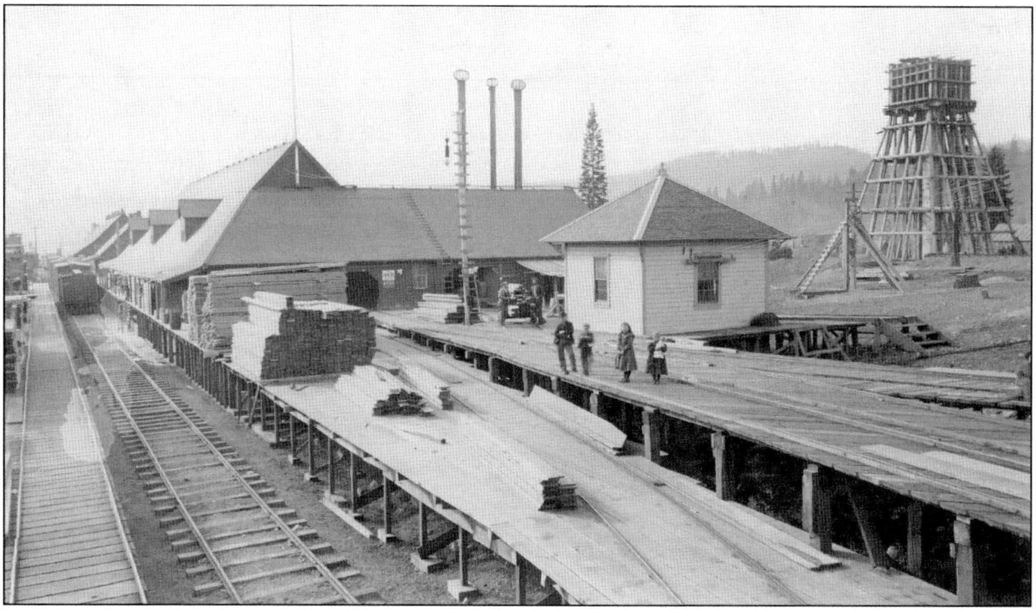

Children are pictured near the railroad tracks in 1903 in front of Upton Mill (above), located near Black Butte. Upton Mill workers pose for a picture with a boy and a woman (below). Abner Weed recruited the good workers from the neighboring mills. Chester Barnum (top center) went to work for Abner Weed in 1905. He lived in one of the new company houses in Rabbit Flat, painted barn red with white trim like all the other houses. Barnum had several jobs during the 47 years he worked at the mill, including being part of the first crew to work in the new door factory. (Both courtesy Harold Barnum.)

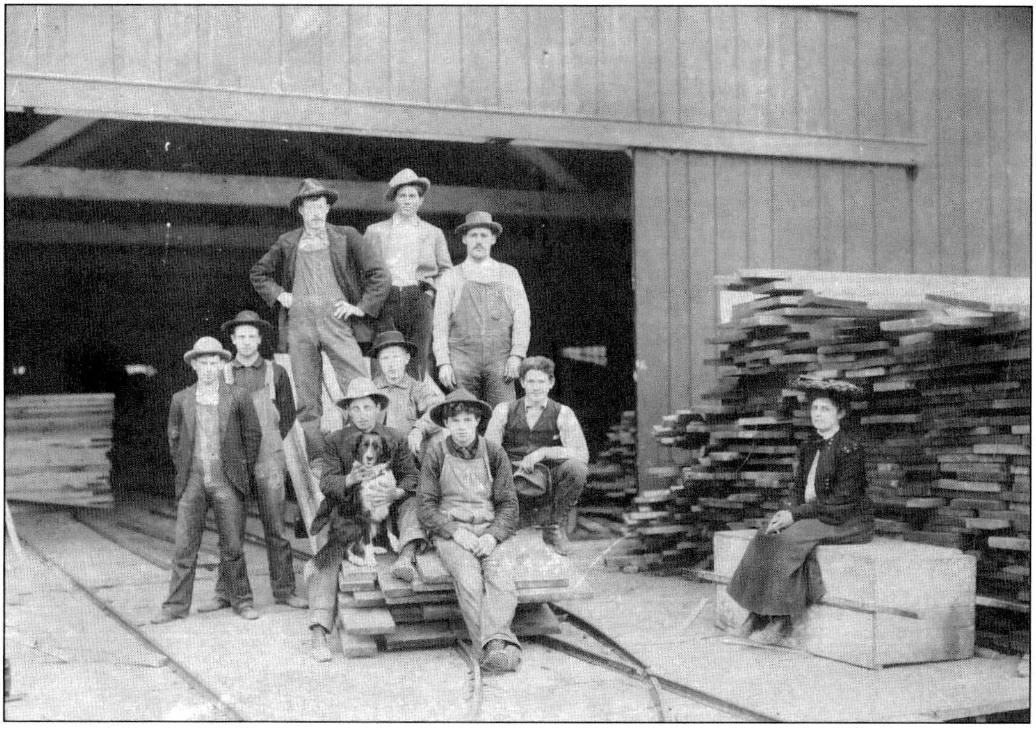

Three

LOGGING IN THE FIELD

The first job in the field is the felling and bucking of trees. A notcher decides which direction to fell the tree and then chops an undercut. Originally an 8-foot, two-man crosscut saw was used to cut down the tree, but electric-powered chainsaws replaced them. A limber chops off the branches and then a bucker cuts the bole into 10- to 18-foot logs.

The logs are skidded to the yard, where they are loaded for transportation. The earliest type of skidding was horse skidding. The forward end of the log is beveled, and sometimes the log is peeled, to make skidding easier. The swamper clears the path, the skinner drives the horses, and the choker-setter fastens the log to the horses.

Another early form of skidding in the Mount Shasta region was big wheel yarding. The knotter removes any missed branches, a gopher digs a hole under each log, and a hooker attaches the chains. When the loaded horses move forward, the chains tighten and lift the logs off the ground, making skidding easier. Stiff-tongue big wheels are used on gentle slopes, while slip-tongues, which require four horses, are used on steeper slopes. By the 1920s, Caterpillars had replaced horses.

Early steam-powered skidding was called donkey-yarding. The "donkey" was mounted on a sled that could winch itself around the field. A horse would haul the cable to a log, the rigger would attach it, and then the donkey-puncher would pull it in. Later high-lead yarding, with aerial cables attached to spar trees, replaced ground-yarding. By 1915, the Clyde Universal skidder and McGiffert loader were used to skid logs. In the early 1920s, Long-Bell Lumber Company purchased the Titanic, one of the largest skidders made, but it was so damaging to the environment that it was outlawed by the U.S. Forest Service.

In the early days, logs were team-loaded onto a wagon and tied down layer by layer. The Clyde skidder and McGiffert loader largely replaced team-loading by 1918. Between 1900 and 1935, at least 14 locomotives were purchased for the Weed mill, but most of them were scrapped by 1956 as trucks replaced locomotives after World War II.

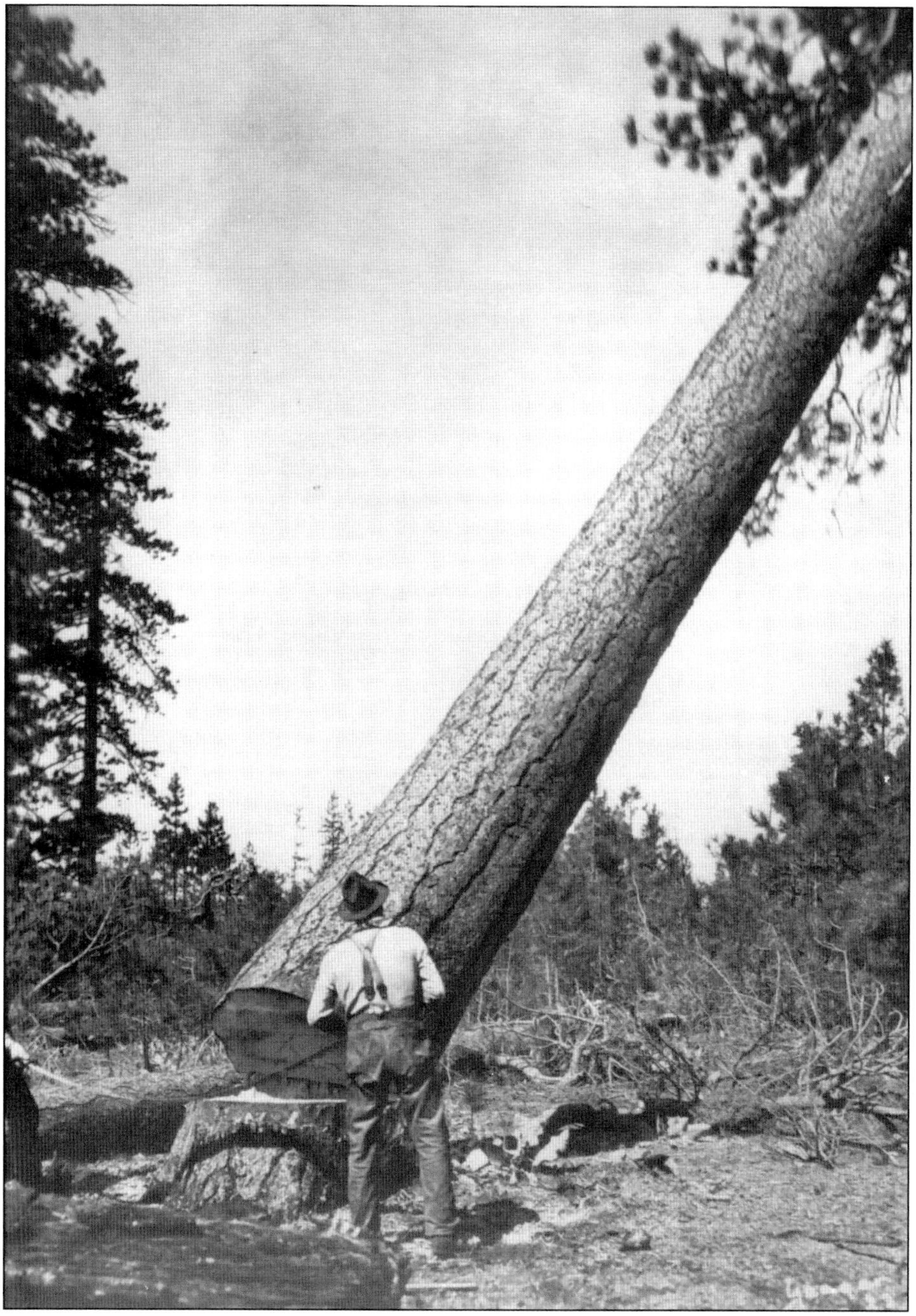

Hand-powered, two-man crosscut saws were used in the field through the 1920s. Crosscut saws cut across the grain of the wood. Two-man crosscut saws were used in the West to cut larger trees. Felling saws, thinner and more flexible, were used to fell the tree, while bucking saws, which were stiffer and heavier, were used to chop off branches after the tree was felled. The cutting teeth of crosscut saws have beveled edges, which act like a knife. After two or more cutter teeth is a raker, which removes the sawdust from the cut. The tree being felled is a ponderosa pine, the most important timber pine in the West. This photograph was taken in Tennant in 1922. (Photograph by C. E. Yeager.)

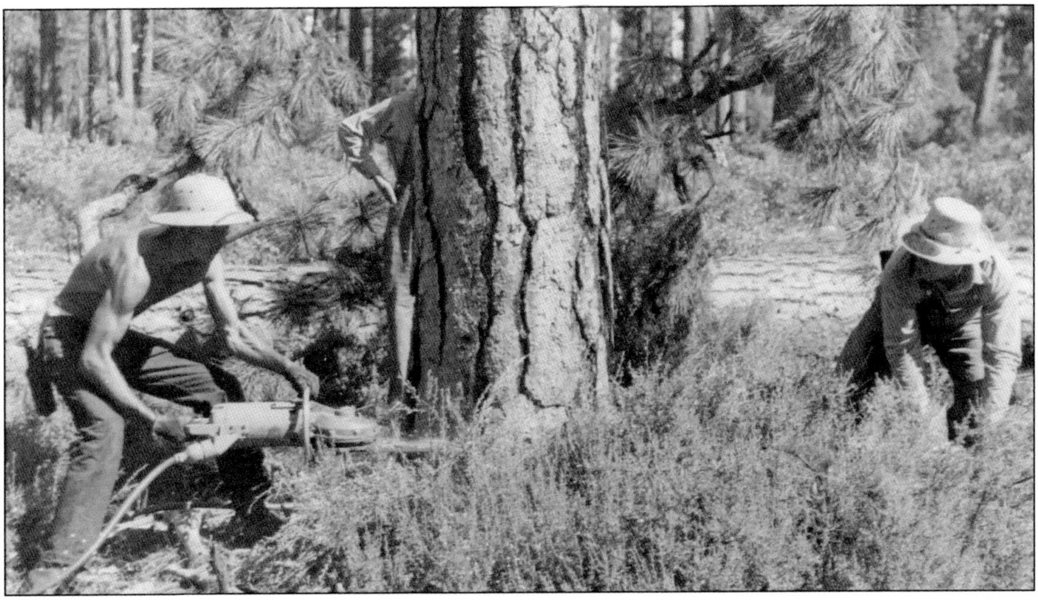

Long-Bell fellers (above) in Modoc County are shown cutting a ponderosa pine tree with an Atkins-Hassler Feller chainsaw powered from a 220-volt high-frequency generator mounted on a tractor. Hard hats were first patented in the United States in 1919, but their use was not required until 1933. Edward D. Bullard founded the E. D. Bullard Company in San Francisco in 1898; the company supplied equipment to miners throughout the American West. When his son Edward W. Bullard returned home from World War I, E. W. modified the design of the company's headgear, producing the "hard-boiled hat," named after the use of steam in the manufacturing process. The early-day Caterpillar (below), from the early 1930s, shows the generator and cord used to power the equipment. (Above courtesy College of the Siskiyous Library Mount Shasta Collection; below photograph by Harvey Gilman, courtesy Madelon G. Gilman.)

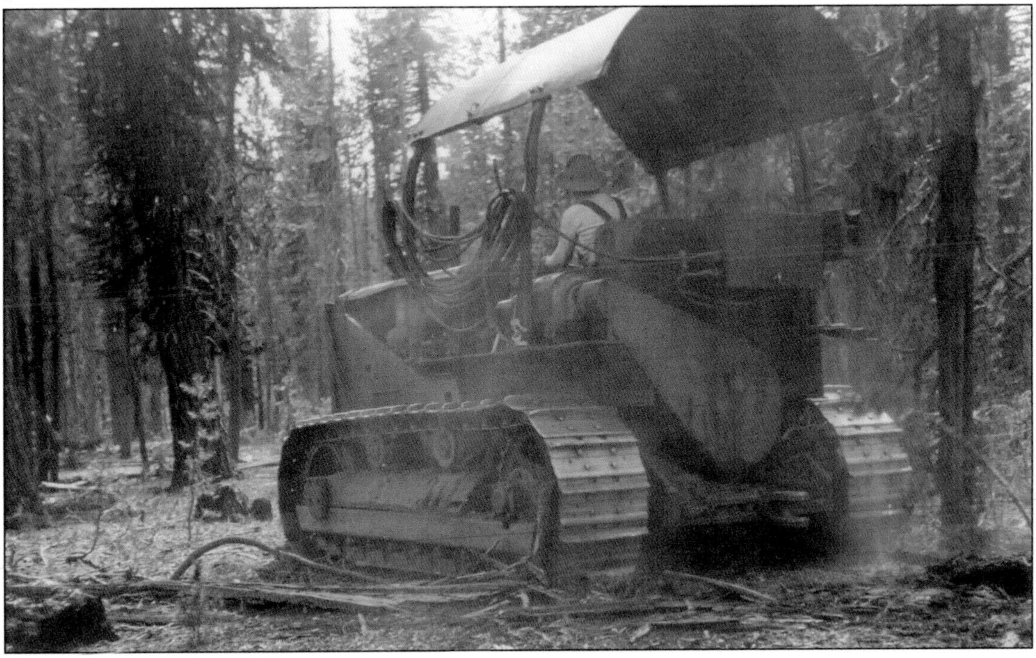

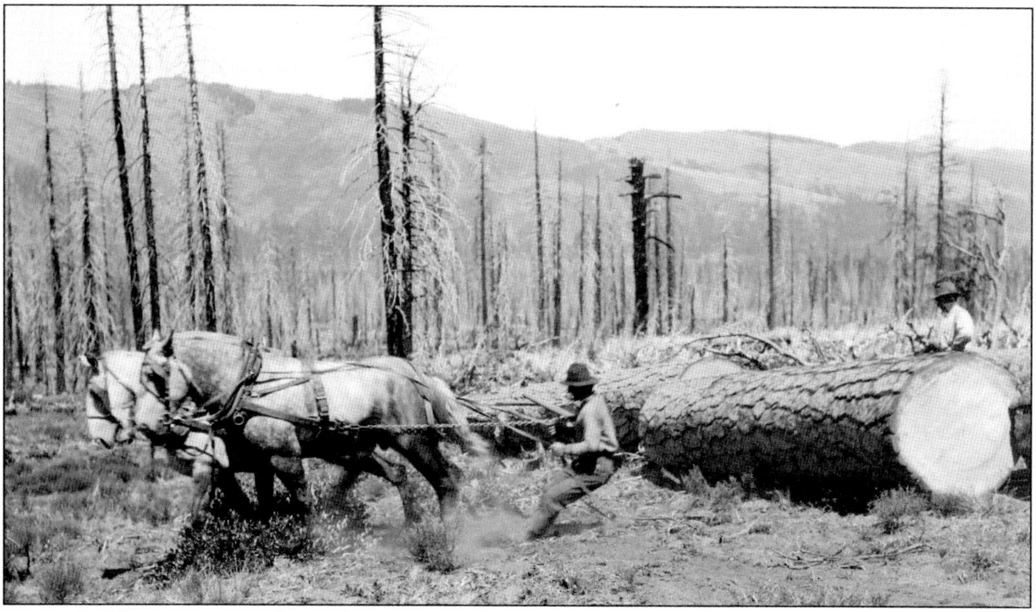

Horse skidding was an early method of yarding the logs. Yarding refers to trees being moved from the place they were felled to the landing site. The roll-out team (above), shown in 1900, is pulling out the log, so it can be aligned for the big wheel skidders (below). The choker setter fastens the logs onto the draft horses, and the skinner drives the horses. Horses could make up to 600-yard hauls. The horses were replaced every four to five years. The two-horse teams from 1910 indicate that these are stiff-tongue big wheels, since the safer slip-tongues big wheels required four horses. (Above photograph by Charles R. Miller.)

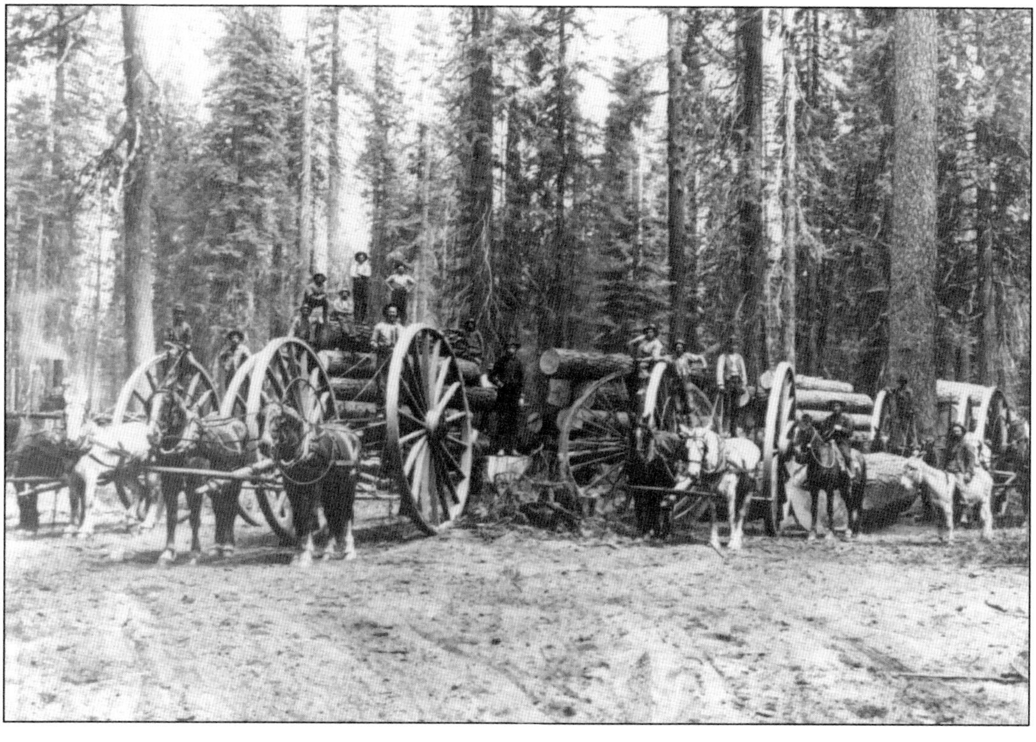

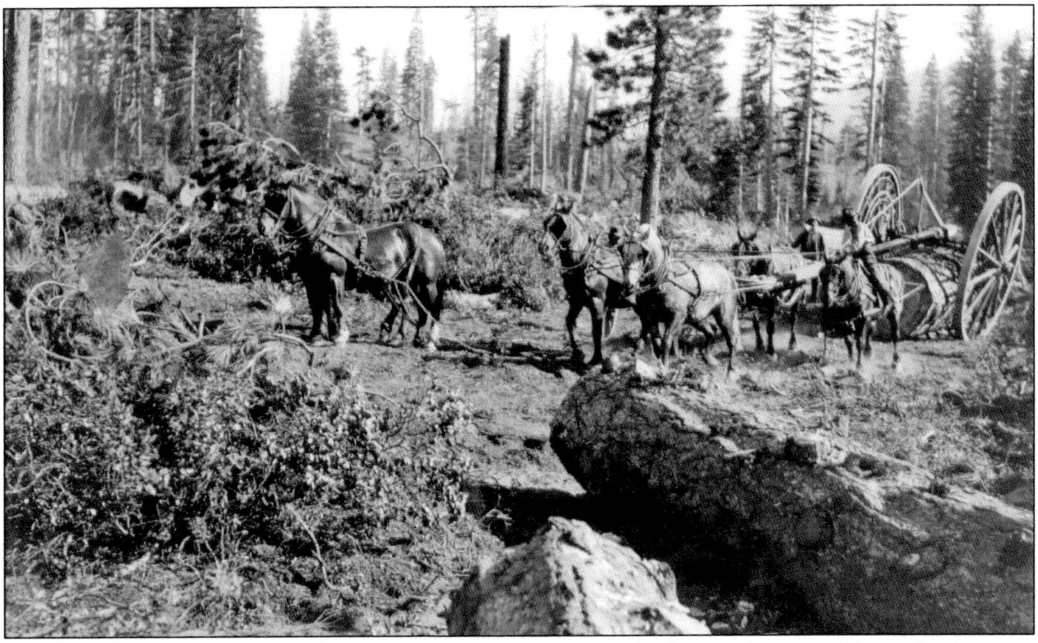

Silas Overpack, a blacksmith from Michigan, designed high wheels in 1875 for the logging industry. Overpack exhibited his red high wheels at the 1893 World's Columbian Exposition in Chicago, which resulted in their rapid spread to the West Coast. By 1894, they were being made in Siskiyou County. John Webb Sr. of the Redding Iron Works improved the high wheel with his slip-tongue big wheel. Although four to six horses were needed to pull the wheels, as shown in this 1905 photograph (above), they could go farther and were safer because the slip-tongue acted as a braking system. A 1924 issue of Long-Bell Lumber Company's monthly magazine, the *Log of Long-Bell* (below), features a Caterpillar pulling big wheels. (Above photograph by Charles R. Miller; below courtesy College of the Siskiyous Library Mount Shasta Collection.)

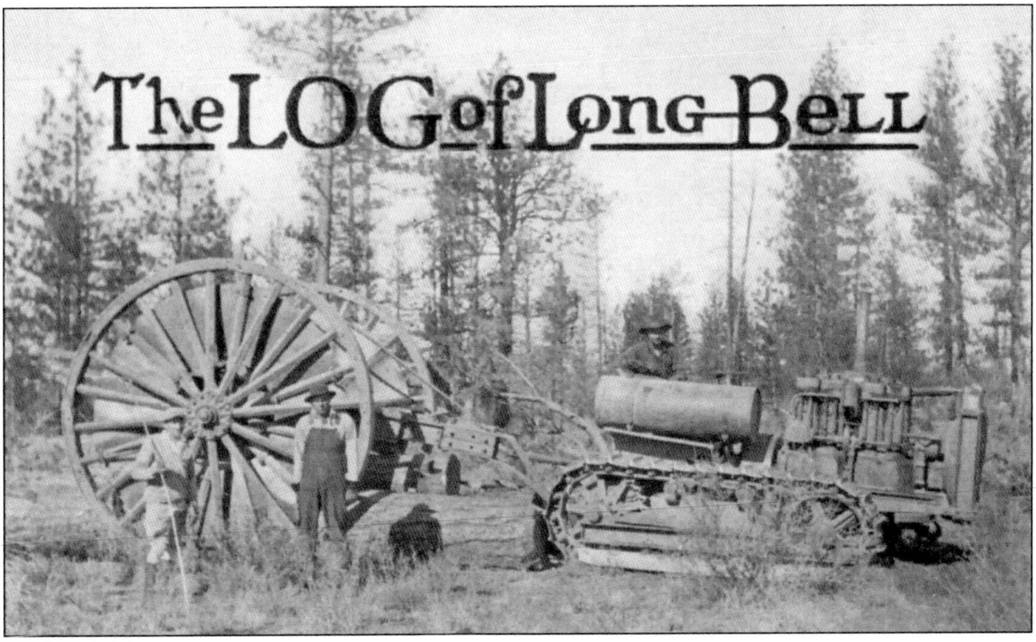

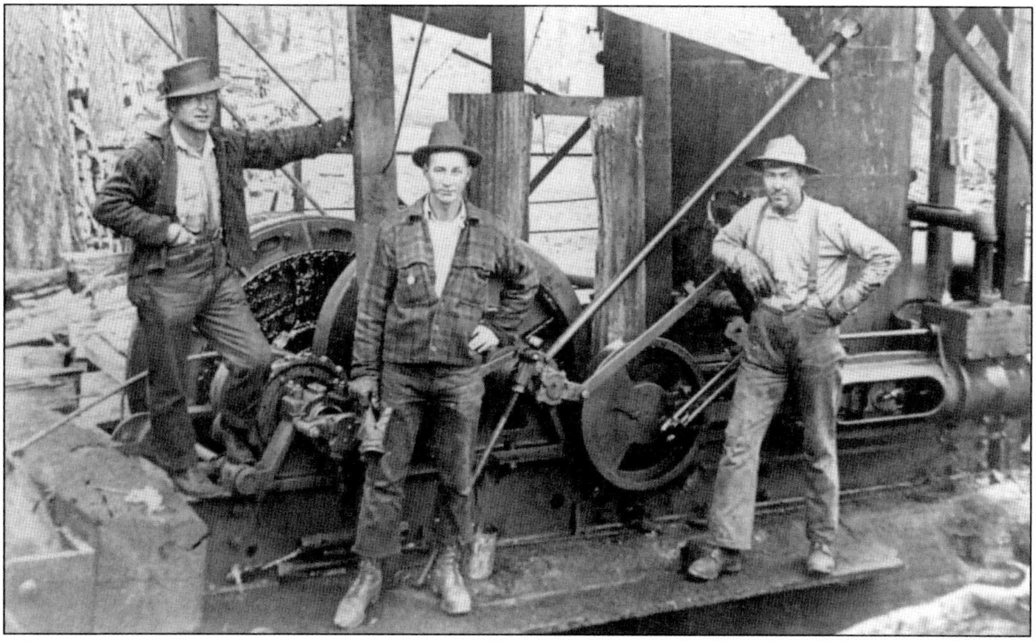

Three men are operating a donkey engine. The rigger attaches the cable to a log, and the donkey puncher (above, left) hauls it in. The short pants are to prevent getting snagged in the branches. Donkey engines were used since their invention in 1881 by John Dolbeer of Eureka, California, until they were replaced by Caterpillars. A donkey engine loader is shown below loading logs onto cars in 1916. Swampers cut the wood for the boiler, two hookers connected bell hooks onto the logs to load into flatcars, and the donkey puncher (second from left) operates the machinery. The Weed Historic Lumber Town Museum has a bell hook on display. (Below photograph by George Schuler.)

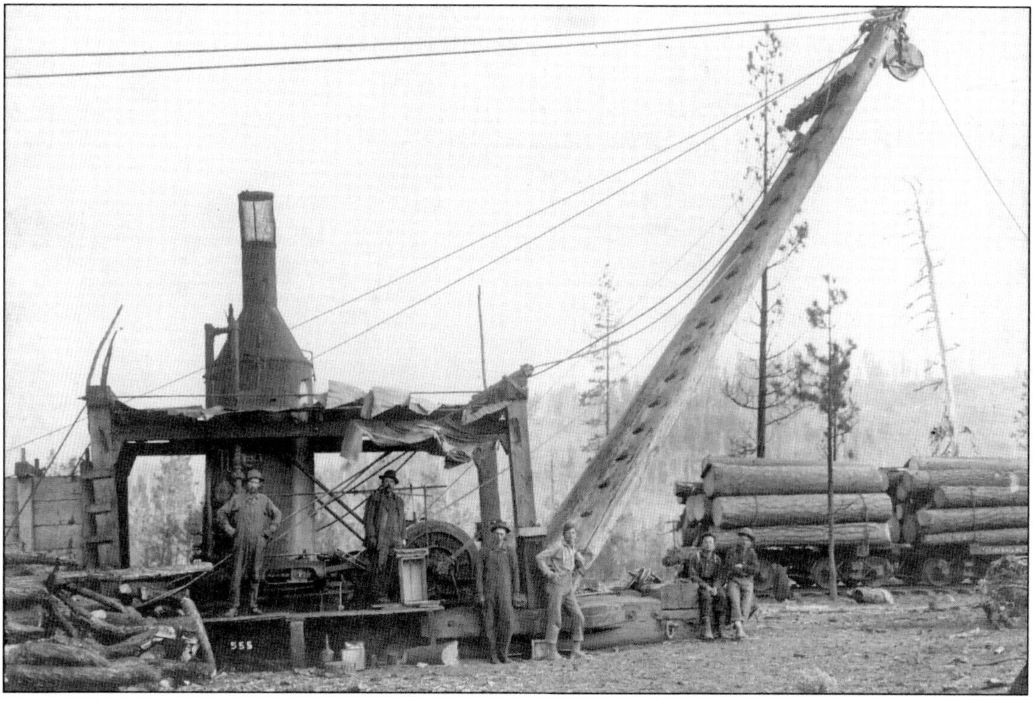

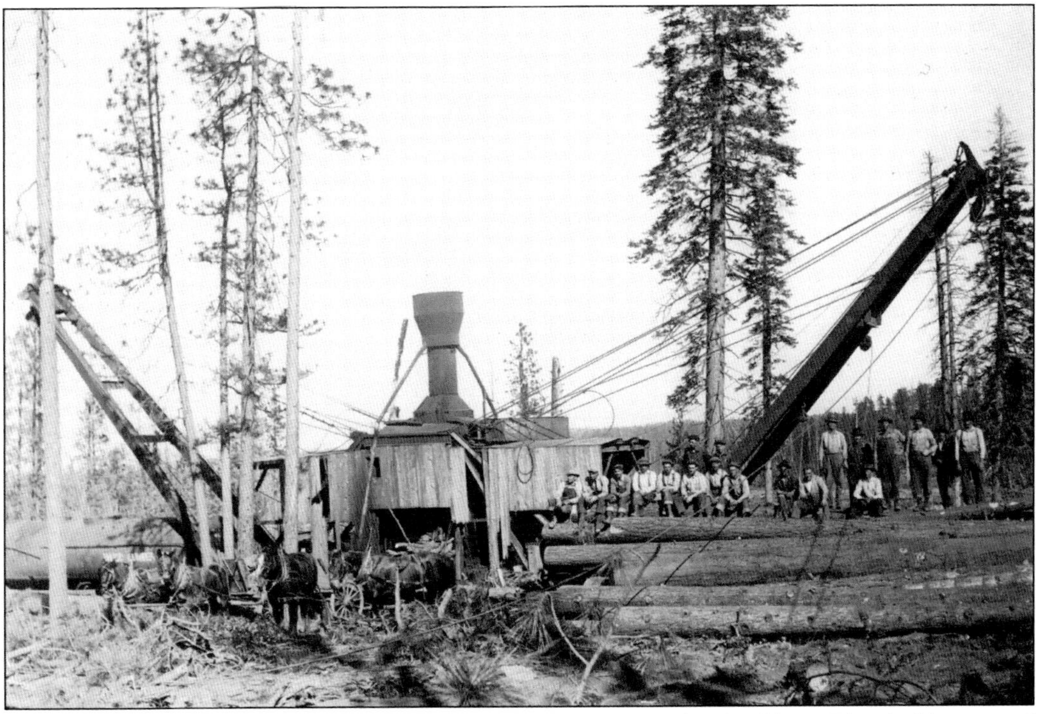

Clyde Double-Ended Skidders (above and below) were also used to load logs. The skidder named Weed Lumber Company No. 5 was used in Tennant during the 1920s. This four-line skidder could haul in logs from both sides at once. A McGiffert loader followed behind the skidder and loaded the logs onto the flatcars.

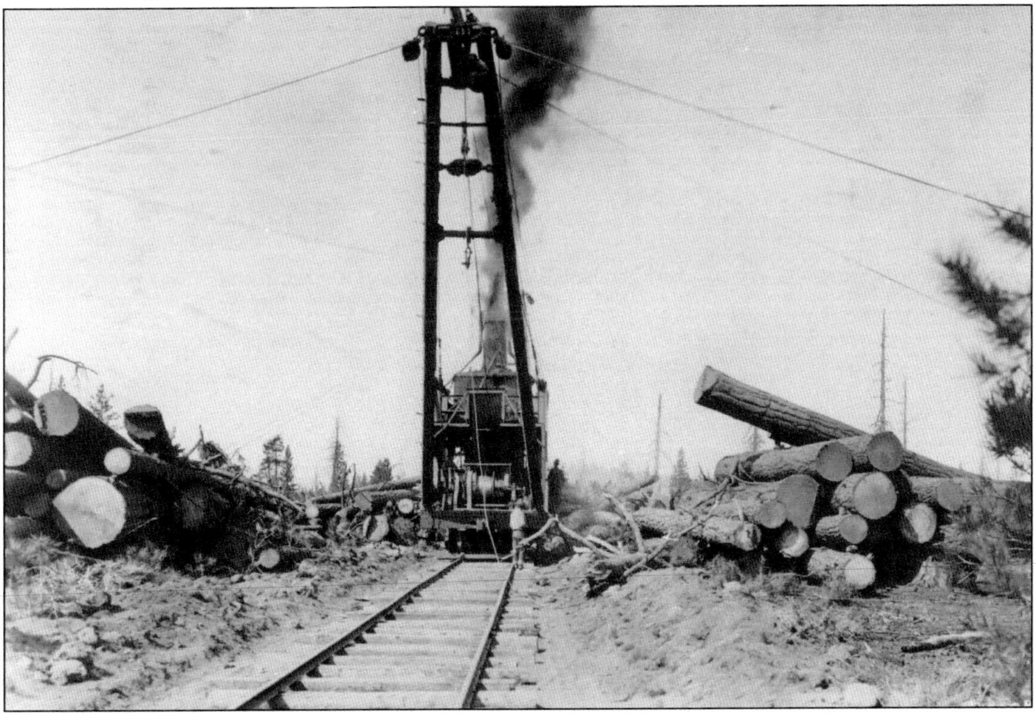

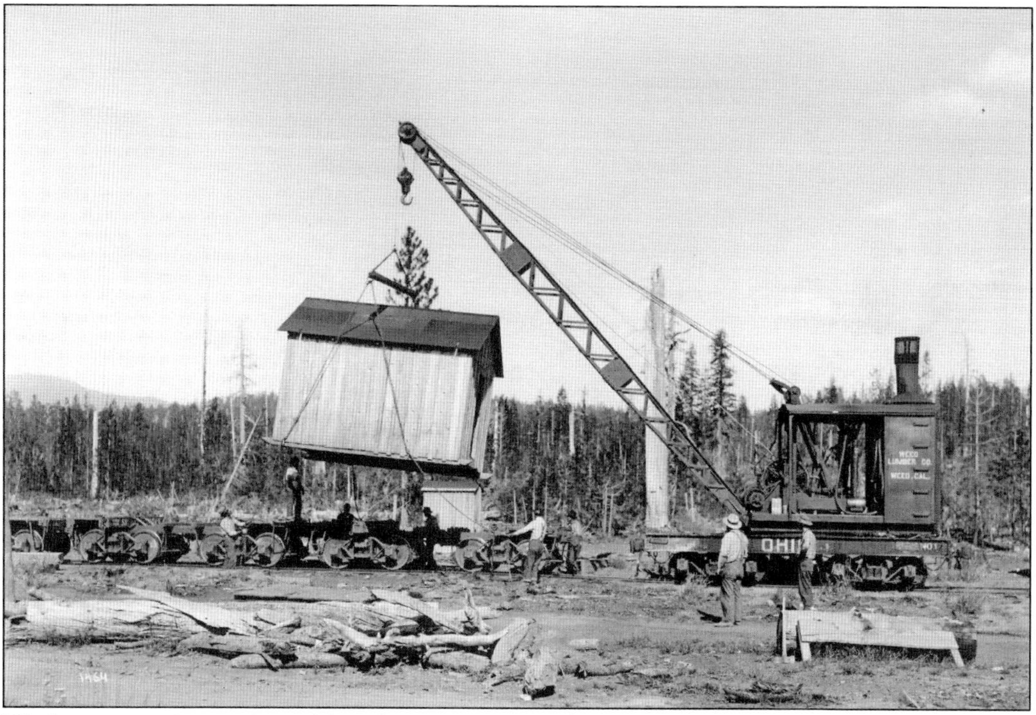

Workers move Camp No. 1 (above) in Tennant in the early 1920s. New Camp No. 1 had 225 two-man, 12-by-18-foot cabins, six supervisor's cabins, and a cabin for the nurse and her husband. The cabins are built on 18-foot skids (below) that can be hauled into place by a donkey engine. (Above courtesy Roger Zwanziger.)

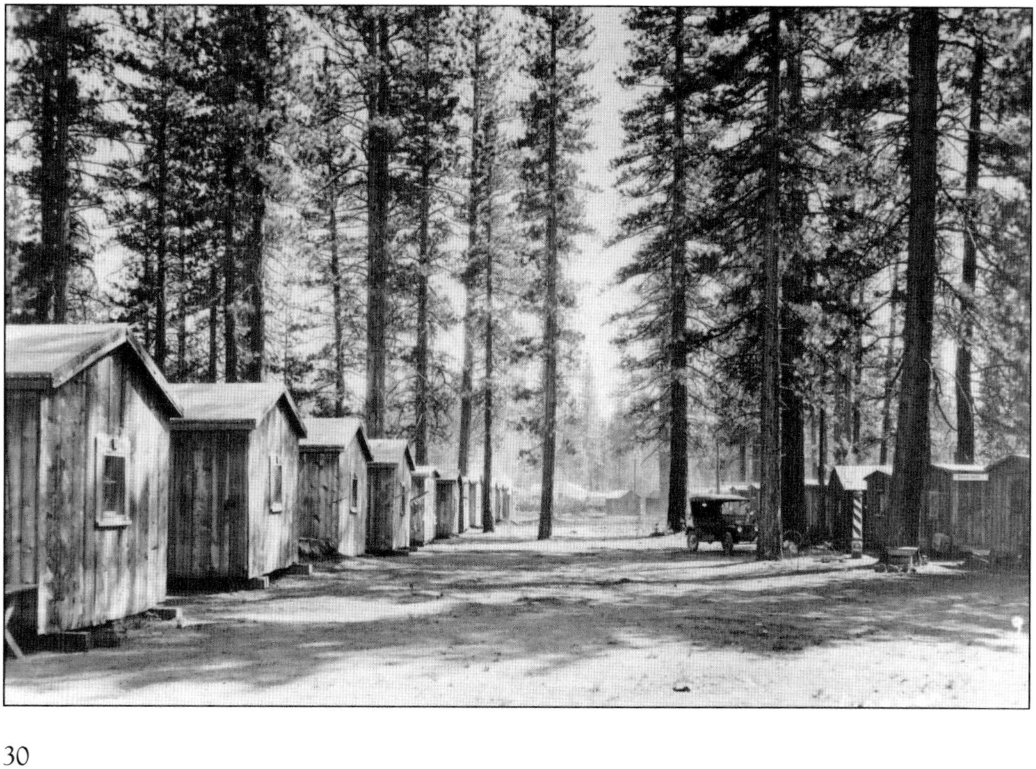

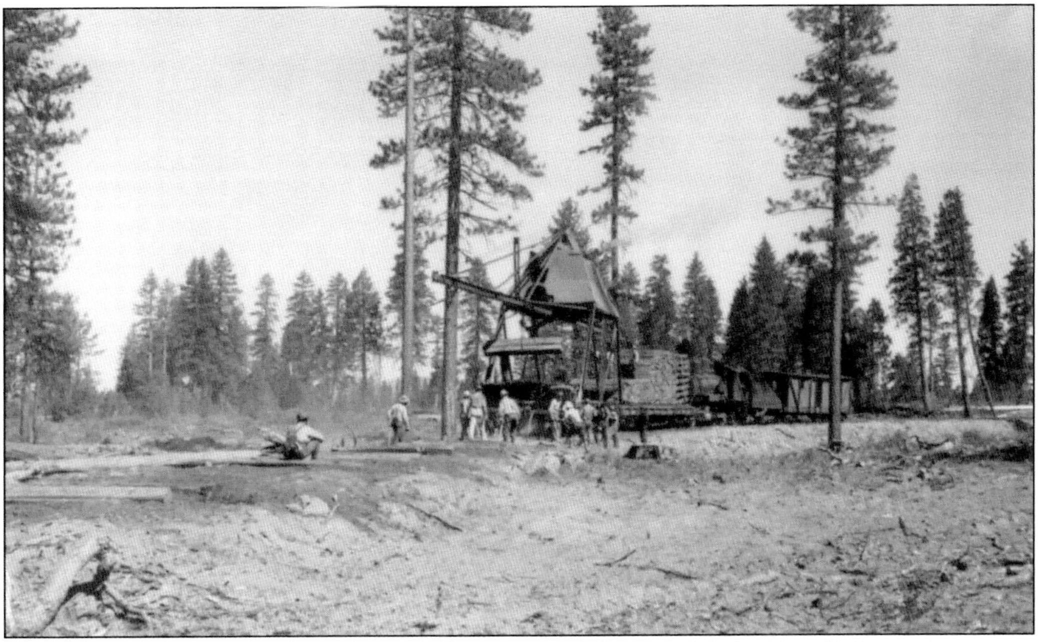

The Long-Bell Lumber Company track-laying crew (above and below), called a track gang, is placing ties and rails in 1938. The steam-powered Clyde Track Layer is mounted on a railroad car, which also carries the rails. Another car, carrying ties, is located behind the track layer. The arm reaches back and hauls the ties forward, placing them on the grade for the gang to lay. Then the rails are laid on the ties and bolted into place. (Above courtesy College of the Siskiyous Library Mount Shasta Collection.)

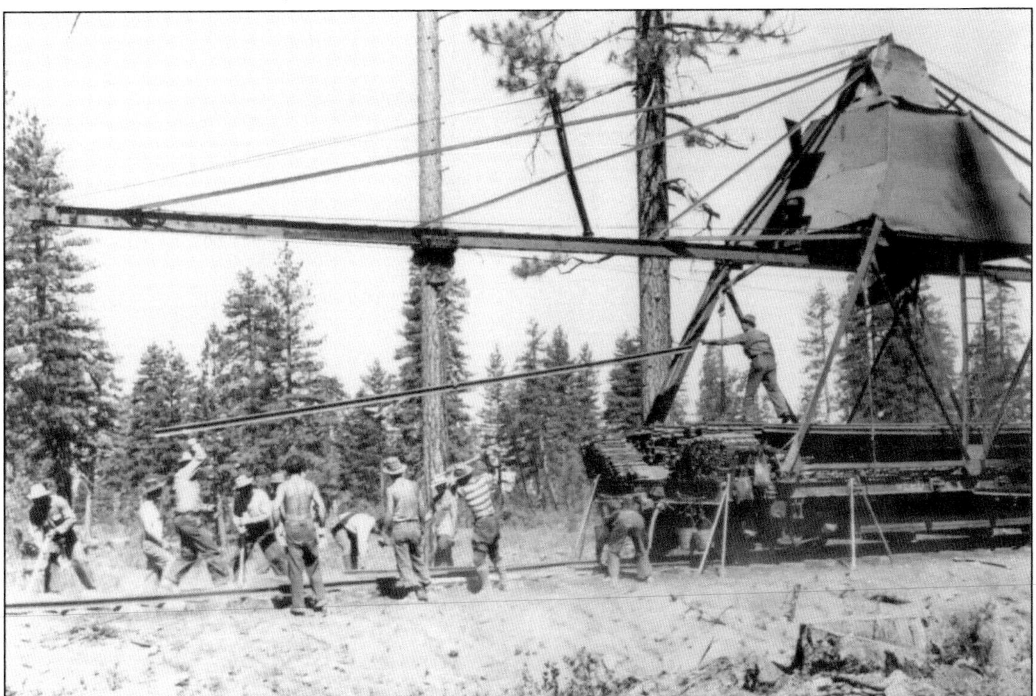

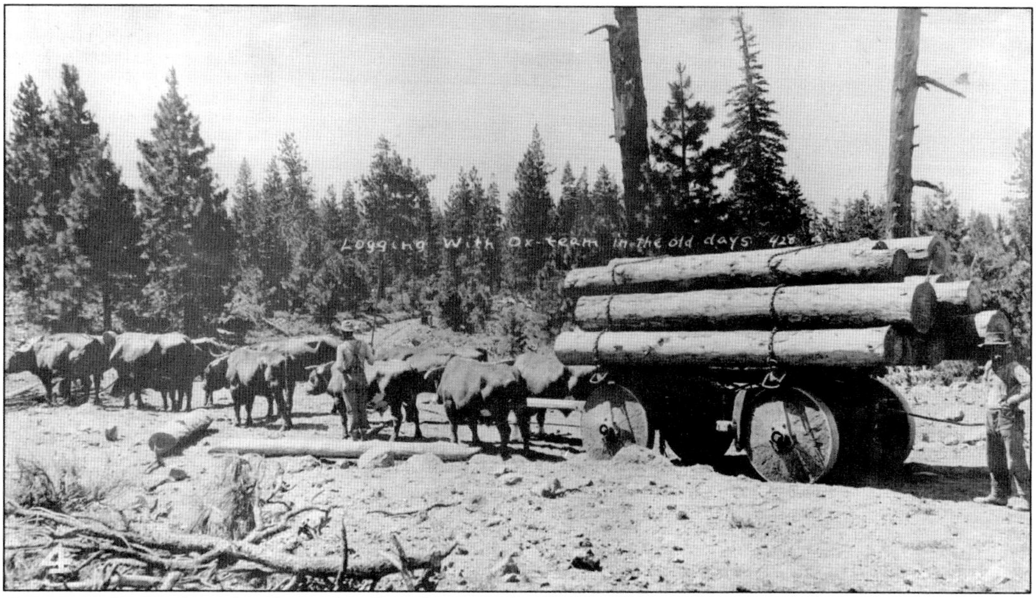

Oxen are shown here hauling a load in the Weed area around 1890. The man who drove the oxen was called a bull skinner. The rimmed wooden wheels are characteristic of the wagons Weed used while at Igerna. Each layer of logs is tied down separately. Logs were then cross-hauled on ramps up to the platform. Horses and oxen were no longer used at the Weed mill after 1920.

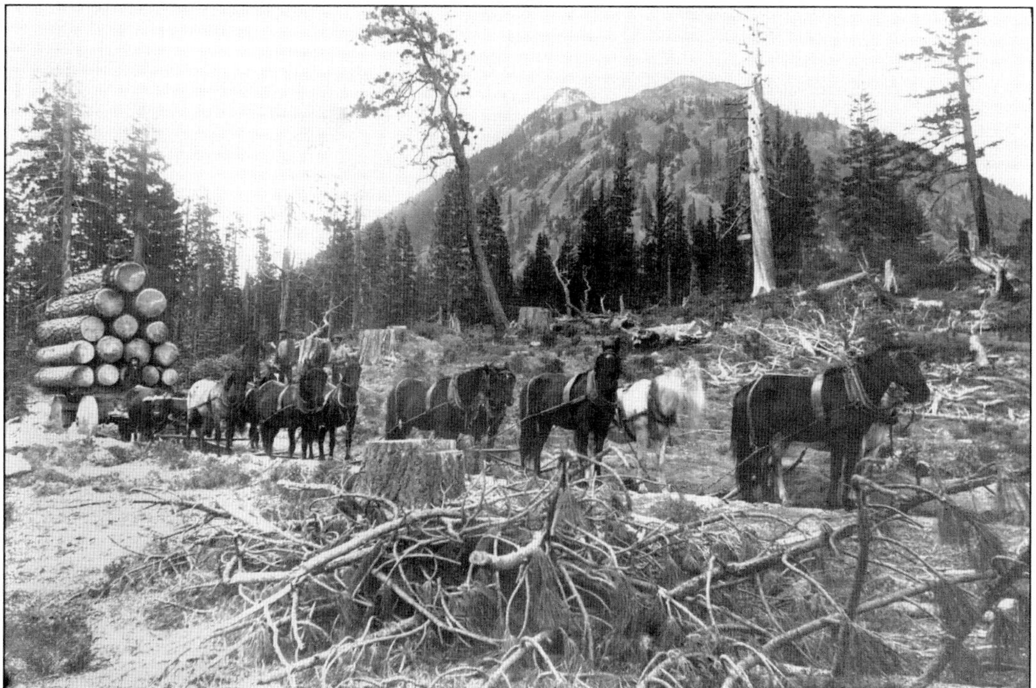

Here is Abner Weed's mixed team of 10 horses and two oxen pulling a load of logs near Black Butte in 1895. Mr. Hedge and Mr. Tibbs built the first mill near Black Butte in 1860. It was called Summit Mill. This mill was later sold to the Maxwell brothers. A huge oxen yoke from early-day logging can be seen at the Weed Historic Lumber Town Museum. (Courtesy Matt Kohn.)

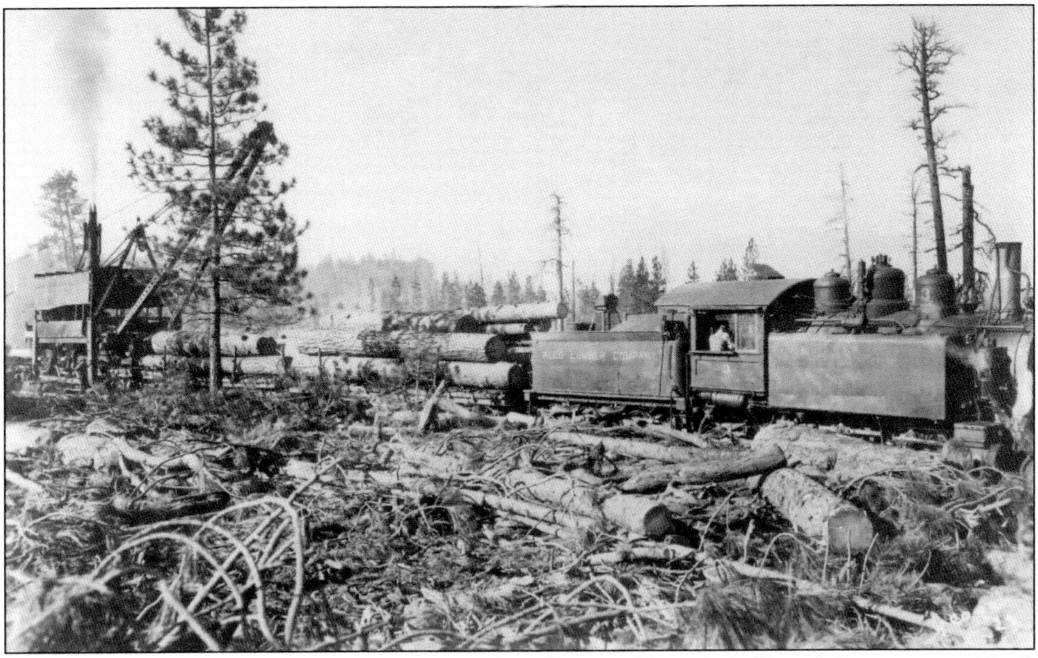

In March 1907, Weed Lumber Company purchased two Baldwin 2-6-2T tank locomotives. No. 3 engine, shown above in its original configuration with side tanks, is being loaded with a McGiffert loader. Both engines were later converted to standard engines with a four-wheel tender. The Baldwin 2-6-2T tank locomotive No. 4 is shown in its original configuration below, with side tanks mounted directly on the engine. The conductor, at center with the bag, carries the mail and payroll to the loggers in the logging camps. (Below photograph by George Schuler.)

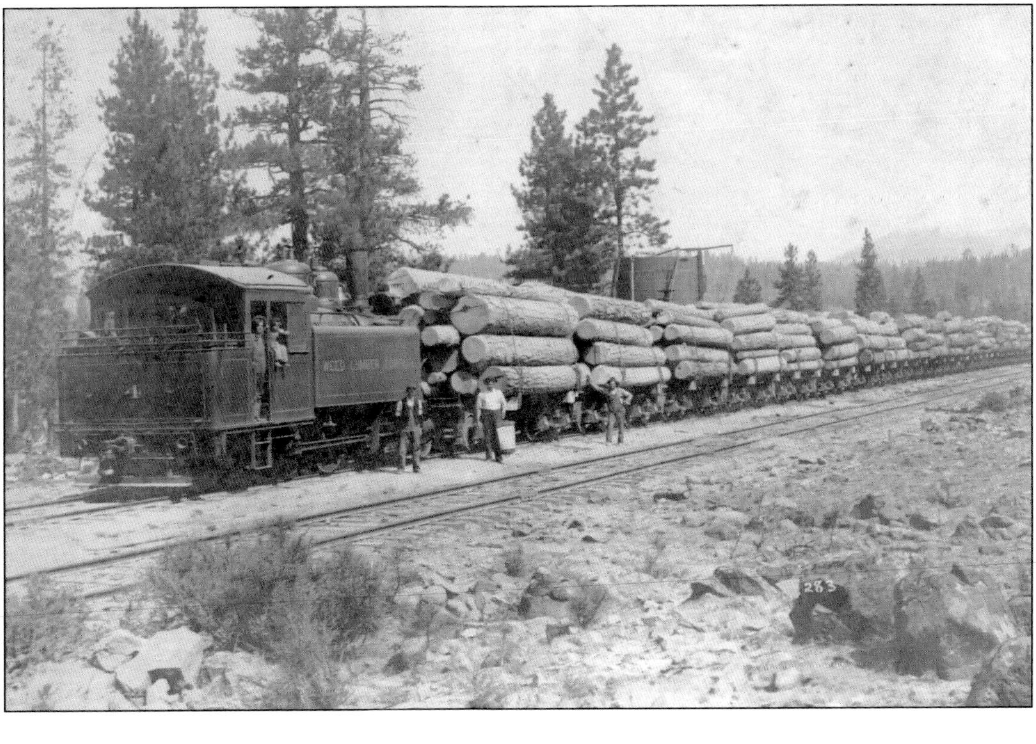

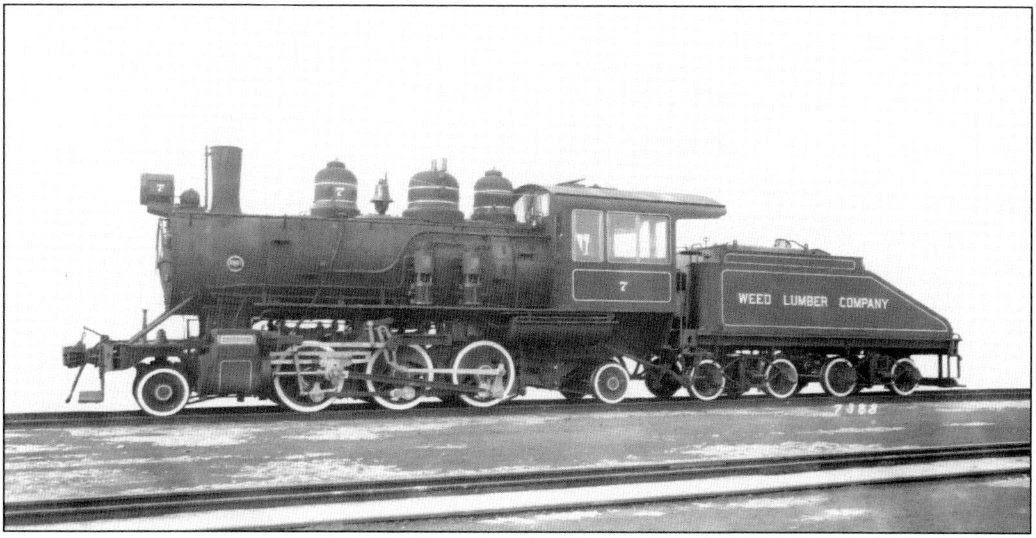

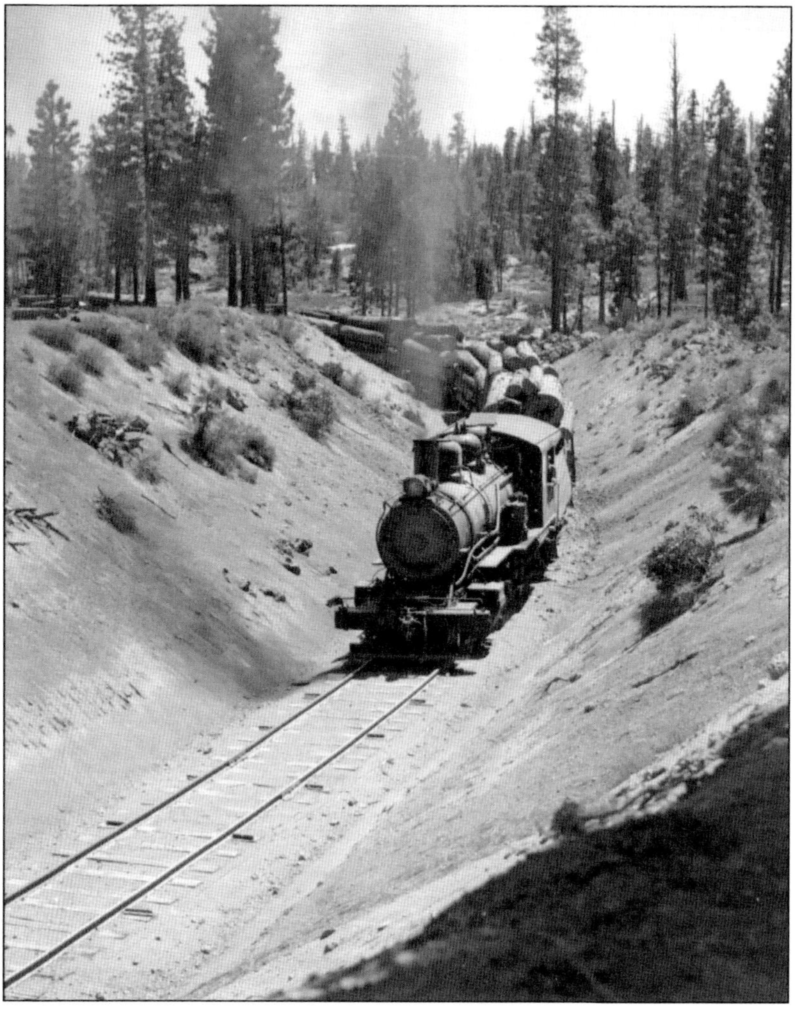

Weed Lumber Company purchased two brand-new Baldwin 2-6-2 steam locomotives, No. 7 and No. 8, in January 1920. The Whyte designation 2-6-2 stands for the wheel arrangement of the locomotive, with two non-powered leading wheels that help negotiate turns, six larger driving wheels coupled together with side rods, and two non-powered trailing wheels. Engine No. 7 (above) shows the tender, the car that holds the fuel. No. 8 (left) is shown hauling logs from Tennant to Weed.

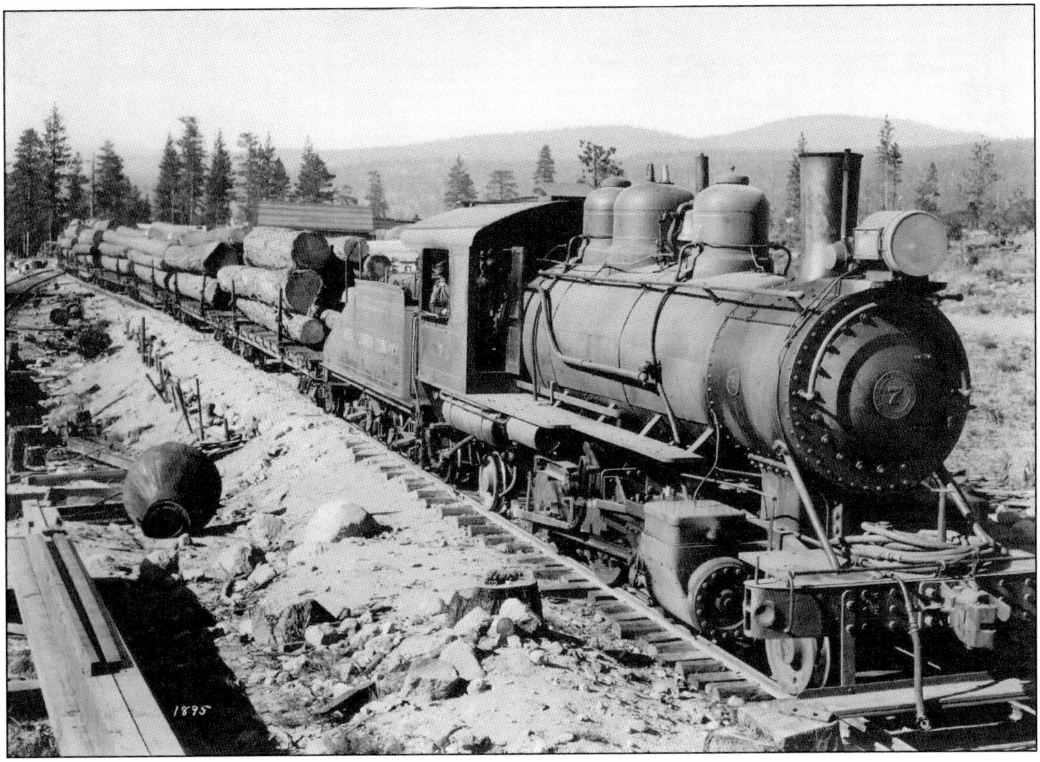

Baldwin engines No. 7 and No. 8 were often called "the twins" because they were both Baldwin 2-6-2 engines purchased at the same time. The tenders were originally labeled with the Weed Lumber Company label, but this was later changed to Long-Bell Lumber Company. Both engines were scrapped in 1956. (Above courtesy Roger Zwanziger.)

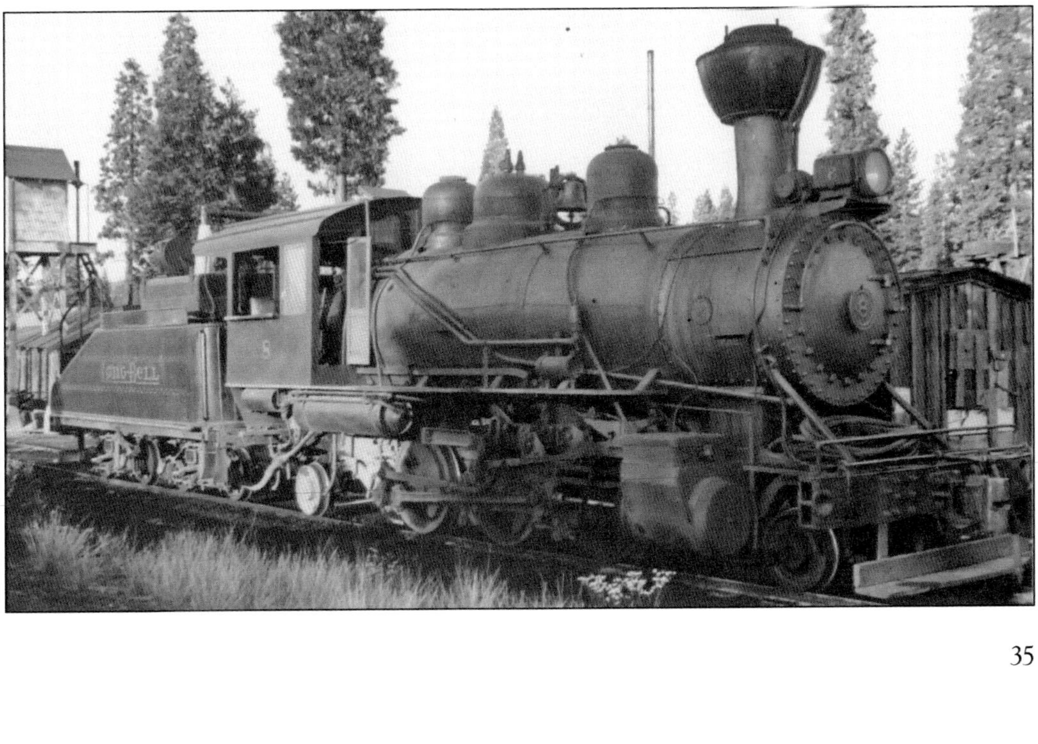

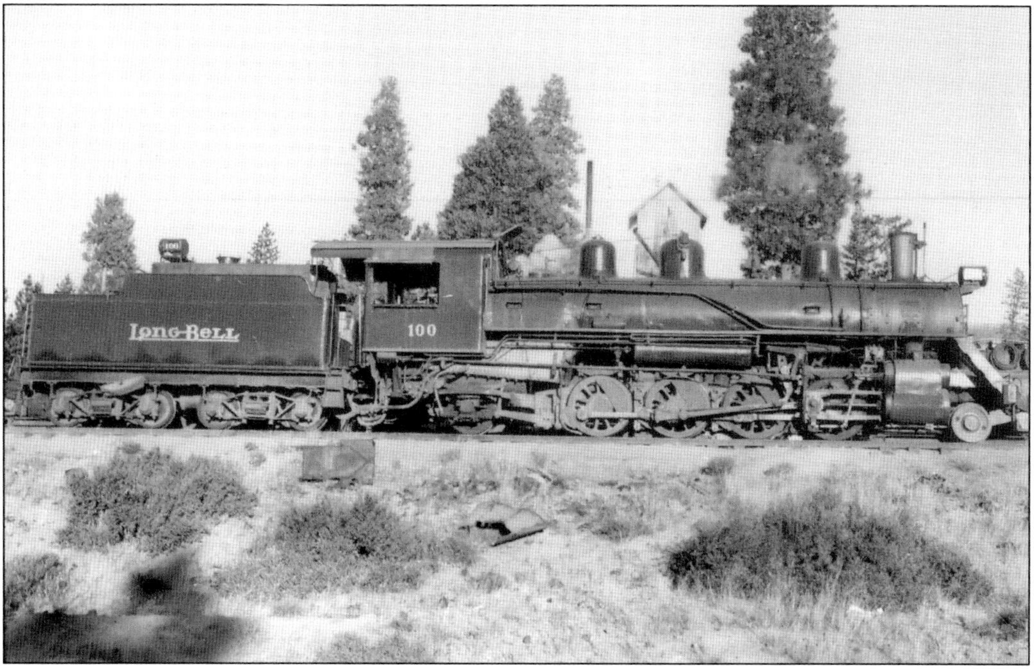

Long-Bell Lumber Company purchased two ALCO Brooks 2-8-2 locomotives. No. 100 (above) was built in 1920 and purchased from Portland, Astoria, and Pacific in the early 1920s. Engine No. 101 (below), purchased new around 1923, is shown here in 1930. These two locomotives were known as loggers, because they hauled loaded cars on the main line. The Brooks Locomotive Works was founded by Horatio Brooks in 1879 in Dunkirk, New York. In 1901, several locomotive companies merged together and formed the American Locomotive Company (ALCO). After 1901, the locomotives produced at the Dunkirk plant were called ALCO Brooks locomotives. (Below courtesy D. E. Warren.)

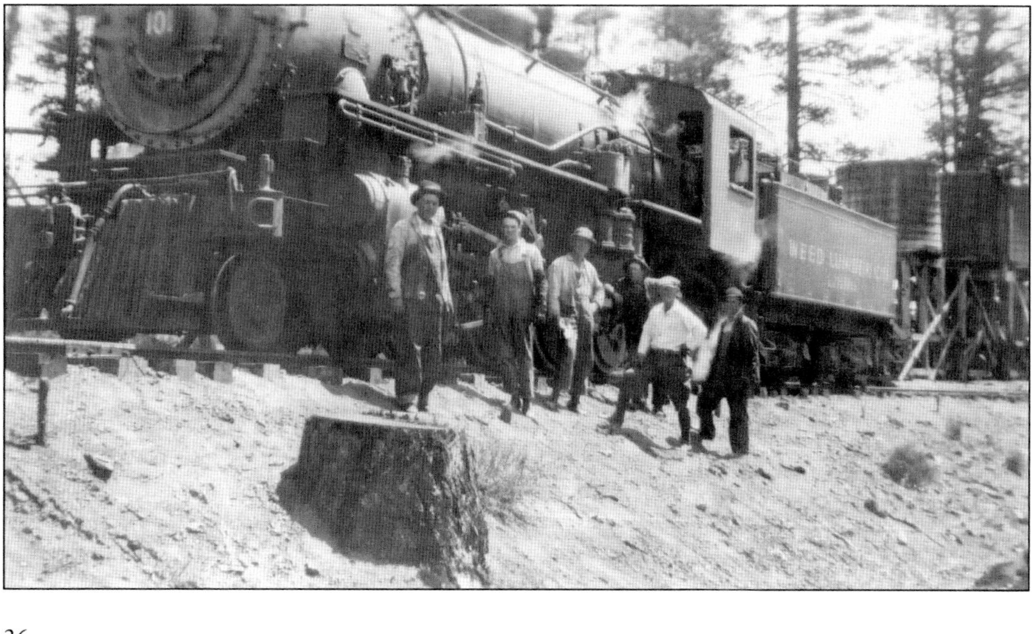

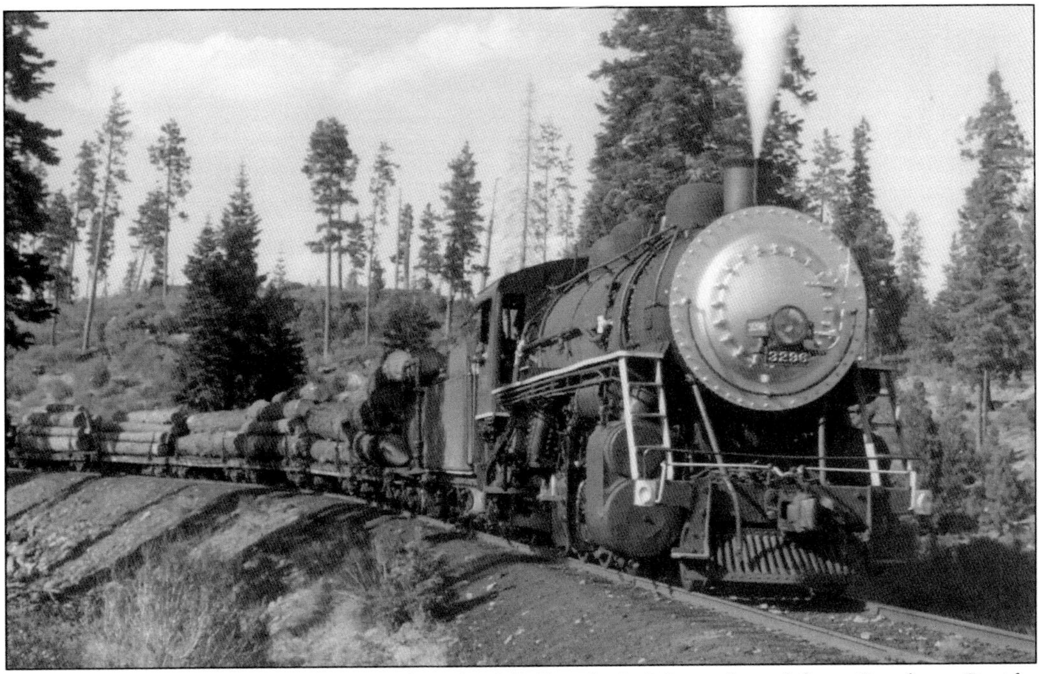

Locomotive No. 3296 (above) is another ALCO Brooks 2-8-2 purchased from Southern Pacific in 1940. This train was not only a logger, it was "the Logger." The train above is hauling logs from Modoc County to Tennant in the 1940s. ALCO Brooks No. 1401 (below) was built in 1926 for the Longview, Portland, and Oregon Railroad; it later sold to Long-Bell Lumber Company. Southern Pacific provided the 22-foot Russell log cars as part of their agreement when Weed sold them the railroad. Weed Lumber Company ran two loggers daily, which hauled 40–60 cars each. (Above photograph by Elmer Zimmerman.)

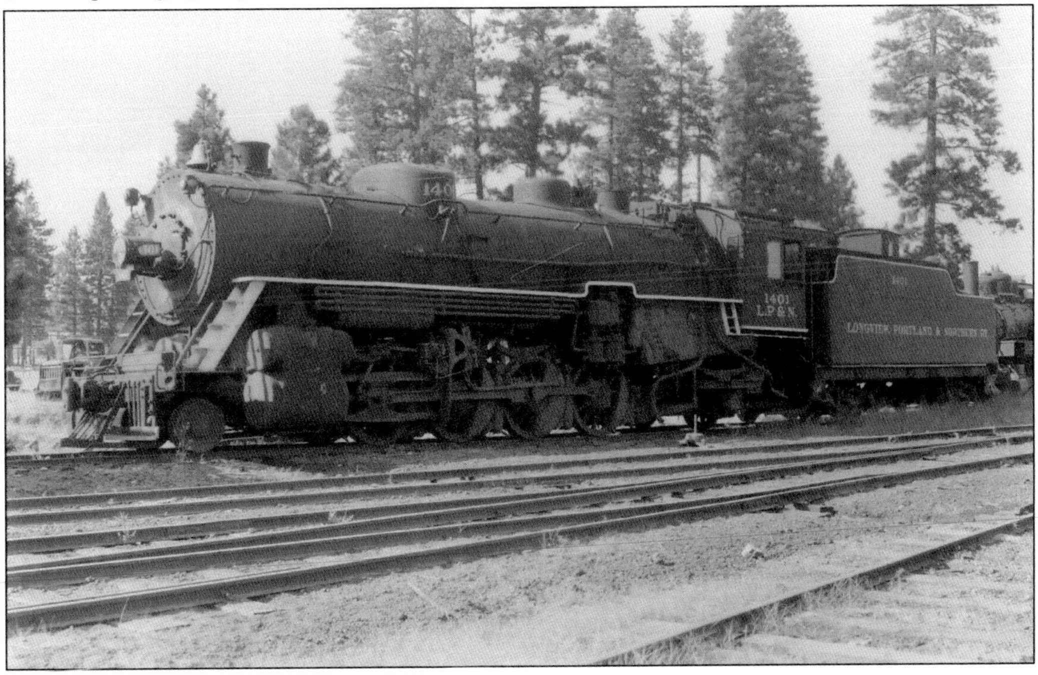

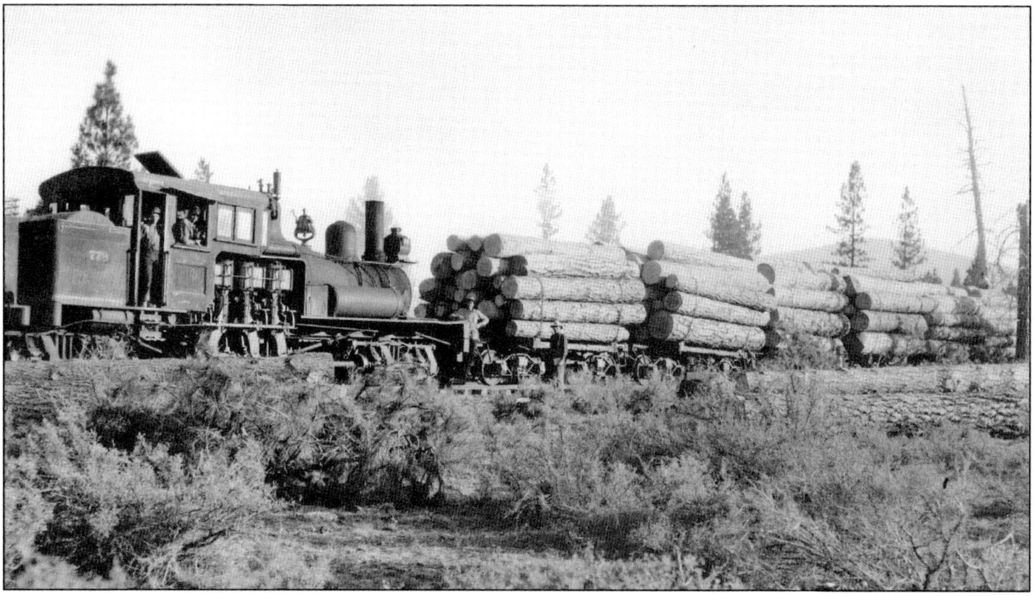

Here is Shay locomotive No. 779 hauling 16-foot logs near Tennant in the 1920s. This three-cylinder, three-truck Shay was built by Lima Locomotive Works in 1903 for the Benson Logging and Lumber Company. It was purchased by Weed Lumber Company in the early 1920s. The Shay engine is also called a "sidewinder" because the wheels that drive the engine are all on one side. (Courtesy Roger Zwanziger.)

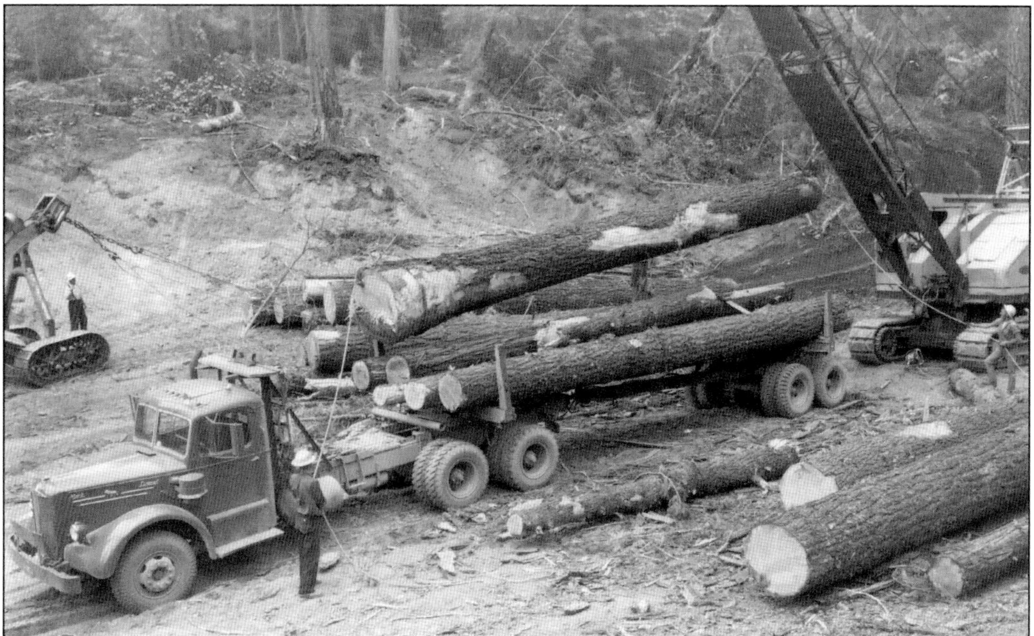

Most of the locomotives were scrapped in the mid-1950s after trucks took over hauling logs. The loggers are loading logs onto a truck with a jammer (far right) using a crane, bridle, and bell hooks in 1957. The arch (far left) was hauled behind a Caterpillar to drag logs in. The Weed Historic Lumber Town Museum has an arch on display in the outer yard. (Courtesy College of the Siskiyous Library Mount Shasta Collection.)

Four

Work in the Mill

In the early 1900s, Abner Weed decided to build his own mill. In 1900, he purchased land from George Decker at Milepost 348 on the Southern Pacific Railroad. A May 6, 1902, newspaper article stated that Weed chose this site "because of the winds, which he knew would quickly and thoroughly dry his lumber." According to old newspaper accounts, Weed began a railroad survey in December 1900, and rails were being laid within a few months. By 1904, it was 13 miles long and reached as far as Haystack and Yellow Butte.

Weed Lumber Company opened for operation in June 1901. By the end of the season, 10.5 million feet had been milled at the new plant. Weed also received a lucrative contract from Southern Pacific to cut ties for their railroad. In May 1902, Weed purchased a band saw. Together with the circular saw, 40 million feet could be produced annually. Weed built a box factory in the summer of 1902. The next year, Weed Lumber Company was incorporated. In 1905, Weed sold his railroad to the California Northeastern Railway Company in exchange for Southern Pacific providing spurs and holding tracks at their expense and allowing Weed Lumber Company right of access to the main line for 40 miles. Between 1905 and 1916, Weed gradually sold his interest to Long-Bell Lumber Company, but they kept the Weed Lumber Company name until 1926.

In 1906, Weed Lumber Company built dry kilns and a new factory. In 1911, the first plywood plant in California was built at Weed. By 1915, Weed Lumber Company was the largest lumber manufacturer between San Francisco and Portland, producing over 90 million board feet annually. In 1917–1918, Long-Bell Lumber Company built a new mill with four band saws, which could produce 1 million board feet every two days. In 1922, the powerhouse was enlarged for a total of four smokestacks and four boilers. A new teepee burner was built in 1928, but the famous Weed winds blew it down in December 1931. By this time, the Depression had taken hold. After swapping cutover land for logging rights with the U.S. Forest Service, Long-Bell sold out to International Paper in 1956.

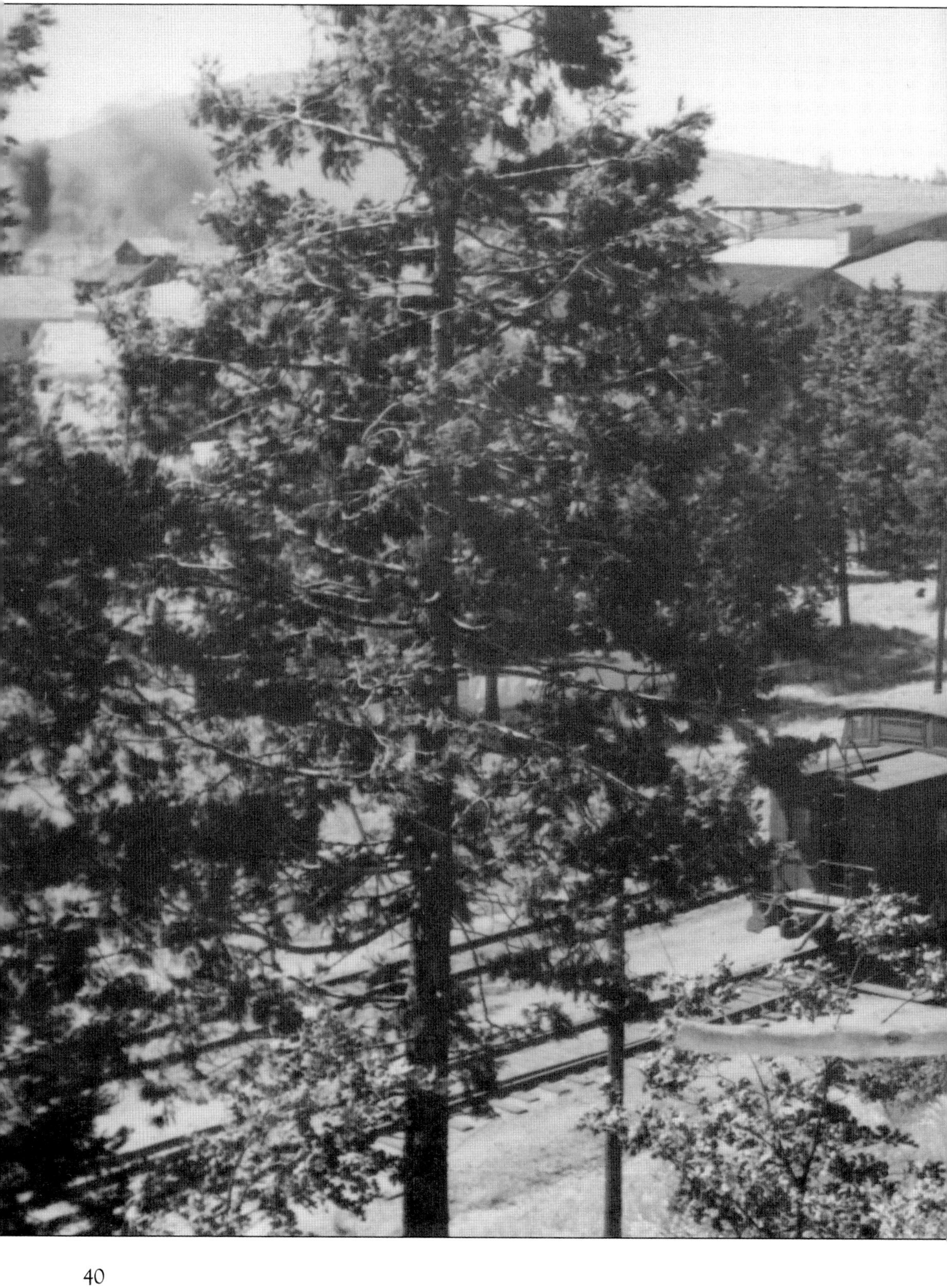

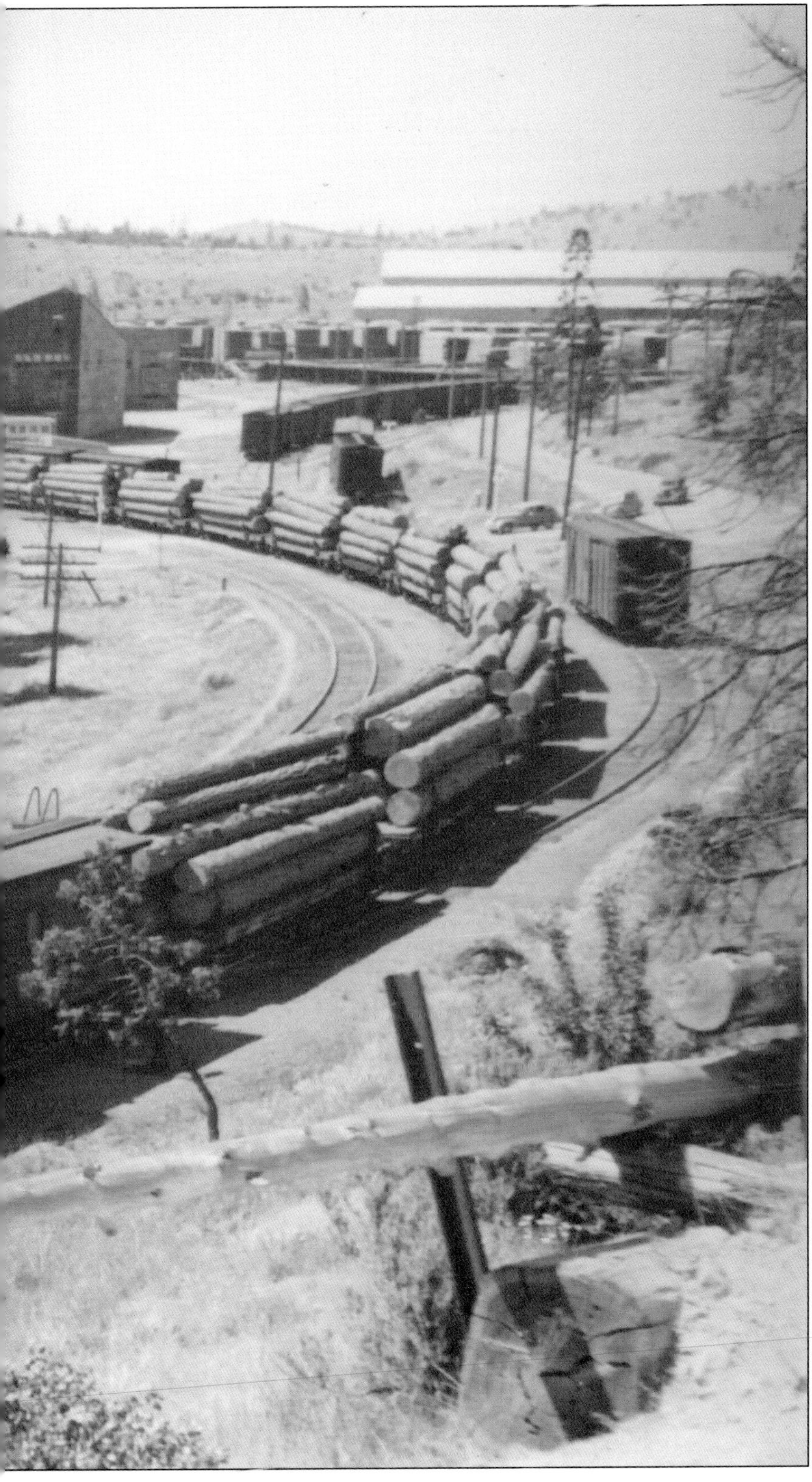

A logger train with a Southern Pacific cupola caboose is shown coming into the Weed Lumber Company mill from Tennant in the 1920s to 1930s. The dark, two-story building to the left of the trees is the blockhouse where block-like wood scraps were stored and later sold to locals for firewood. The large building in the center is the box factory. Beyond the box factory towards the right is Yard No. 1, where the lumber was stored. The track between Yard No. 1 and the main track went directly into the factory, where doors and windows were loaded. This photograph was taken from Schoolhouse Hill near the hairpin curve on Hillside Drive.

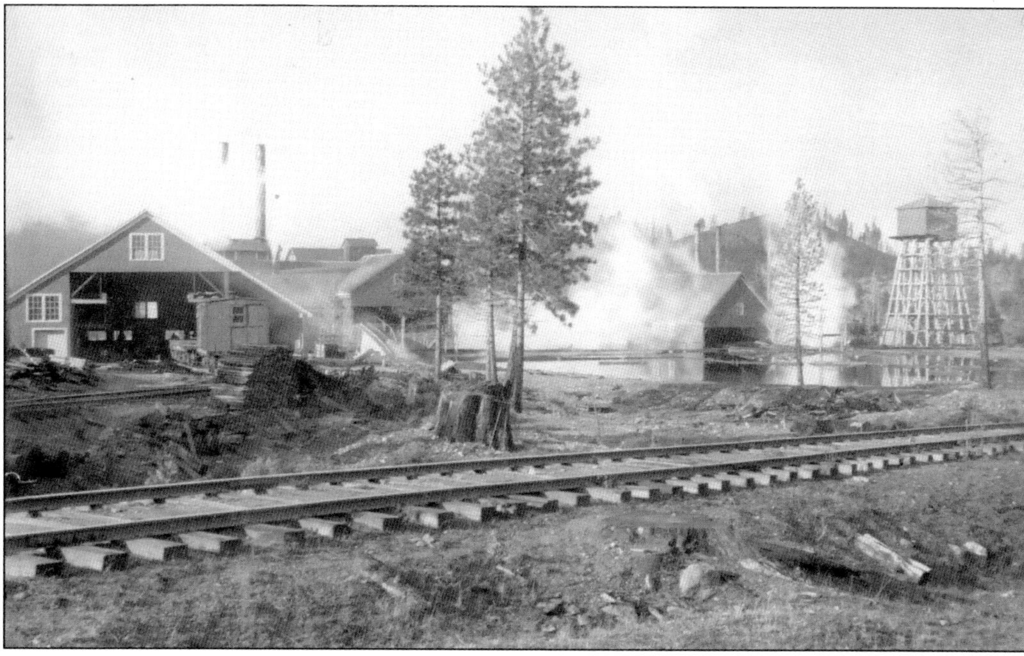

The machine shop (above, left), the first building in Weed, was built in 1900 and is still standing today. In 1902, Abner Weed purchased a band saw (below), which was more efficient than the circular saw, although they both cut about 20 million board feet annually. The band saw cut the logs into 12-to-14-inch cants, or square logs. The cants were then sent to the gang saw, which made simultaneous parallel cuts into boards. The log carriage holds the log, the man holding onto the levers (left) rotates the log, and the block setter (front right) determines the size of the cant. The block setter is Tom McGonigal. The toothed piece at the end of the equipment he is holding is called a dog.

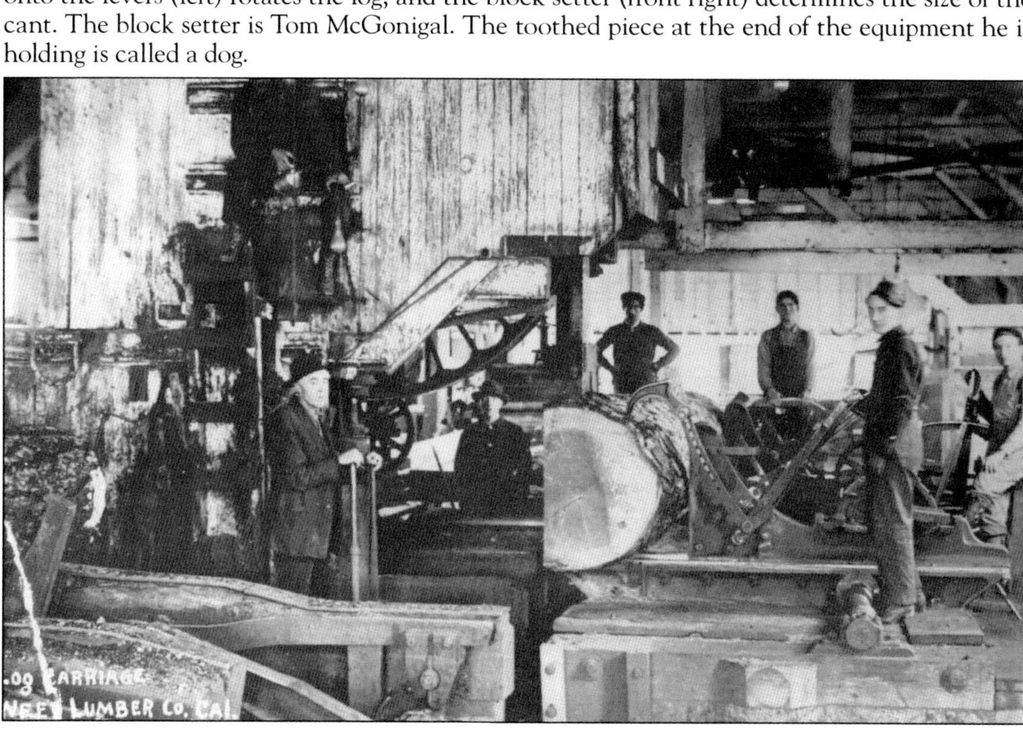

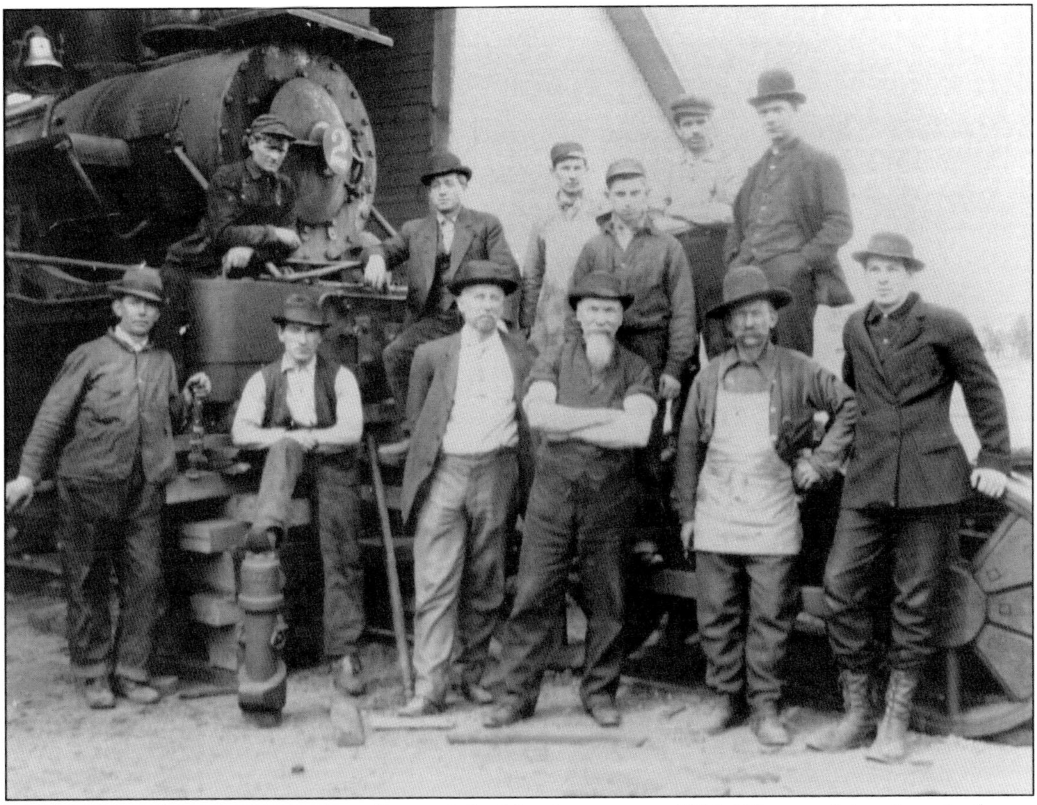

The machine shop crew stands in front of the No. 2 engine in 1910. The machine shop is always the first building constructed because metal parts necessary to build the mill were made and repaired here. The crew also repaired the locomotives and other equipment.

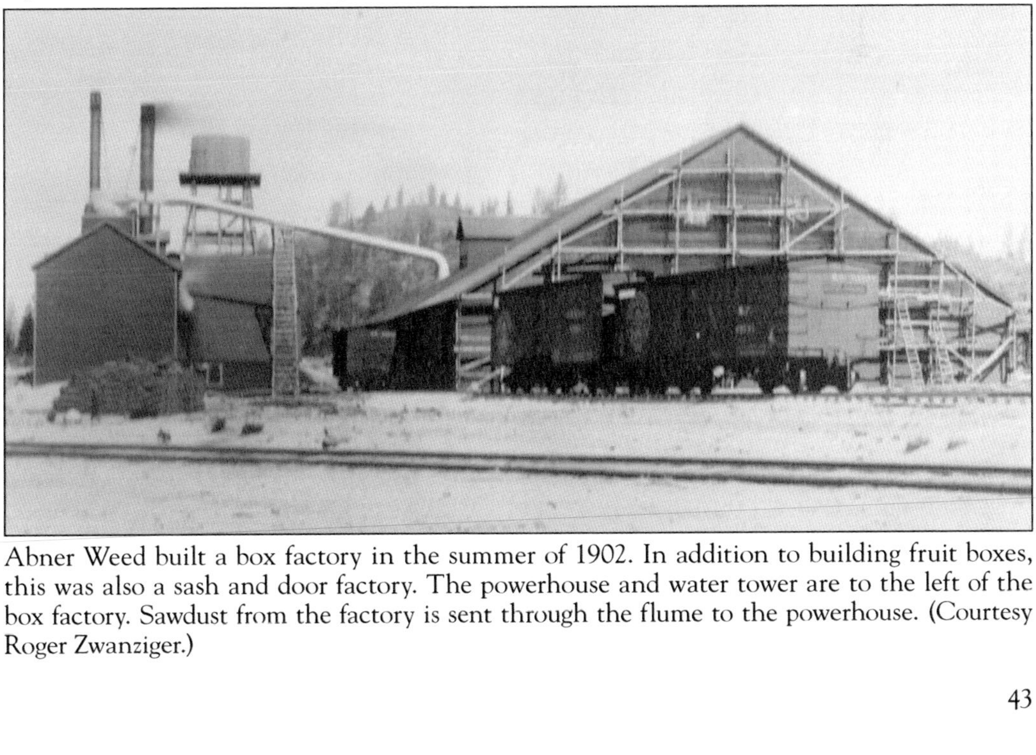

Abner Weed built a box factory in the summer of 1902. In addition to building fruit boxes, this was also a sash and door factory. The powerhouse and water tower are to the left of the box factory. Sawdust from the factory is sent through the flume to the powerhouse. (Courtesy Roger Zwanziger.)

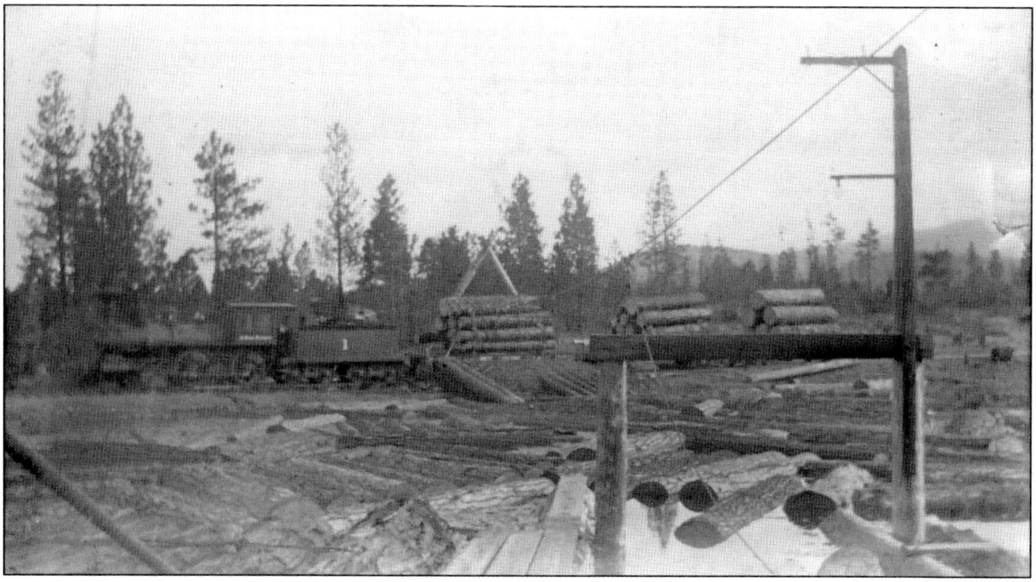

Shown here is a No. 1 engine, a 4-4-0 Portland Locomotive Works steam locomotive built in 1881, at the Weed mill sometime between 1901 and 1903. The Whyte designation 4-4-0 means that it had a two-axle bogie with four small wheels on the front axle, which negotiated curves, and four large wheels on the back axle. Locomotives with this configuration were also called an American, Standard, or eight-wheeler. No. 1 is unloading logs at the log dump. The A-frame has a cable attached to a donkey engine, which helps with the unloading. The same scene from the other side of the track (below) can be seen in this 1901 photograph. In the background is Mill No. 1 with three stacks on the powerhouse. (Below photograph by Mel Carpenter.)

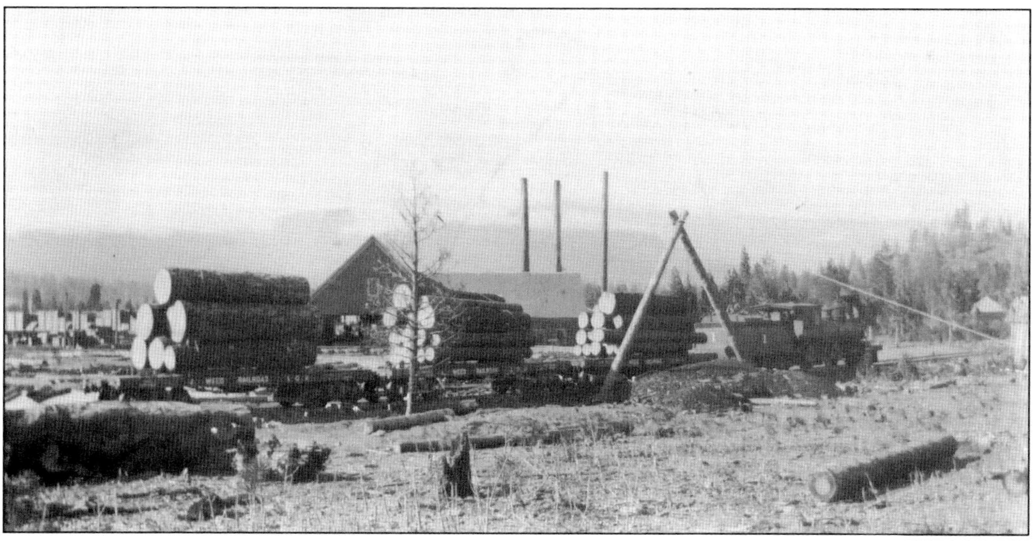

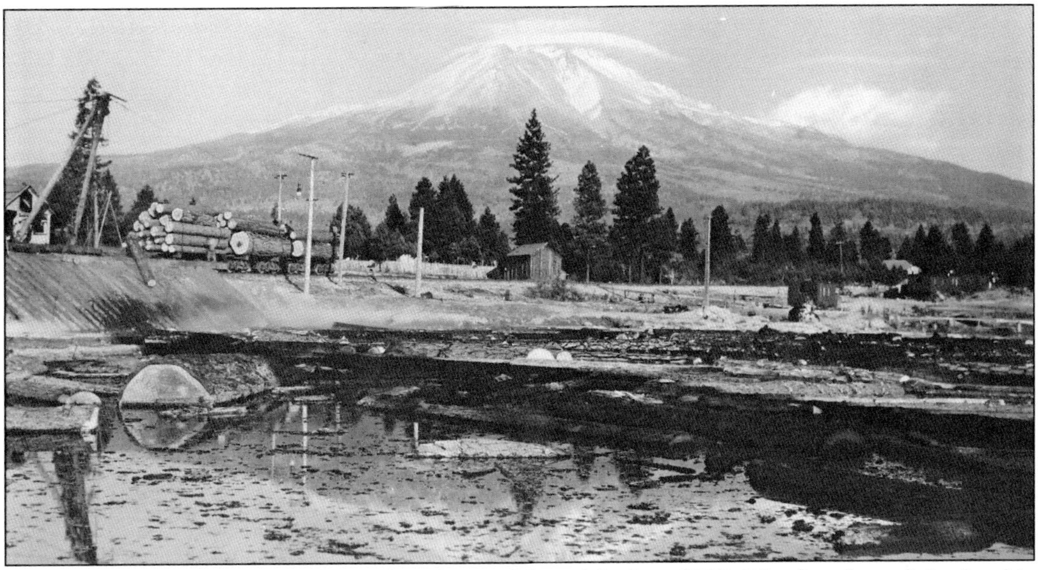

The log dump at the old millpond is shown (above) before 1918. The last log of the load is sliding down the log dump while three more loads wait to be dumped. Mount Shasta looms in the background. The photograph below provides a side view of the unloading landing and log dump in 1922, showing the A-frame and shack that holds the steam donkey. Straps are fastened around the load and then the main line from the donkey is lifted, which dumps the logs into the pond. The man on the right is Louis Welch. (Below photograph by C. E. Yeager; courtesy Louis Welch.)

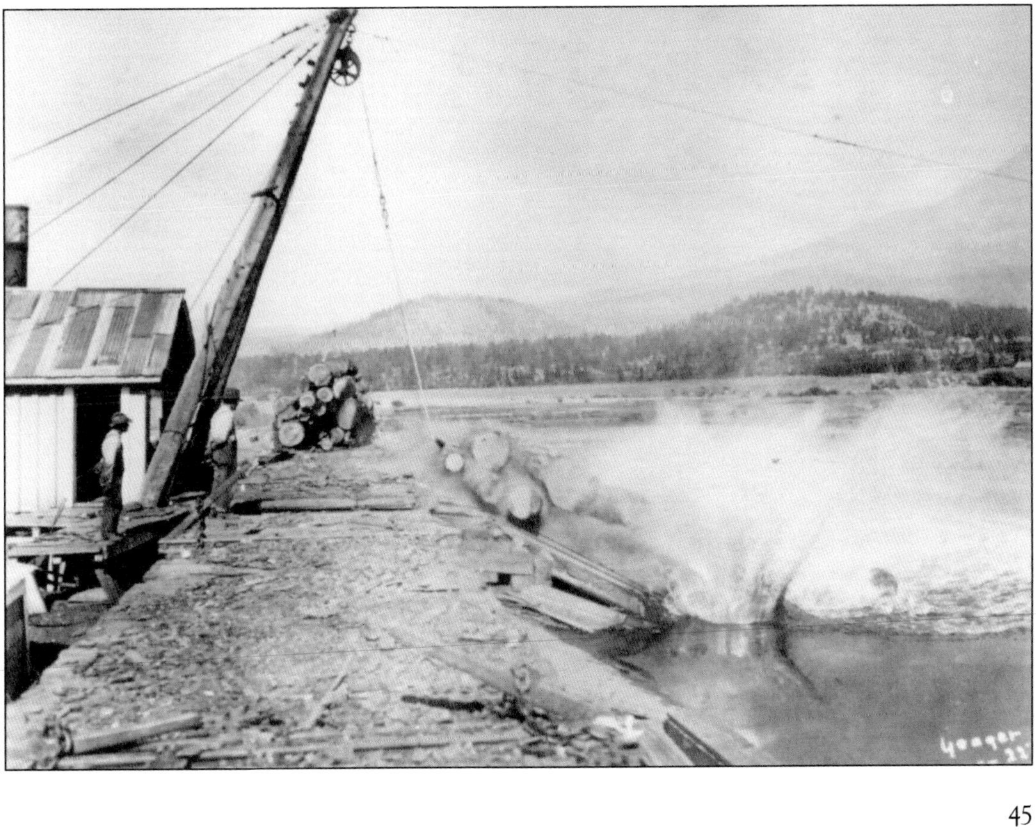

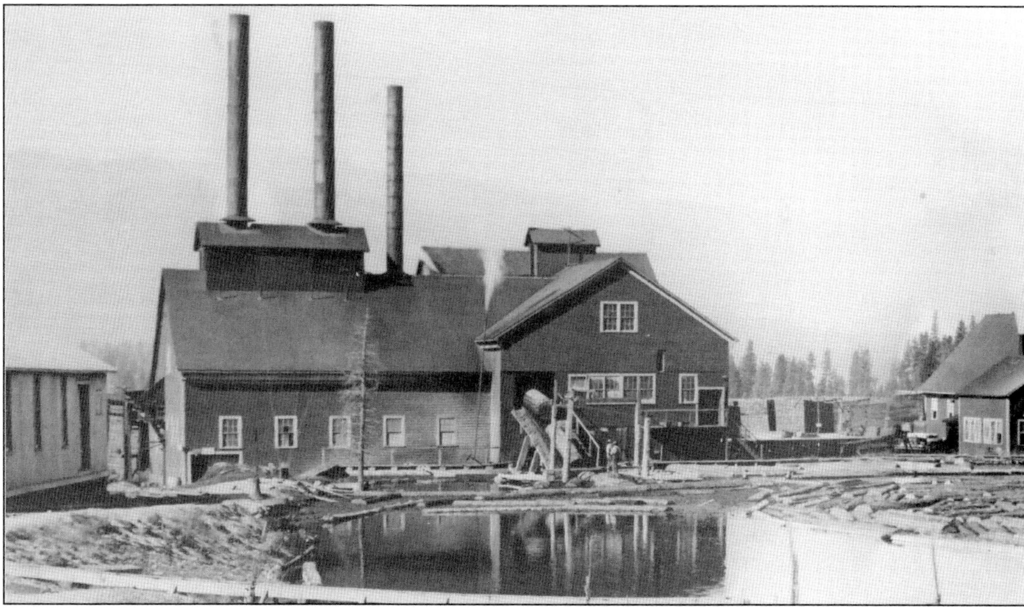

Mill No. 2 (above) is on the left side of a panoramic photograph taken around 1905 (see other half on opposite page). A slip feeder and pond man are standing below the slip on Mill No. 2. The pond man lines up the logs in the pond, so they are ready to feed into the slip. The slip feeder guides the logs onto the slip, which has a chain with teeth called dogs that hauls the logs from the pond into the mill. The photograph below, taken a couple years later, has a burner beside Mill No. 2. Excess wood scraps not used in the powerhouse are burned here. Rooming House No. 1 is to the left of the burner, and the fire lookout is on Schoolhouse Hill. The lookout was torn down in 1921.

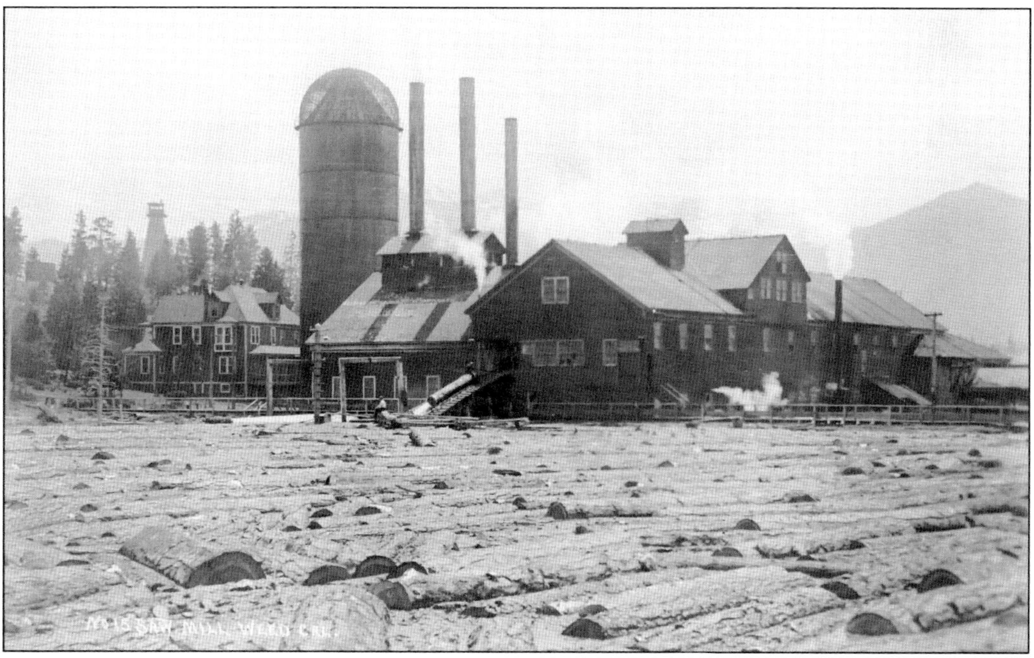

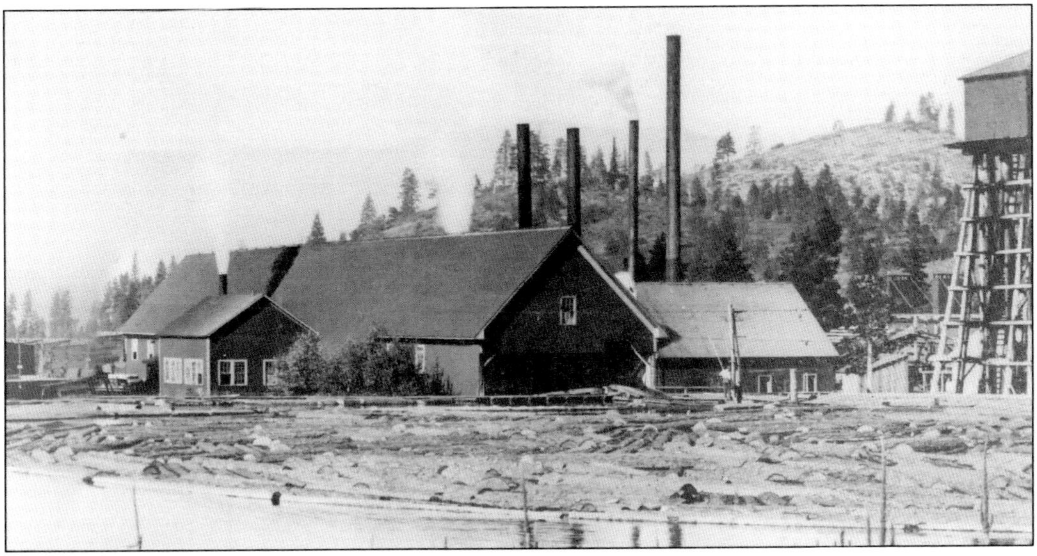

Abner Weed's first mill site was located where the fire station now stands in Weed. There was only one pond, which served both mills. Mill No. 1 (above) has a little "time shack" in front, where paperwork was taken care of. To the right is a water tank, which is 40 feet tall in order to provide pressure. The hill behind Mill No. 1 is called Reservoir Hill, where more water was stored in case of fires. The power plant is the extension attached to the back side of Mill No. 1. It housed an Allis Chalmers steam generator that ran the plant (below).

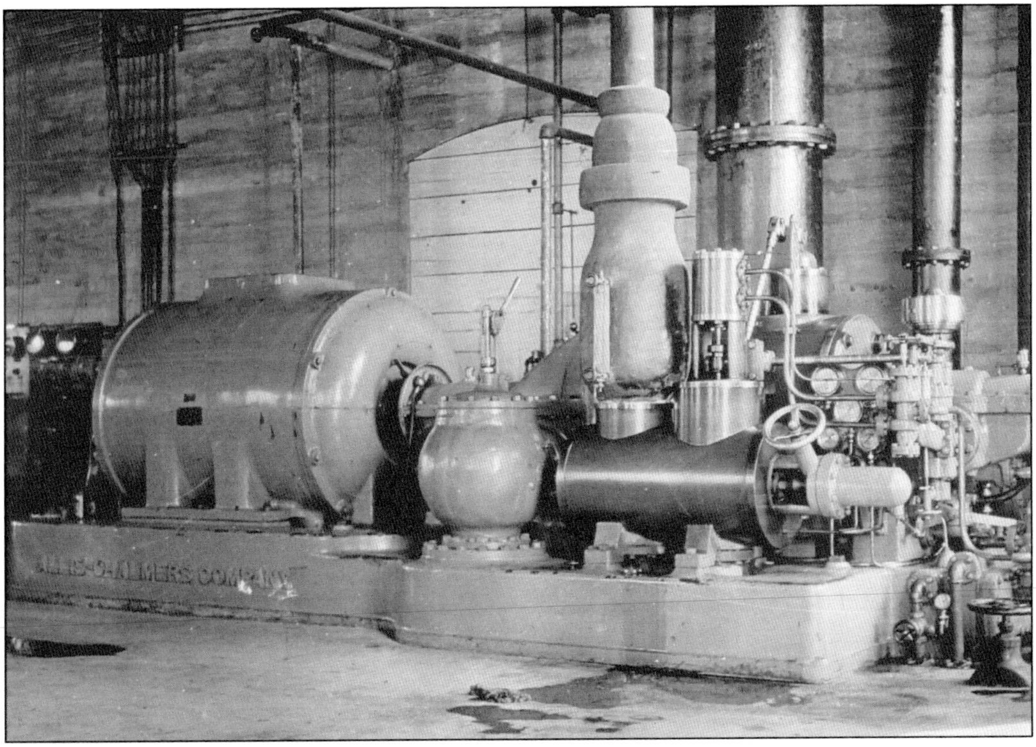

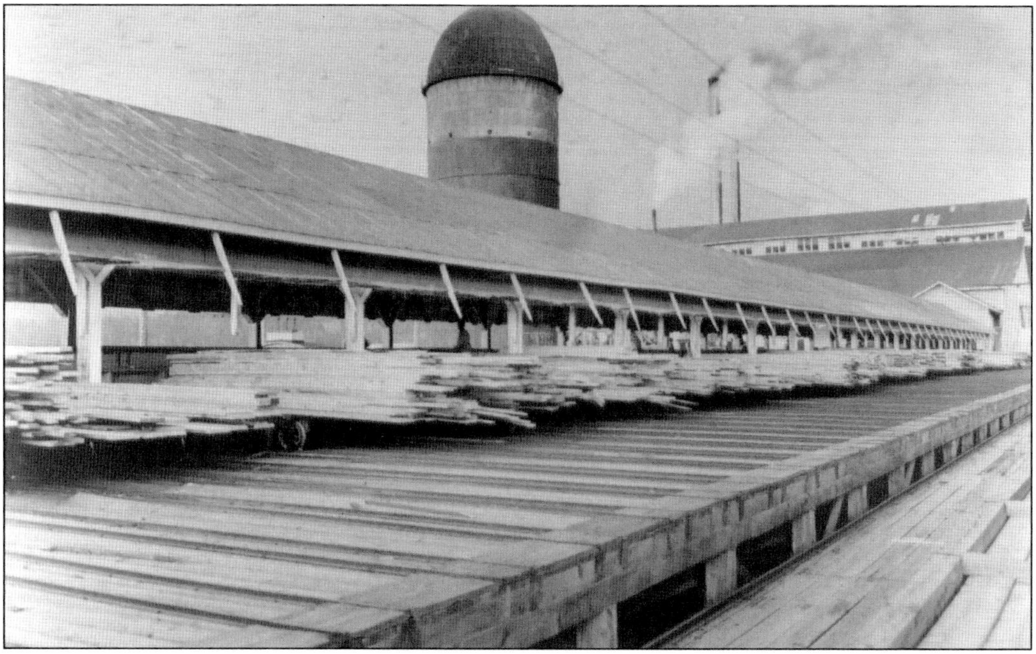

The lumber waiting to head to the kiln was called the green chain (above). The 1922 photograph shows the burner and sawmill in the background and the recessed transfer tracks in the foreground. Twenty or so pullers load the green lumber onto the cars based on grade and thickness. Graded green lumber is being loaded into the stacker (below) in 1922. The boards on the right are "stacked on edge" and ready for the dry kilns. C. E. Yeager was a Medford, Oregon, photographer who came to Weed in 1922. He took photographs for Weed Lumber Company in Tennant and Weed as well as family portraits. After this date, Long-Bell Lumber Company hired Harvey Gilman, who worked at Long-Bell, to take photographs of new projects. (Both photographs by C. E. Yeager.)

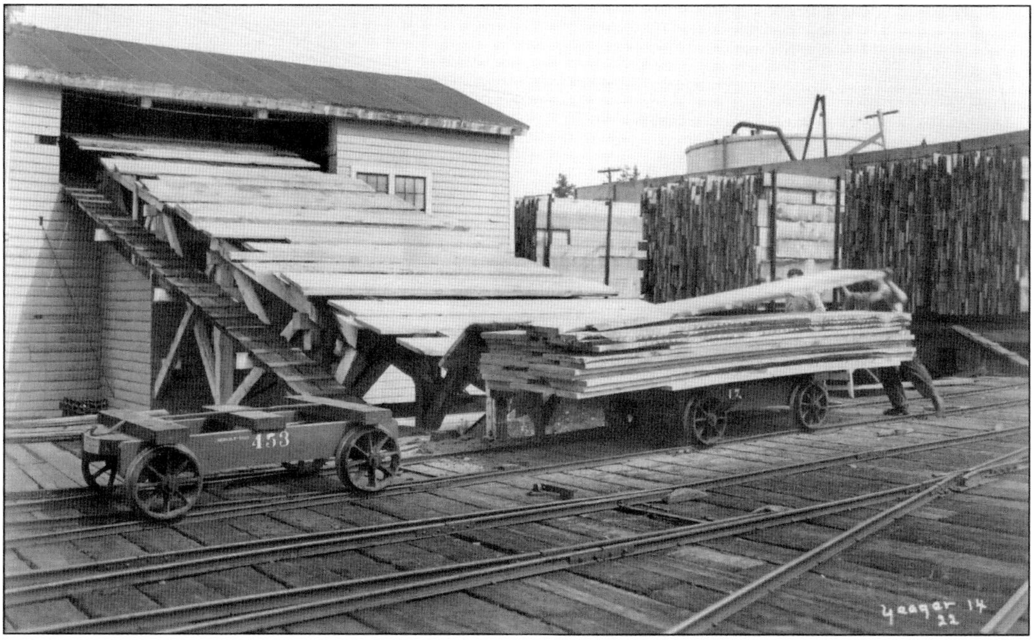

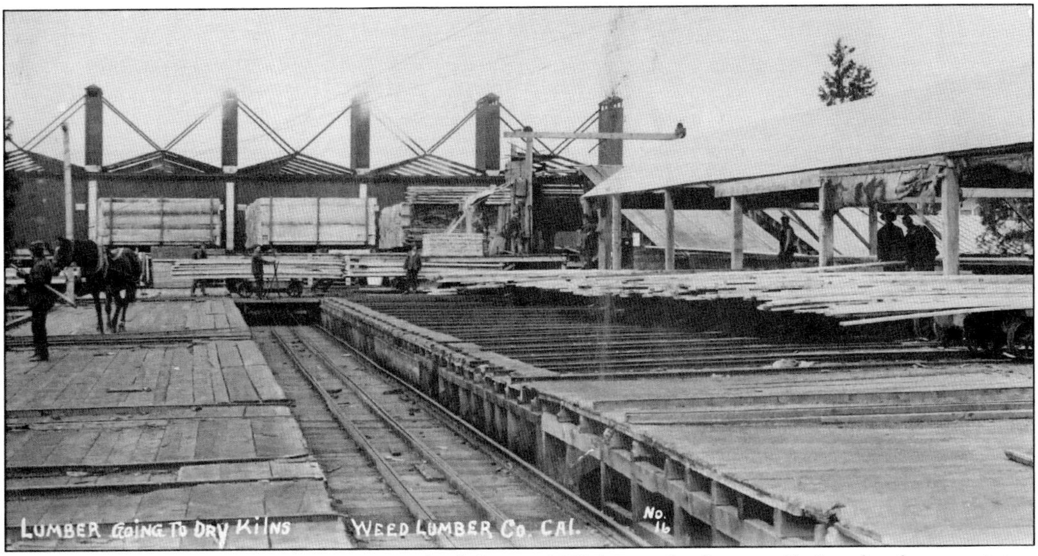

Long-Bell Lumber Company built some dry kilns in 1917 (above background) shortly after acquiring Weed Lumber Company. The green chain is to the right in this photograph. The transfer operator (above and below) rolls "empties" (empty tramcars) into the loading shed along special transfer tracks, which are at a lower level (above foreground). After the tramcars are stacked to a certain height (below), the transfer moves the lumber to the yards or into the dry kiln where they dry for two to seven days. The green chain, with the burner and mill beyond, are in the background. The transfer, or small building (below), and transfer operator are on this side of the transfer tracks. (Above courtesy Roger Zwanziger; below photograph by C. E. Yeager.)

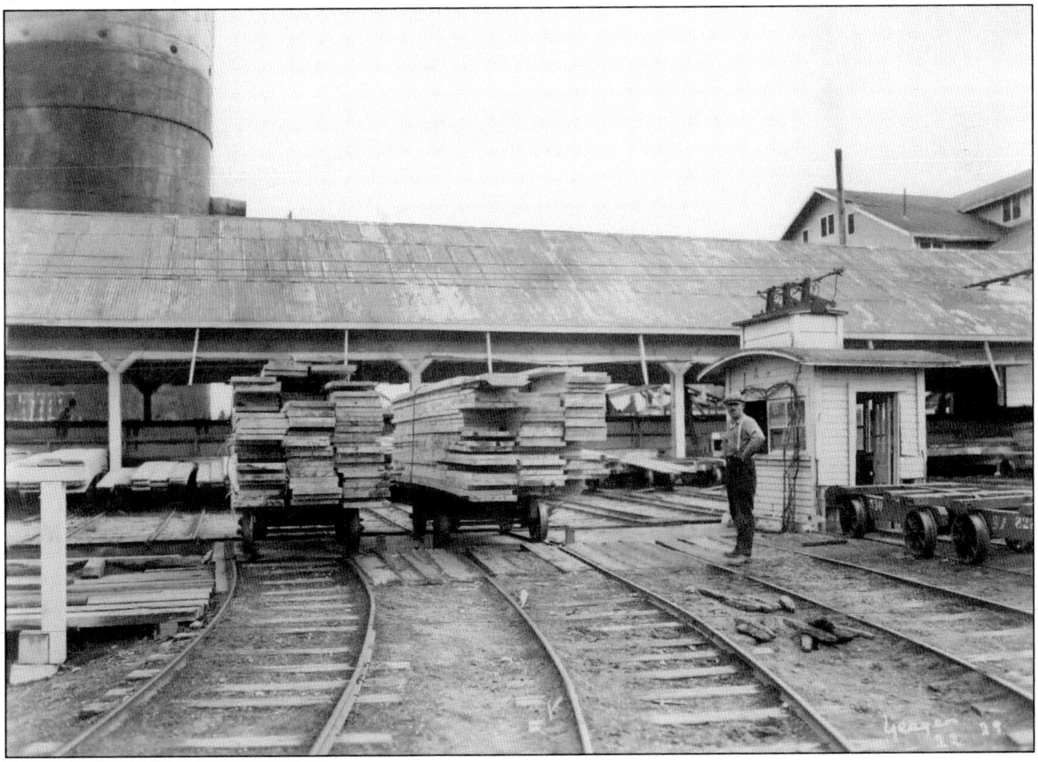

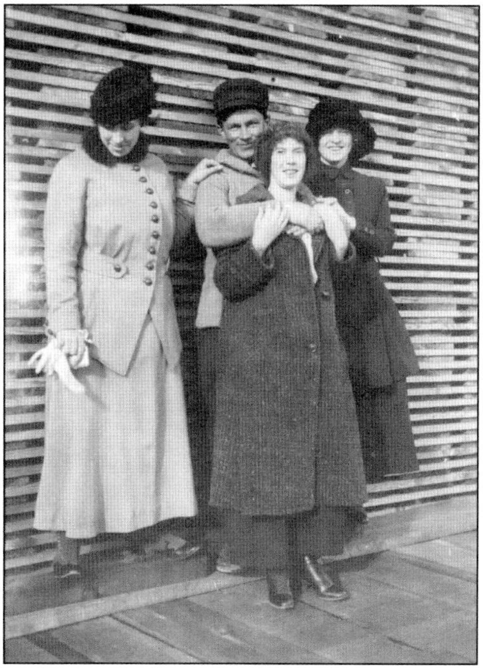

Green lumber foreman George Zwanziger with three women (left) is in front of a stack of drying lumber in the 1910s. Two-by-four fir "stickers" were used as spacers, so the air would circulate and dry the lumber. Fir was used because it did not discolor the pine. In the 1940s, after there were enough dry kilns to dry the lumber, the lumberyards were removed. Lumber was shipped out on trains every day.

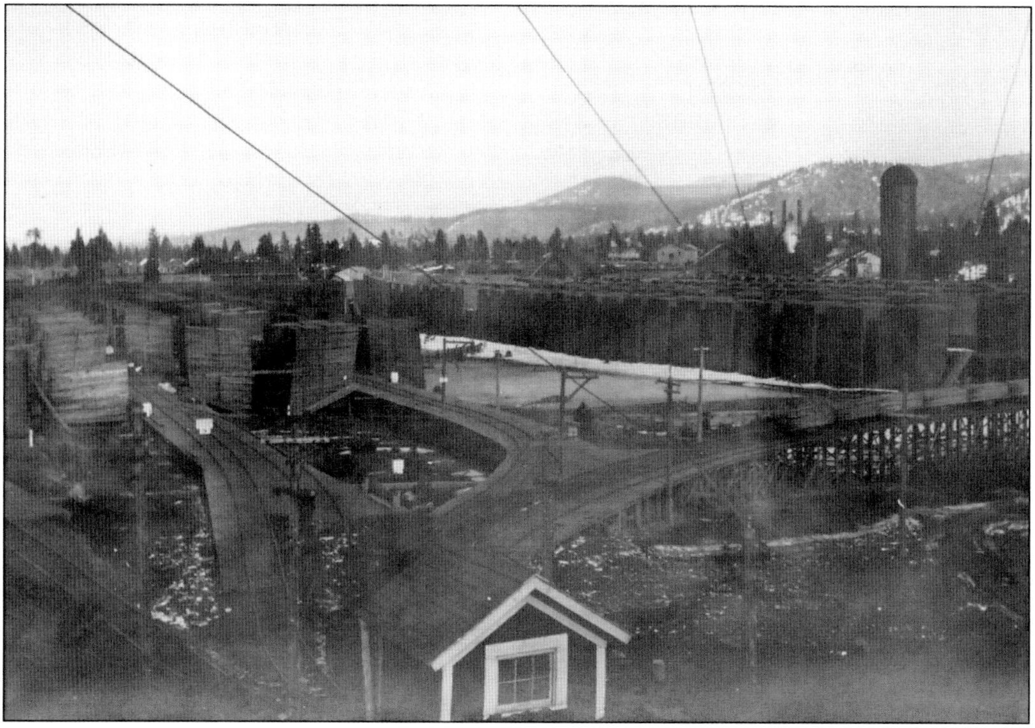

Tram tracks in 1905 were used for hauling dried lumber from the yards to the planing mill or factory. Mill No. 2 is the dark building with a steep roof in the center beyond Yard No. 1. The original burner is to the right. Mill No. 1 is about halfway between Mill No. 2 and the burner. The small building (front center) is one of several hose houses that surround the perimeter of the yard. Many early buildings were painted barn red with white trim. (Courtesy Roger Zwanziger.)

Pictured is George Zwanziger (right) and a friend in the early 1920s standing beside the drying lumber in the yard. George would later marry Camille Albee, the granddaughter of Abner Weed.

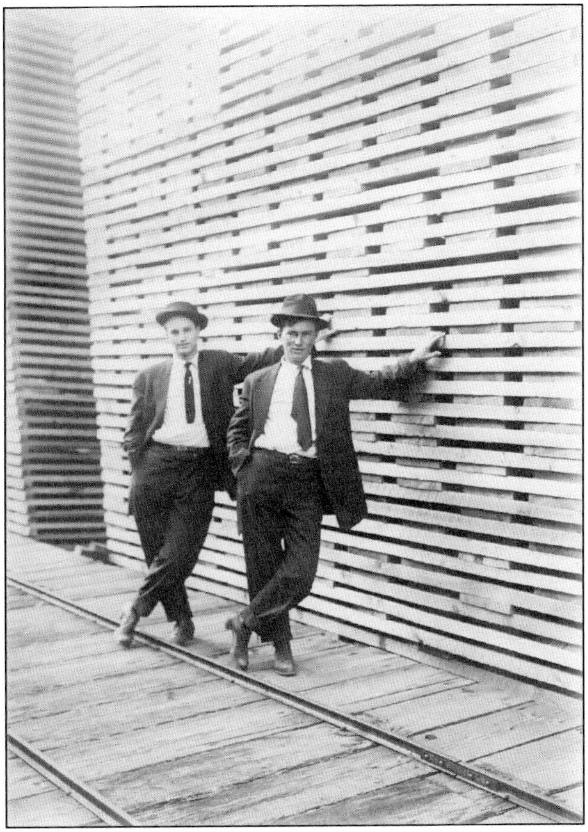

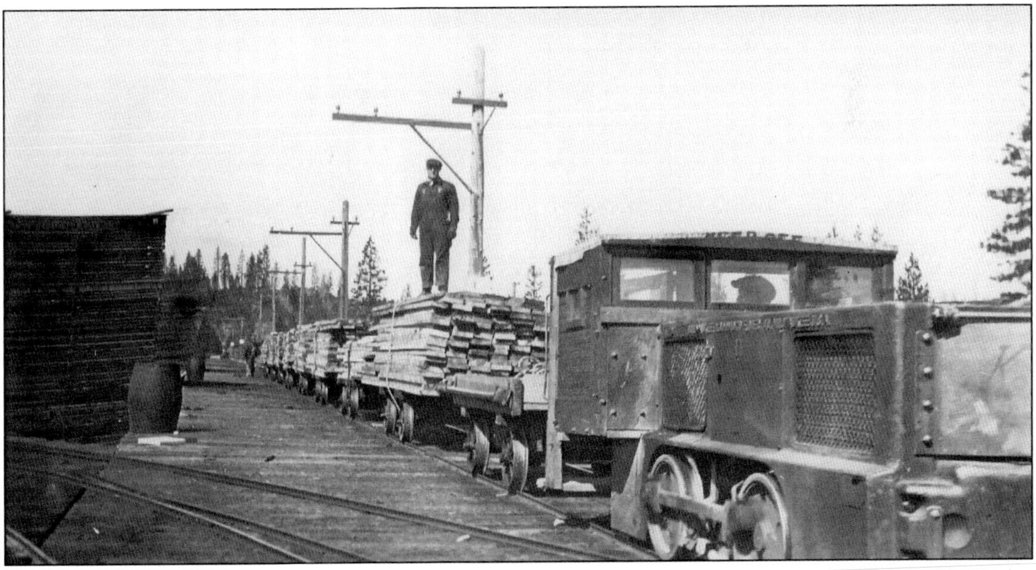

The 1920s tram engine was used to move the lumber from the dry kilns and lumberyards to the planing mill and box factory. On Sundays, boys from town would ride the empty cars all the way from the sawmill to Highway 97 after making sure the switches were all set correctly, so there would not be any collisions. Several tramcars can be seen at the Weed Historic Lumber Town Museum. (Both courtesy Roger Zwanziger.)

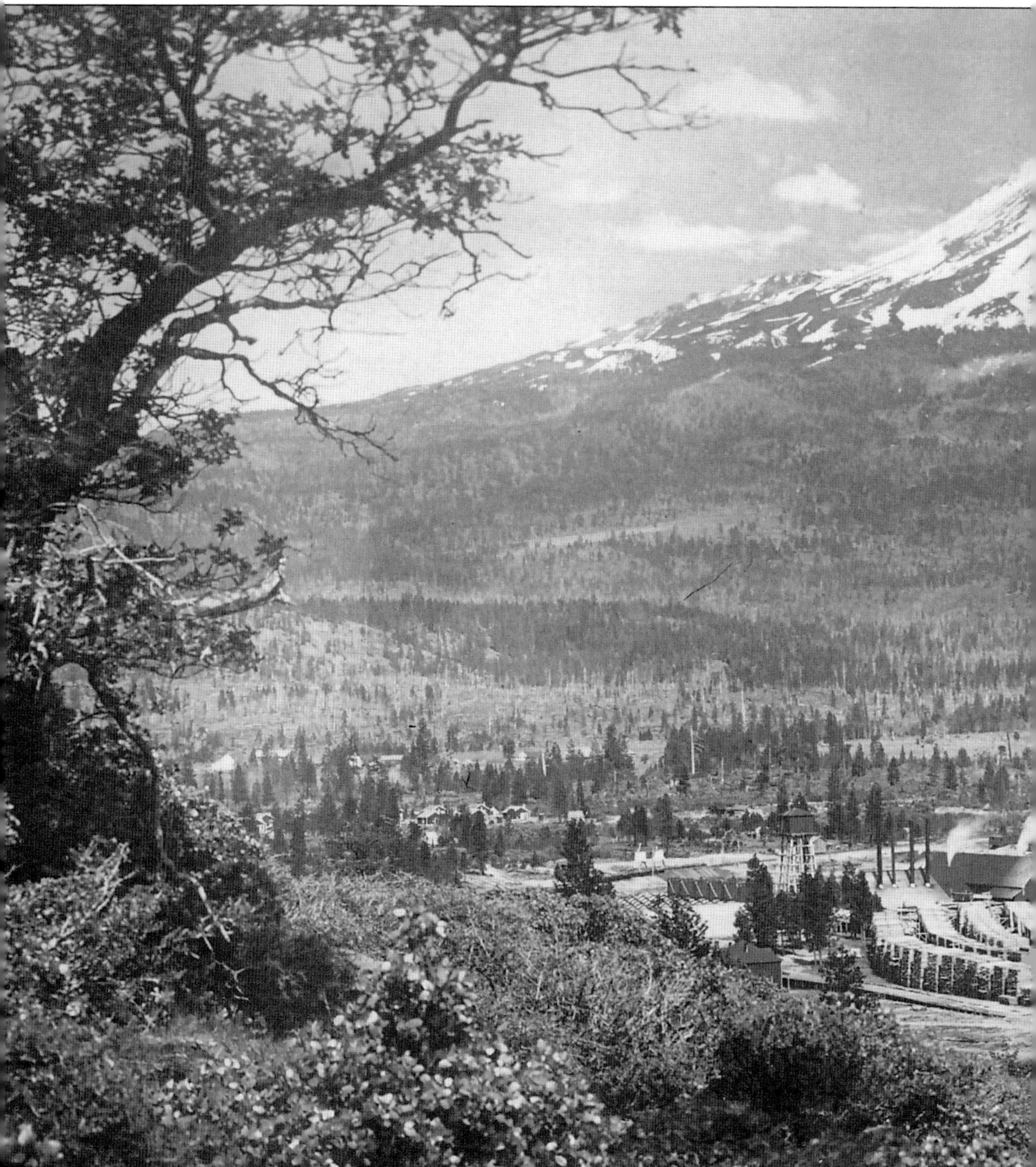

This is an early view of Weed Lumber Company, located at the base of Mount Shasta, in 1907. Beyond Yard No. 1, from left to right, are the water tower, the powerhouse attached to Mill No. 1, Mill No. 2, Rooming House No. 1 with a cookhouse on the lower floor, and Rooming House No. 2. In the background to the left are some company houses. Mount Shasta is one of the major peaks in the Cascade Range. This volcanic range is a result of the subduction of some small oceanic plates off the coast of Oregon, Washington, and Northern California, below the North

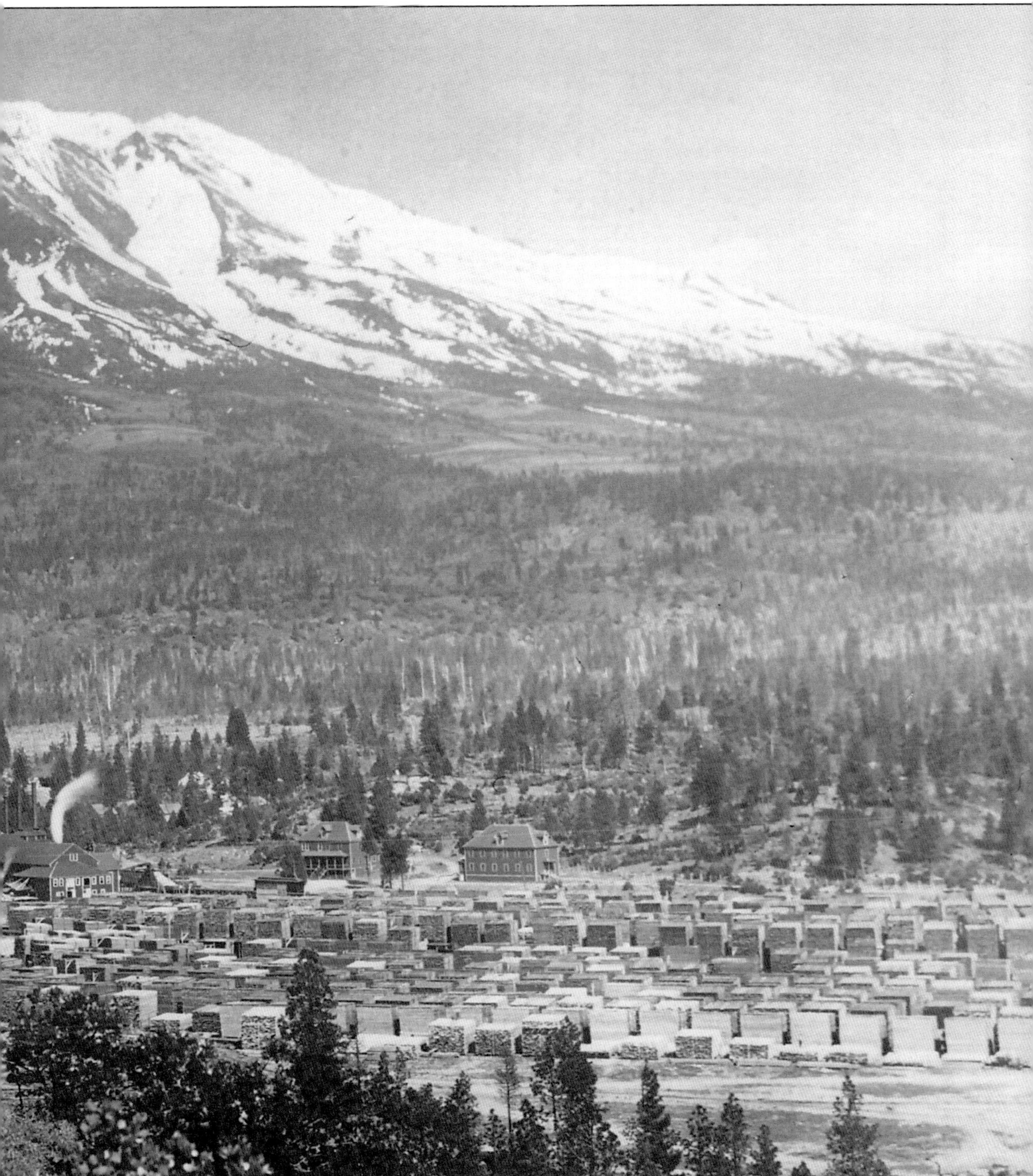

American continent. As the plates subduct, they get hotter and melt. The molten material rises to the surface, forming a volcanic range that stretches from Mount Lassen north to Mount Garibaldi in British Columbia. Shastina is one of four volcanic cones on Mount Shasta. The gash on its western slope is Diller Canyon, named after J. S. Diller, who photographed the glaciers during a USGS survey of Mount Shasta in 1883–1884. The hill behind the two rooming houses (right) would become known as Schoolhouse Hill after a school was built there in 1908.

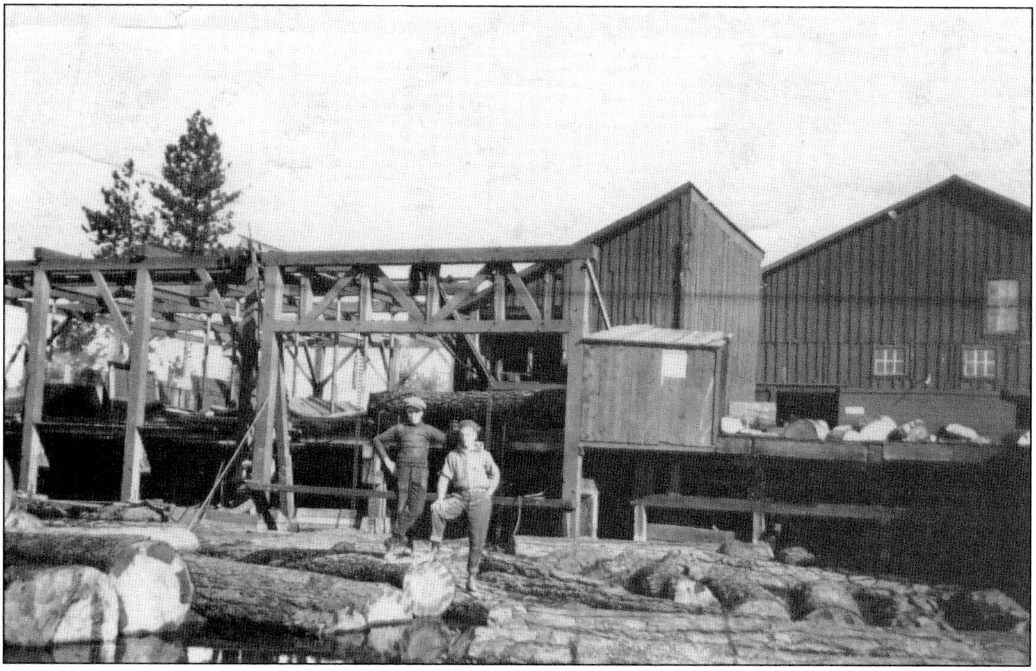

Two men are standing on logs in the log pond at the plywood plant, also called the veneer plant, around 1914 (above). The plywood plant at Weed was the first built in California, in 1911, and the third on the West Coast. By the 1960s, it was the oldest plywood plant in operation in the western United States. It produced panels made of ponderosa. The logs in the pond are cut in 8-foot lengths. The two men load the logs onto the platform behind them. The logs are boiled in a vat for two days to soften them for peeling. In 1919, under the auspices of Bruce Clark, the plywood plant was upgraded with new equipment, including a Proctor Dryer, shown below in 1922. Bruce Clark was the superintendent of the veneer and plywood plant. The green veneer was placed in the dryers and steam-dried for 24 hours. (Photograph by Harold Frodsham; courtesy Carole Steele.)

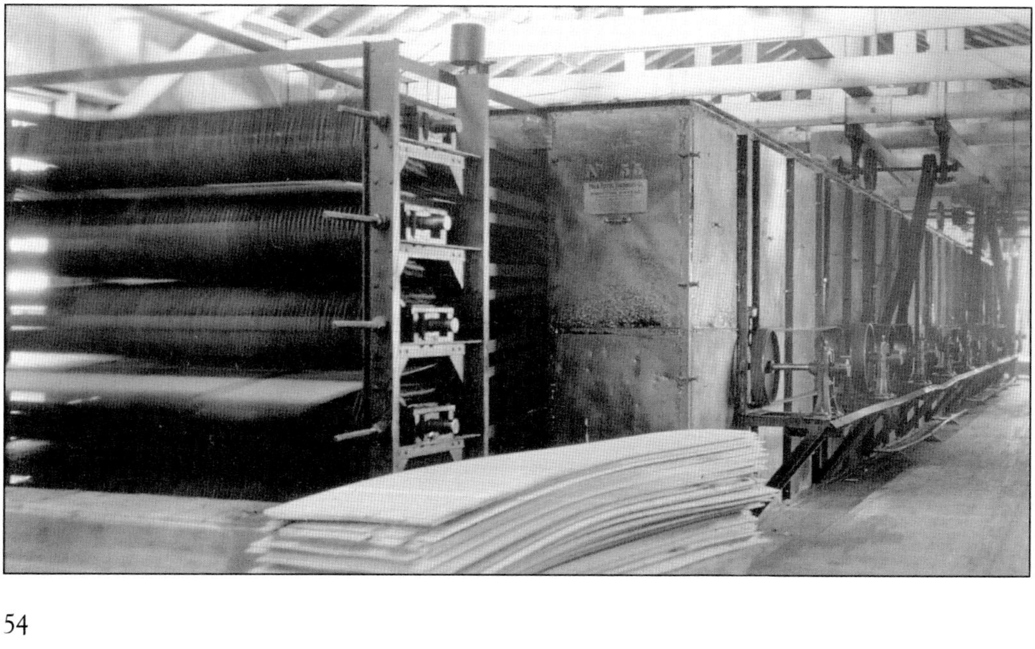

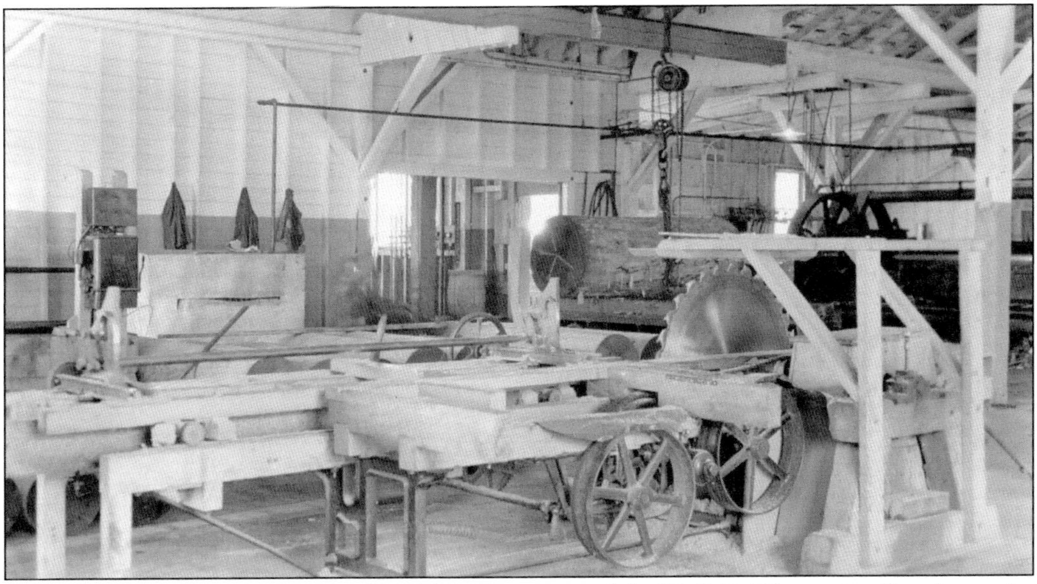

This is the interior of the veneer plant (above) as seen on July 25, 1922. The ripsaw (front) cuts the plywood to size. The table beyond it is where the edges of the ripped plywood are trimmed. Beyond that are logs waiting to be peeled. (Photograph by Harold Frodsham; courtesy Carole Steele.)

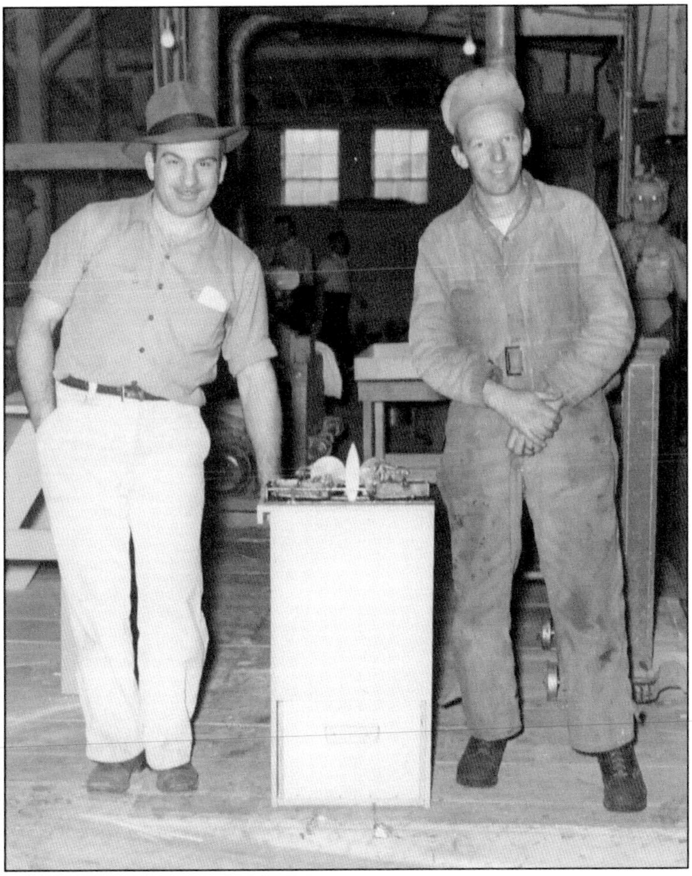

Mario Marchi (left) and Hap de Long are shown with their 1950 boat-tail patch invention, which repairs the knots in the plywood. Mario started working for Long-Bell in 1930 and became the assistant plywood superintendent in 1954. When his boss, John Dohrn Sr., was promoted to plant superintendent in 1967, Mario became the new plywood superintendent.

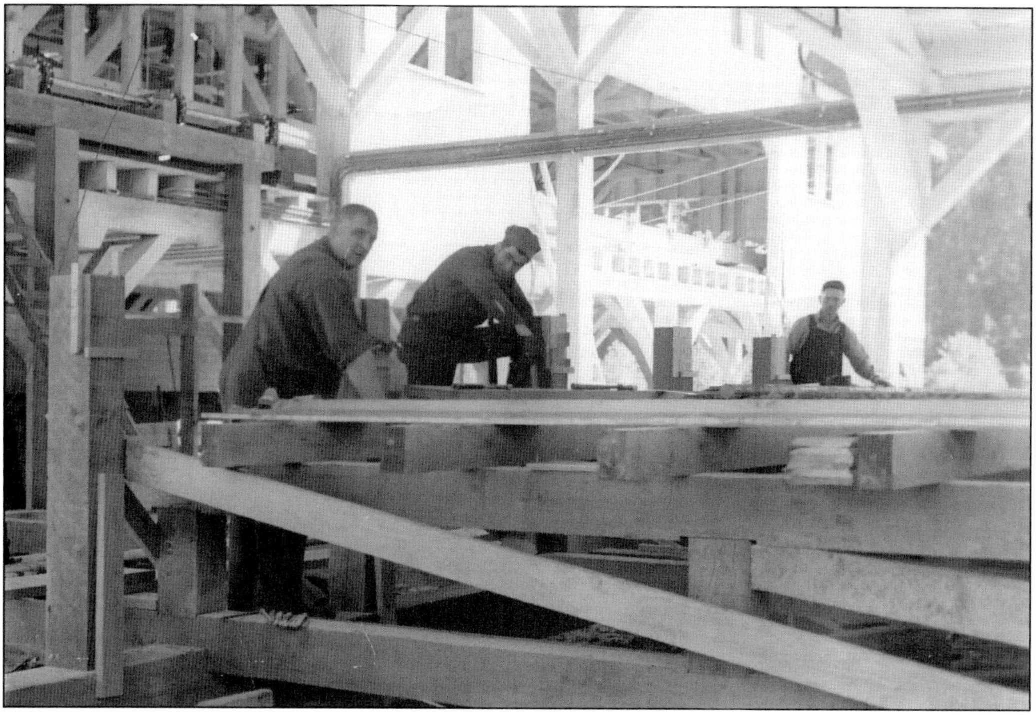

This photograph shows the construction of the new mill at the new site in 1917–1918. This building was still called the New Mill until it was torn down in 1983. Ed Dickey (left) was a machinist at the mill.

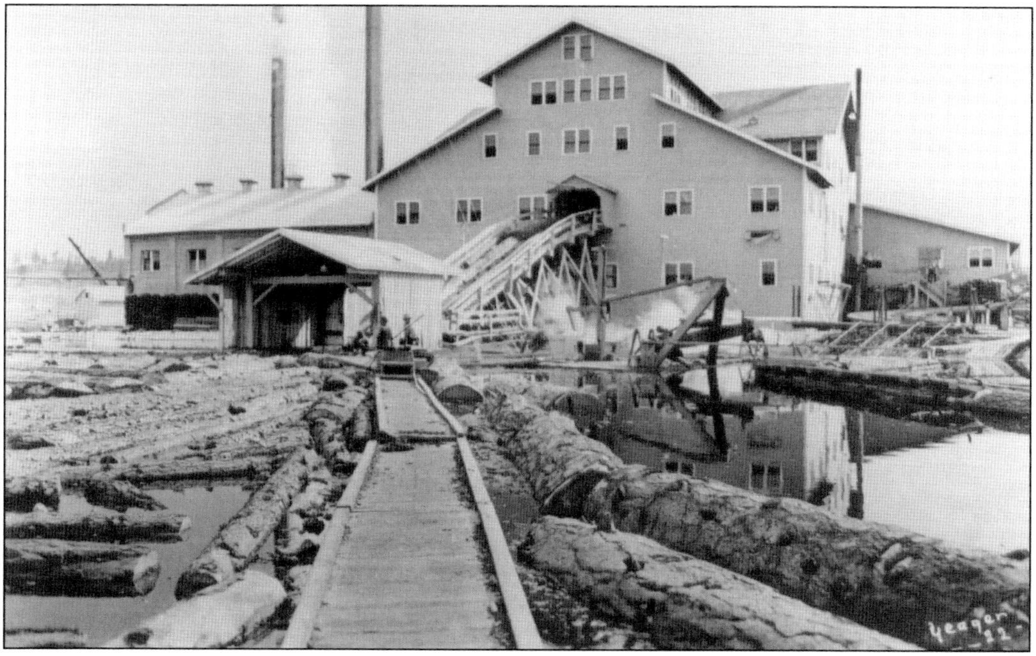

Pictured is the New Mill in 1922 with logs in the pond waiting to go up into the mill on the slip chain. The slip chain, which hauls the logs up the slip, is also called the "endless chain." (Photograph by C. E. Yeager.)

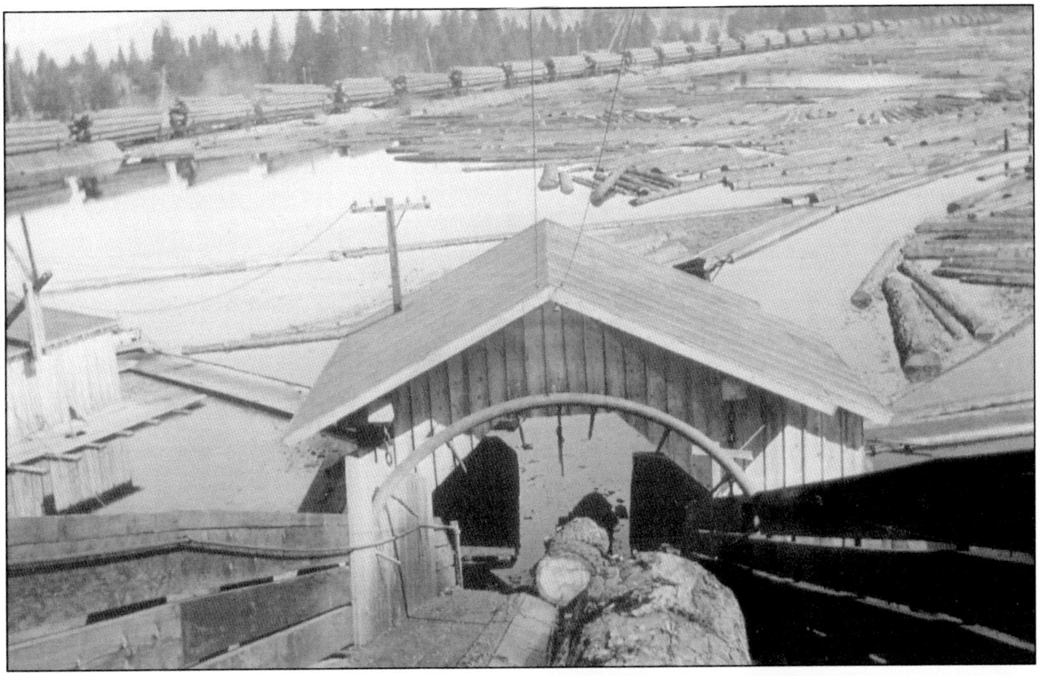

The slip (above) is shown as seen from the New Mill around 1955. Notice the logger train in the background, dropping off logs at the log dump (upper left). (Photograph by Alford Linville.)

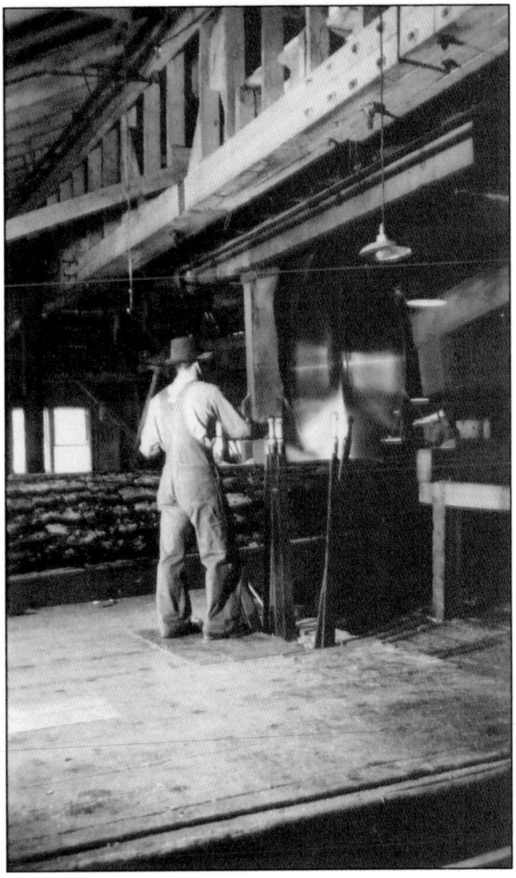

The lever man operates the levers that bring the logs up the slip into the sawmill. The 32-foot logs were then cut into 16-foot lengths on the deck saw. The 1938 photograph shows Alford Linville at the levers. Alford says his favorite job was when he was "a ramblin wreck from the sawmill deck and a helluva leverman." (Photograph by Harvey Gilman; courtesy Alford Linville.)

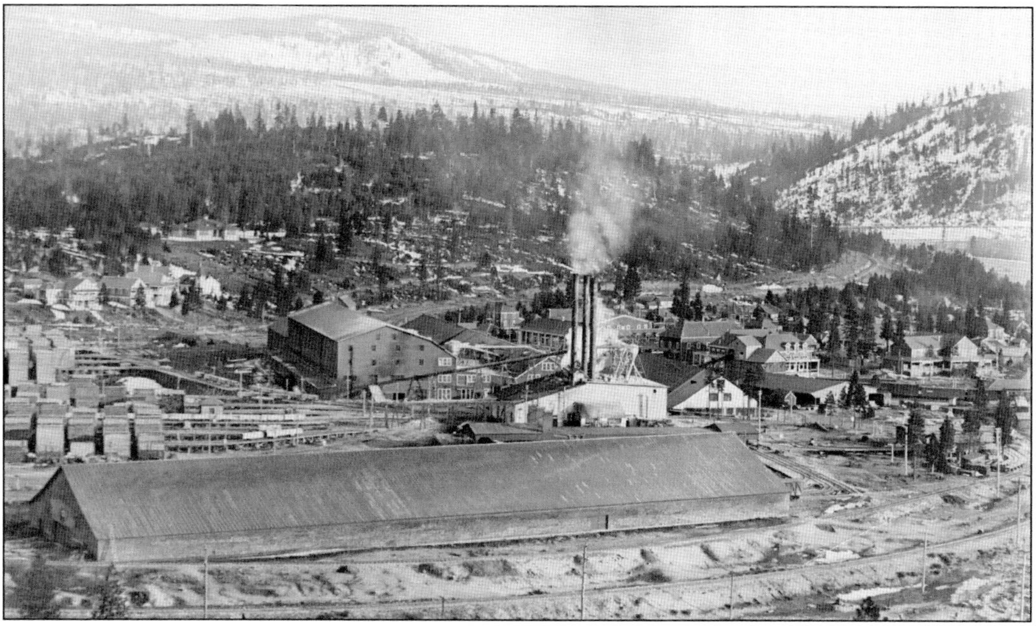

Weed in the 1920s is pictured above. The long building in the foreground is the planing mill. The light building near the center with the three stacks is the powerhouse. The building to the left is the sash and door factory built in 1909. To the right of the factory, just behind the stacks, is the Weed Mercantile. Between the "Merc" and the railroad tracks is Grandma White's house, mother of Jude White and grandmother of Julian White, but called Grandma White by all. At the base of Schoolhouse Hill, beyond the railroad tracks, is the schoolhouse built in 1922. The fancy building below and to the left of the school are the houses of the upper management, often called "Nob Hill" by the workers in the mill. Long-Bell Lumber Mill (below) is shown in front of Mount Shasta. The structure on the far left used to take refuse to the burner, which is no longer standing. (Above photograph by Pres Fidler, courtesy Roger Zwanziger; below photograph by J. H. Eastman, courtesy College of the Siskiyous Library Mount Shasta Collection.)

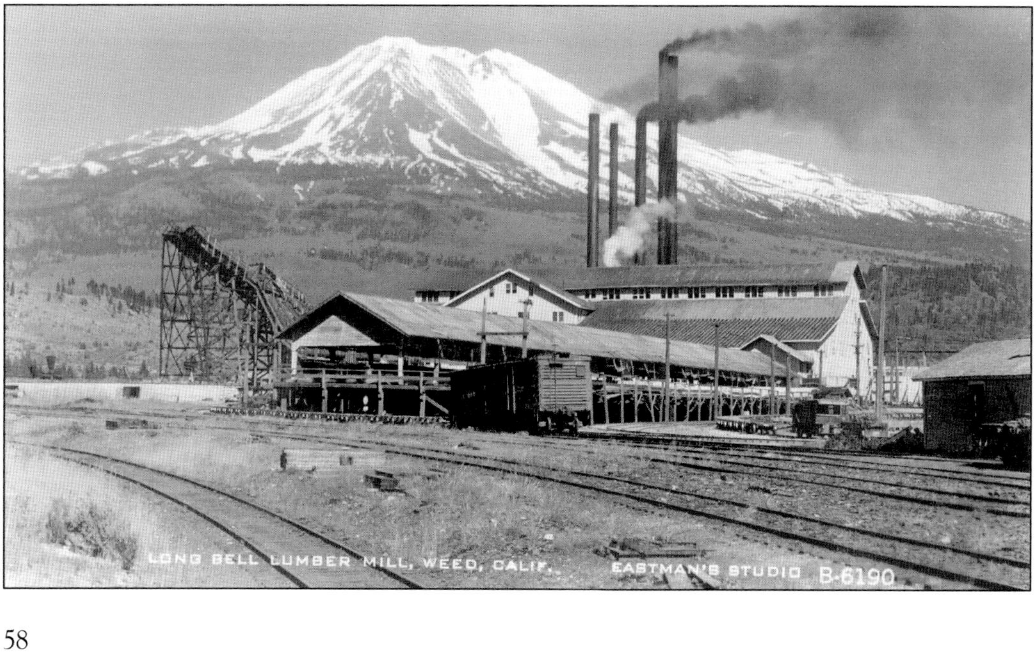

A new Teepee Burner (right), purchased in 1928, was 220 feet high, the tallest burner in the world at the time. The conveyor, to the right of the burner, cut scrap wood into 16-foot lengths for selling as firewood; it was dropped into a car below. The rest of the scraps went into the burner.

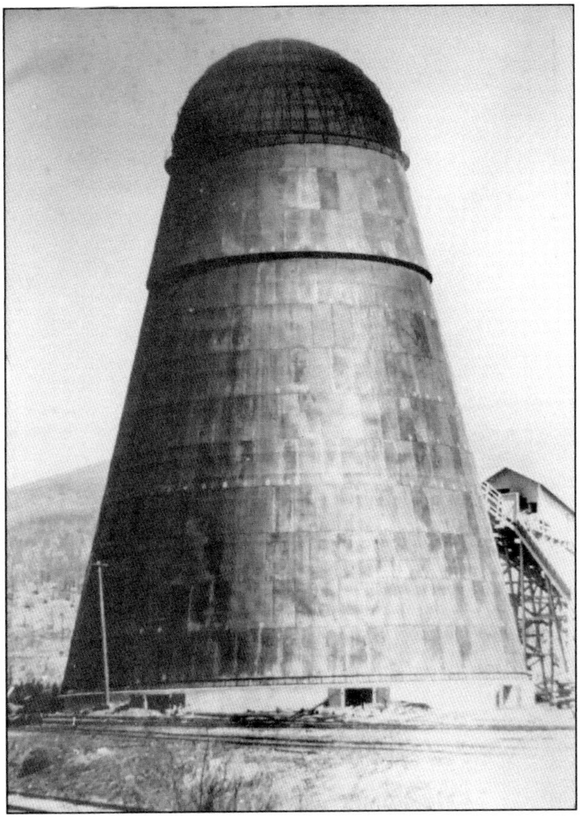

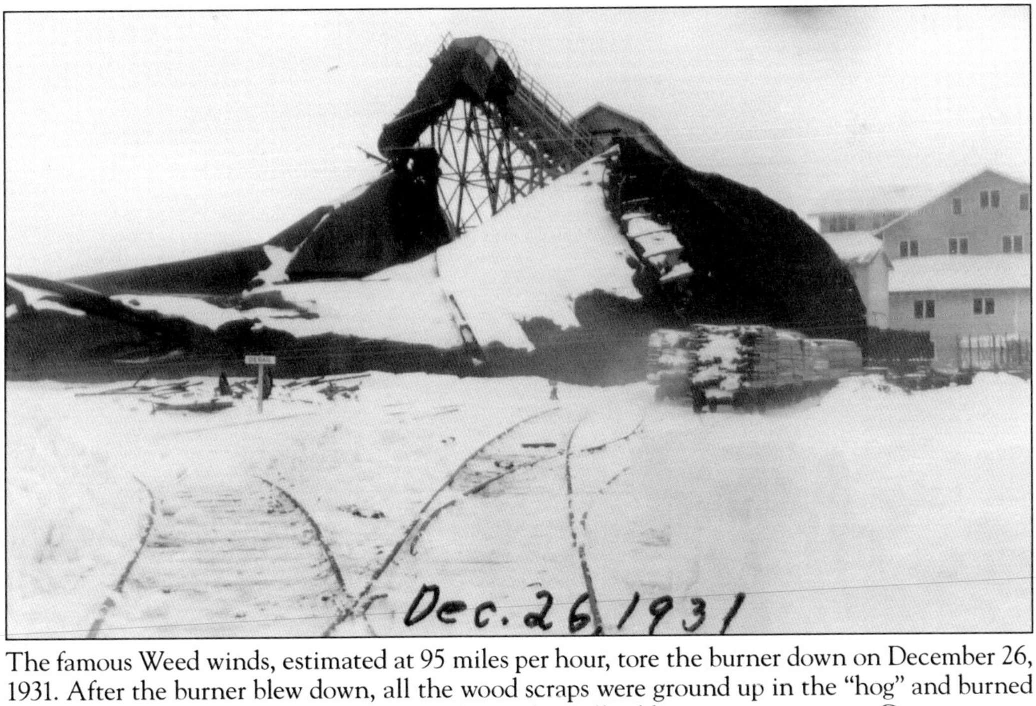

The famous Weed winds, estimated at 95 miles per hour, tore the burner down on December 26, 1931. After the burner blew down, all the wood scraps were ground up in the "hog" and burned in the powerhouse for energy to run the plant. The mill sold its excess energy to Copco.

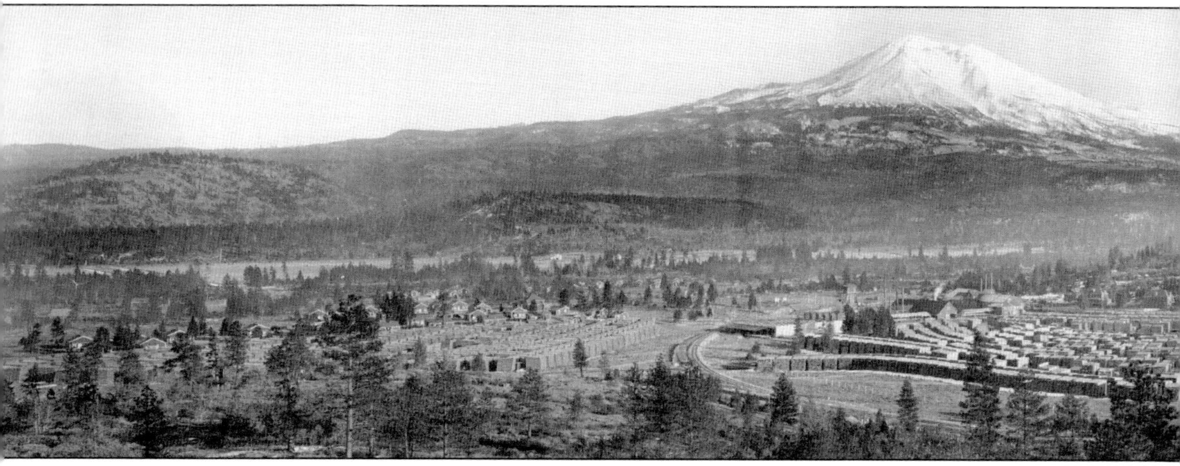

Pictured is a July 27, 1931, panorama of the Long-Bell Lumber Company. Mount Shasta and Black Butte are the two main peaks in the distance. Schoolhouse Hill and Dogwood Hill, where

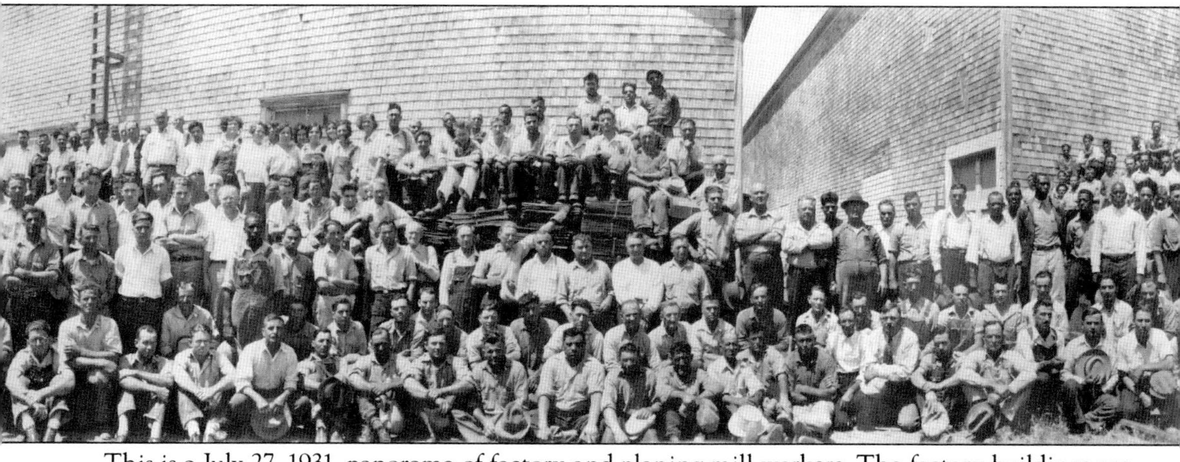

This is a July 27, 1931, panorama of factory and planing mill workers. The factory buildings are behind the workers, and the two houses are on Nob Hill, now known as Schoolhouse Hill. Ted

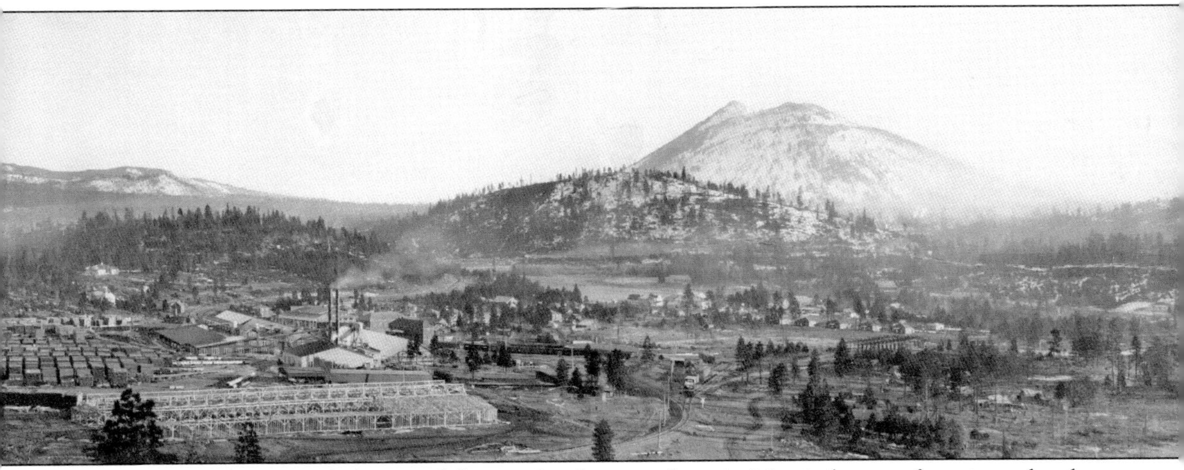

schoolboys would go to pick dogwood flowers for their teachers in May in hopes of passing school in June, are the two large hills between Mount Shasta and Black Butte.

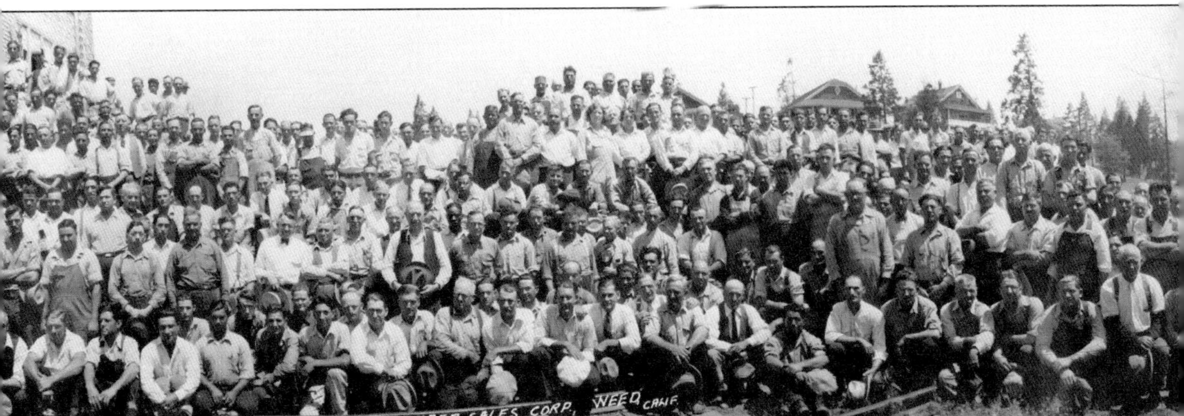

Garrett is in the front row near the center to the right of the man with glasses in the dark vest.

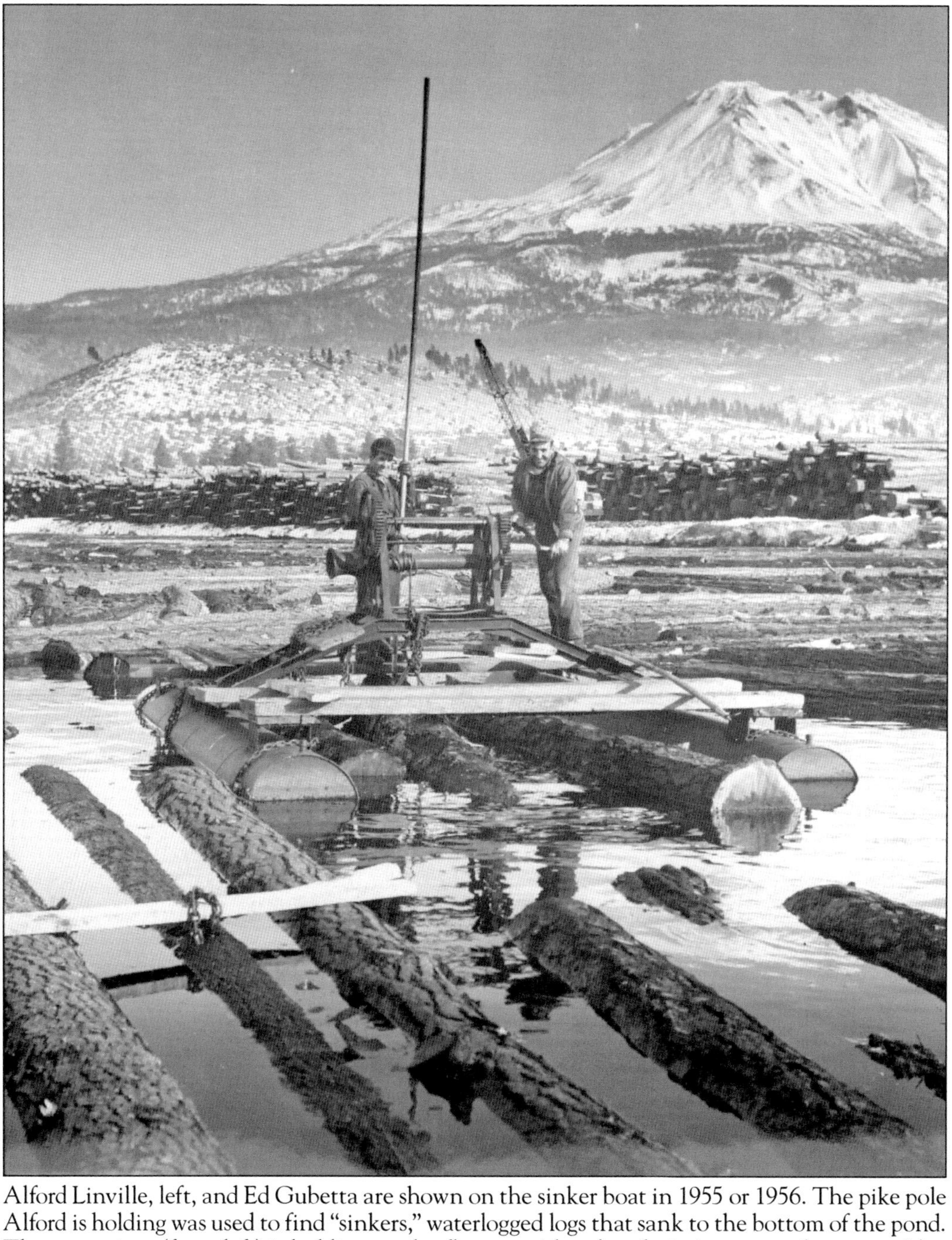

Alford Linville, left, and Ed Gubetta are shown on the sinker boat in 1955 or 1956. The pike pole Alford is holding was used to find "sinkers," waterlogged logs that sank to the bottom of the pond. The cross-piece (front left) is holding up the floaters with a dog chain in a set-up known as "dog to log." The logs were sent through the slip house and up the chute to the sawmill. (Courtesy Alford Linville.)

Alford Linville (right) is shown in 1936 with his new "Bone Dry" logging boots, which he purchased for his first job at the mill as a pond man. The boots had steel caulks, or spikes, on the bottom so that the log roller could keep a good footing. Ideally, the boots would keep the pond man's feet "bone dry," but it did not always work that way. Alford said, "Nothing was colder than a pair of wet boots in the wintertime." These selfsame boots are part of the exhibit at the Weed Historic Lumber Town Museum. (Courtesy Alford Linville.)

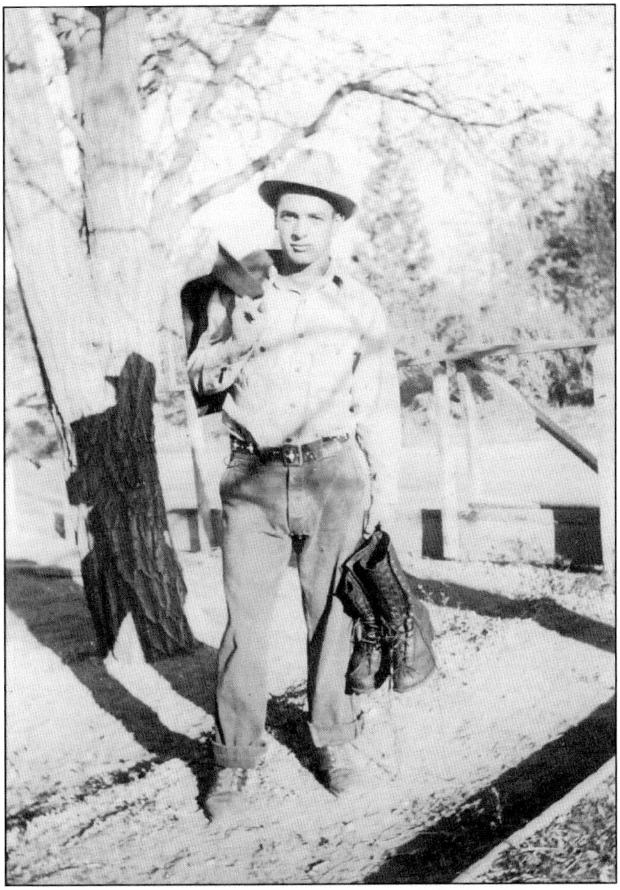

Pete Bernardi (below, left) and Roy Barnum (third from right) are shown working inside the factory in 1929. Bernardi is running the sticker machine, which packages box kits for California Fruit Growers Exchange. The boxes for shipping produce are assembled in the field. (Courtesy Pete Bernardi.)

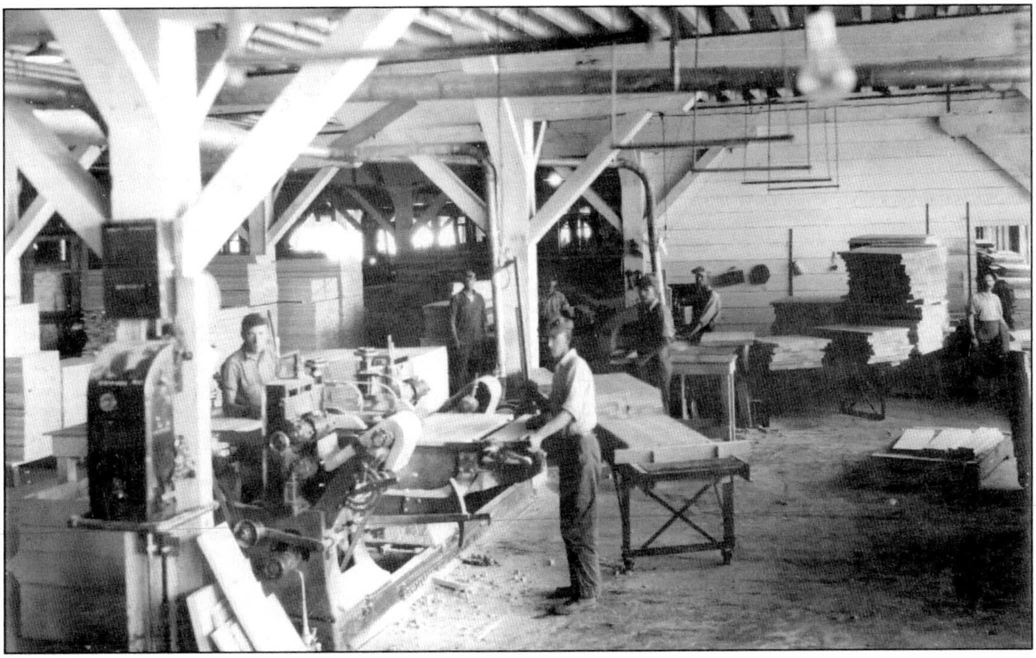

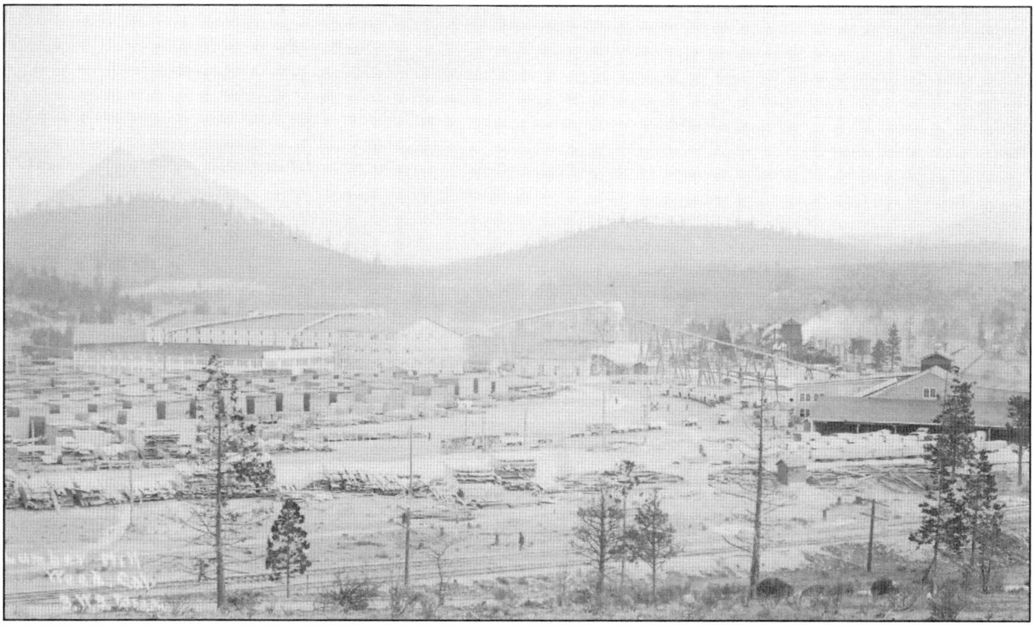

This late 1920s–1930s photograph was taken from Reservoir Hill. The factory is to the left, the powerhouse is in the center, and the planing mill is on the right. The pipes carry sawdust from the planing mill to the powerhouse, which generates power for the plant. (Photograph by Frank Paterson.)

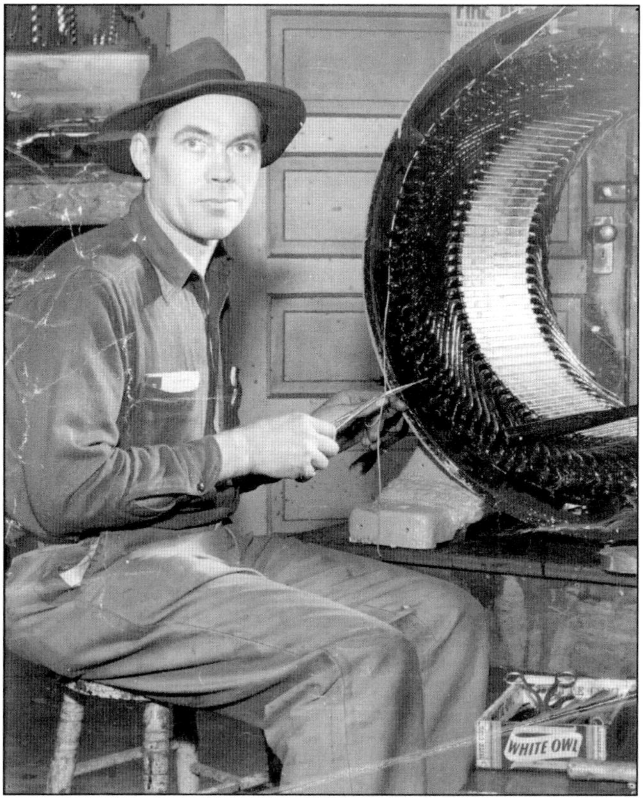

Shown here is Leslie Robert "Les" Kyle (left) working on the generator in the 1940s. Kyle moved to Weed in the 1920s and was an electrician for Long-Bell and International Paper. During World War II, Kyle and Roger Zwanziger were scoutmasters for the Boy Scouts. Kyle served as the Weed chairman during the 1942 nationwide rubber-salvage campaign. Troops 31 and 32 collected 28,600 pounds in three days. (Courtesy Etta Ruth Kyle.)

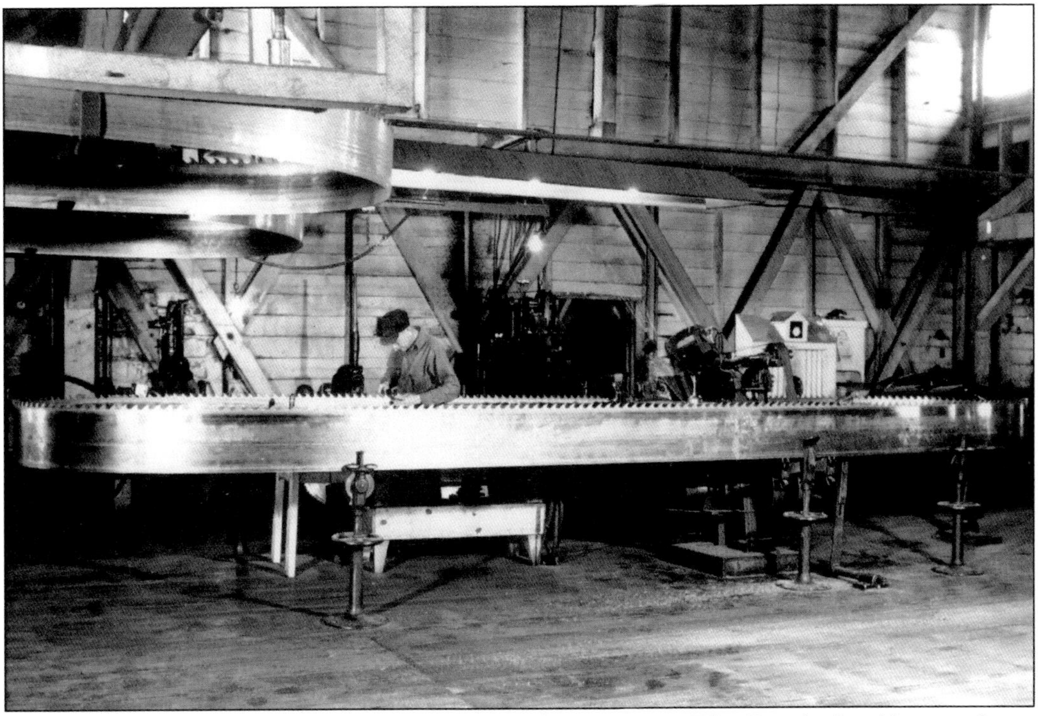

The filing room in the loft of the sawmill is shown here in 1940. "The Grinder," or filing machine, slowly filed each tooth. The fitter sets the teeth as they go by, alternating the teeth to the inside and outside. (Photograph by Harvey Gilman; courtesy Madelon G. Gilman.)

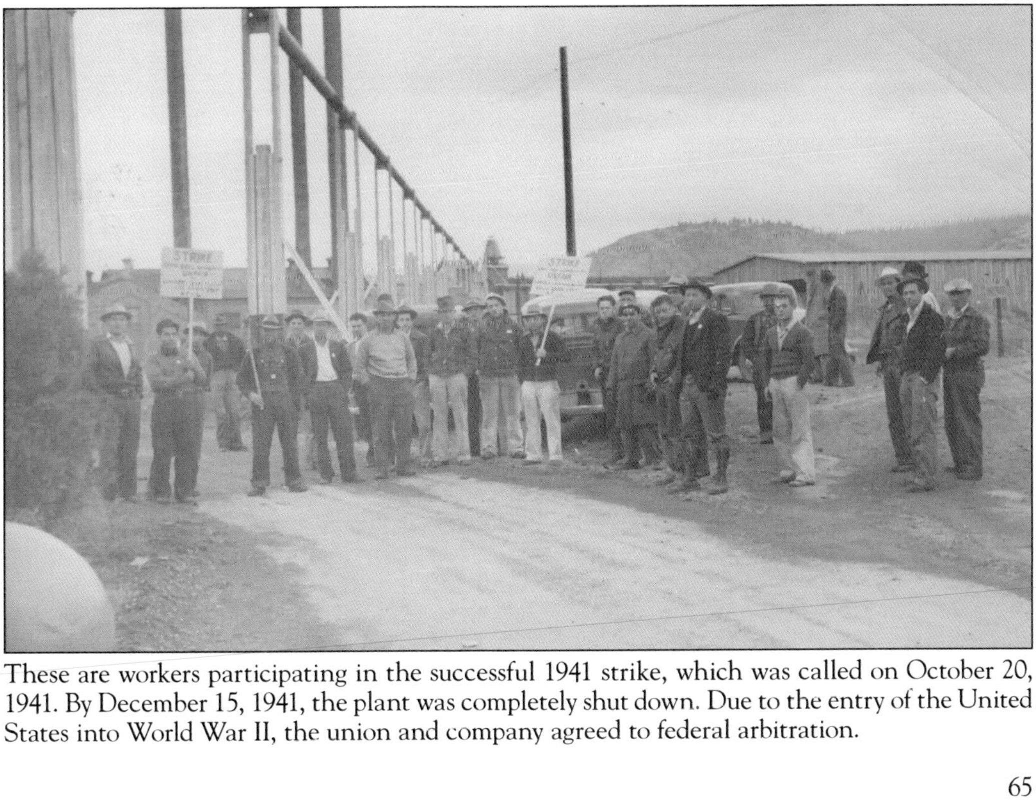

These are workers participating in the successful 1941 strike, which was called on October 20, 1941. By December 15, 1941, the plant was completely shut down. Due to the entry of the United States into World War II, the union and company agreed to federal arbitration.

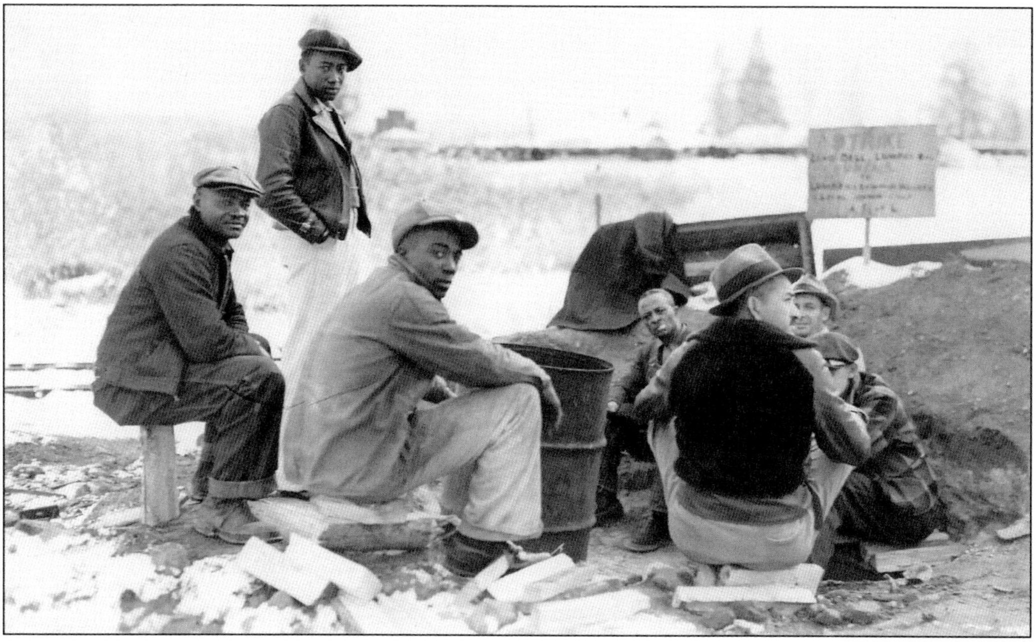

The Weed mill workers successfully unionized in 1919 into the International Union of Timber Workers, Local No. 114. Long-Bell Lumber Company brought over favored black workers from its mill in Louisiana in 1920–1921 in an attempt to break a strike. Dr. Laurence H. Shoup, professional historian, points out that the entire workforce "including Black Americans, Greeks, and Italians, went out at the beginning." It lasted for six weeks but was ultimately unsuccessful. The 1941 strike (above and below) was successful because of the interracial solidarity among the workers. Even though the union treated all members equally, the company enforced a hierarchy with the managers living in large houses on Nob Hill; the department heads on Main Street, Gilman Avenue, and Camino Row; and the rest of the employees largely segregated into ethnic neighborhoods. Roy Barnum (below, second from left) is helping pass out food during the 1941 strike.

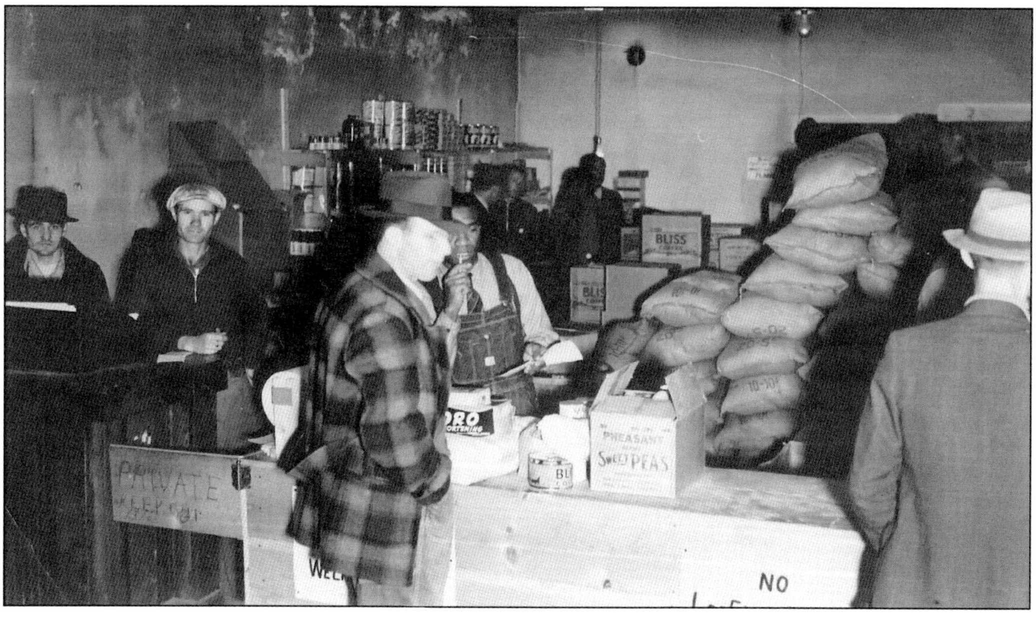

Five

Tennant

Tennant is named after J. D. Tennant, the vice president in charge of Long-Bell's operations in the Pacific Northwest, who helped plan the town. Tennant was the modern, fast-paced "highball" logging headquarters for Long-Bell from the early 1920s until 1956, when it sold out to International Paper. During this time, over 3 billion board feet of ponderosa pine was removed from the surrounding forests and processed at the Weed mill. Tennant is located 8 miles from Bray Wye, renamed Leaf, along an old spur. Leaf is about 30 miles from Weed, and Bray is a couple miles up the road from Leaf. In 1923, all the other Weed Lumber Company spurs on the mainline were closed down.

Tennant was a thriving community with a hospital, nurse's house, cemetery, library, church, post office, mercantile store, elementary school, barbershop, power plant, one phone, cookhouse, dining hall, a 100-room lodging house, 100 two-bedroom company homes, and 1 six-bedroom home for the superintendent. There were even tennis courts, a swimming pool, and a nine-hole golf course at Tennant.

The engine house, called the Round House, housed six engines, including the Baldwin 2-6-2 "twins," No. 7 and No. 8; a Baldwin 2-6-6-2 No. 1001; and the ALCO Brooks 2-8-2 engines No. 100, No. 101, and No. 3296. No. 101 was purchased brand new around 1923 for the Tennant operation. In addition, "Big Red," a 1918 Meister and Sons motorcar, ran twice daily between Tennant and Leaf for mail, newspapers, goods, and passengers from the mainline.

Camp No. 1 was located 40 miles from Tennant, just inside the Modoc County line. It was later moved 20 miles south, becoming New Camp No. 1. While drilling a well for the new camp, pockets of cool air were found in the basalt. This air was piped to the camp kitchen and dining room for air-conditioning in the hot summers. As with earlier operations, 100 miles of railroad spurs were in operation at any given time. A large map showing the railroad spurs of Weed Lumber Company/Long-Bell Lumber Company can be seen in the Weed Historic Lumber Town Museum.

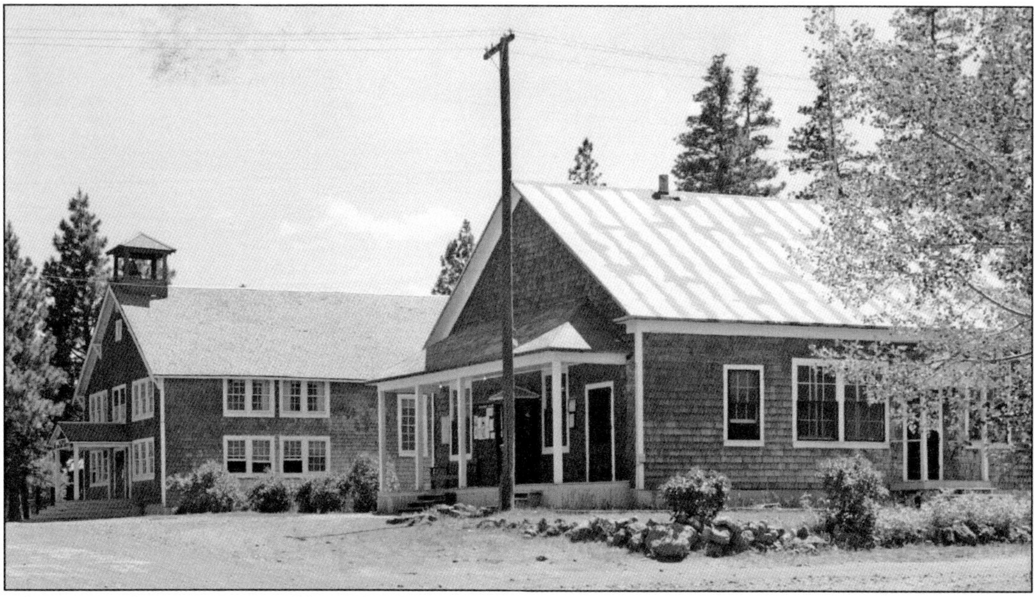

Above are the Tennant Wildwood Christian Church (left), which is also the community center, and the Tennant branch of the Weed Lumber Company Office, as seen in 1922 through 1925.

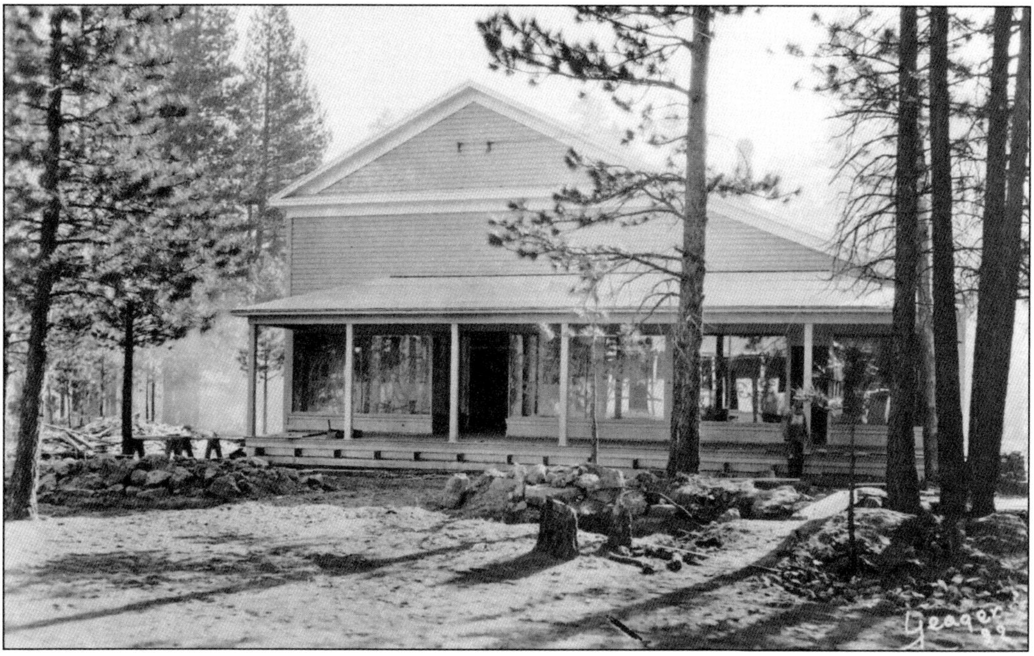

The new company store in Tennant, also called the "Merc," was the main source of food and other supplies. The motorcar "Big Red" supplied perishables on a daily basis. Dry goods were brought in weekly by George Linville and Bob Bowen, who drove the Weed Wholesale Company truck. The Tadina Dairy ran the Company Ranch and supplied milk to both Weed and Tennant as part of its lease payment. During the winter, the Tadina Dairy also butchered six to eight hogs every two weeks for Long-Bell Lumber Company. The Tadina Dairy was operated by John Tadina Sr. and his son Gerald Tadina, who took over the business in 1937. They sold the business to the Belcastro brothers, Pete, Tom, and Joe, in 1946. (Photograph by C. E. Yeager.)

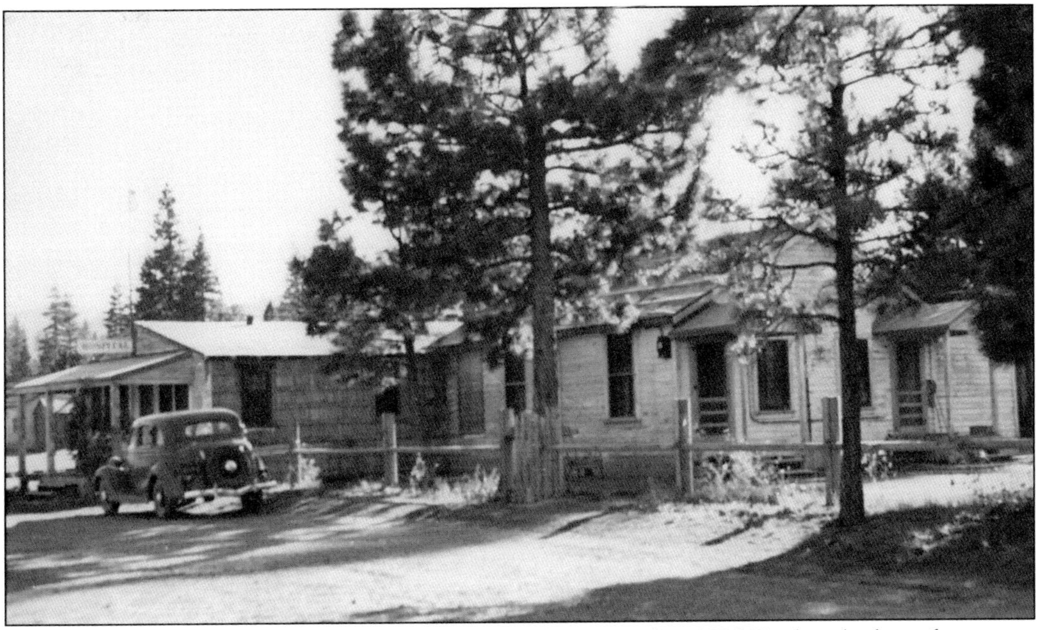

The two-bed Tennant Hospital (left) and nurses' home, with a 1935 Ford parked out front, was tended by a group of nurses, including Estelle Dollarhide, until 1935, when Dr. Dragi Todorovic worked for Long-Bell Lumber Company at Tennant. Dr. Todorovic's brother, Valerian Todorovic, was the veterinarian for Long-Bell Lumber Company.

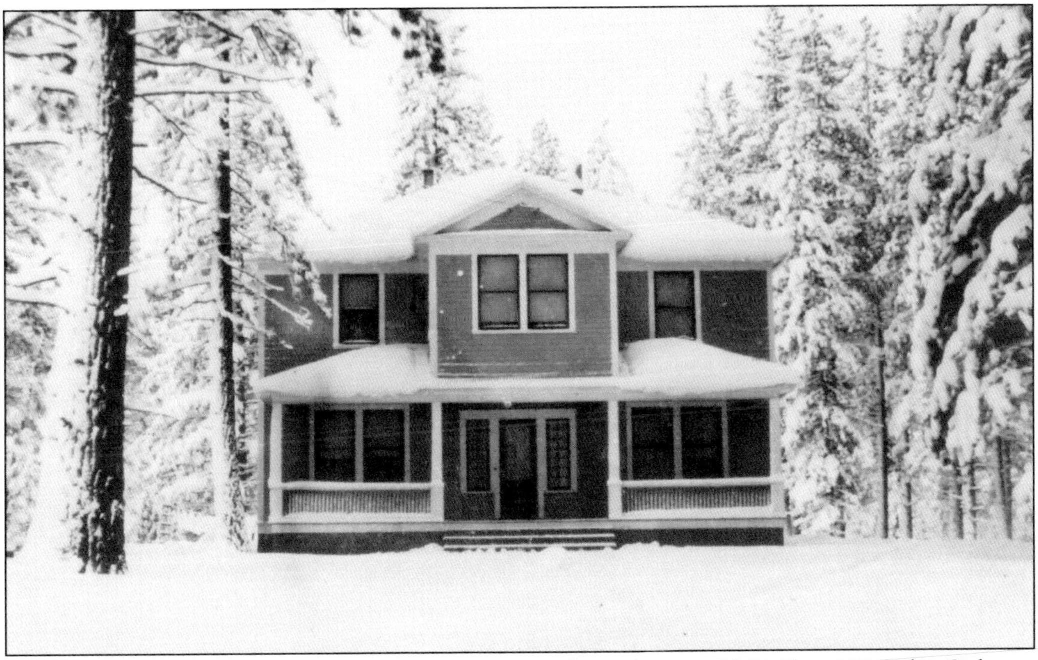

Elmer and Gladys Zimmerman's home in Tennant is shown here in 1940. Elmer moved to Siskiyou County in 1930 and got a job at Tennant, where he worked as a choker setter, tractor operator, and "cat doctor," eventually becoming logging superintendent in 1948. Gladys and Elmer Zimmerman established a scholarship for Weed High School graduates, whose parents or grandparents worked in the lumber industry, in order to further their education. (Courtesy Donna Steffenson Sartor.)

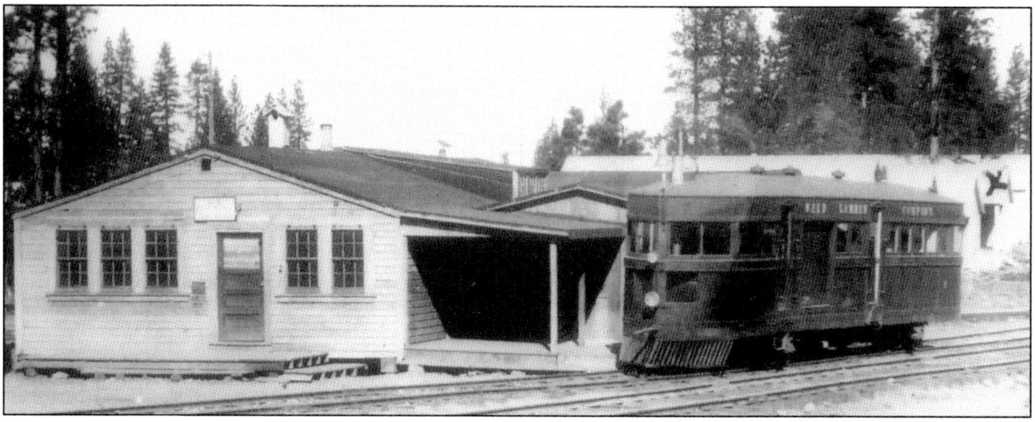

Here is "Big Red" parked in front of the Tennant Post Office in 1920. This motorcar, along with its twin, was built in 1918 by Meister and Sons of Sacramento. They were originally used on the Ocean Shore Railway south of San Francisco, but No. 61 was soon sold to Long-Bell Lumber Company. It was used as the twice-daily car between Leaf and Tennant, picking up mail, passengers, and goods from Southern Pacific's passenger trains No. 39 and No. 40. Postmaster Max Filson operated "Big Red," which once got stuck out in a snowstorm during the winter of 1936–1937. (Courtesy Donna Steffenson Sartor.)

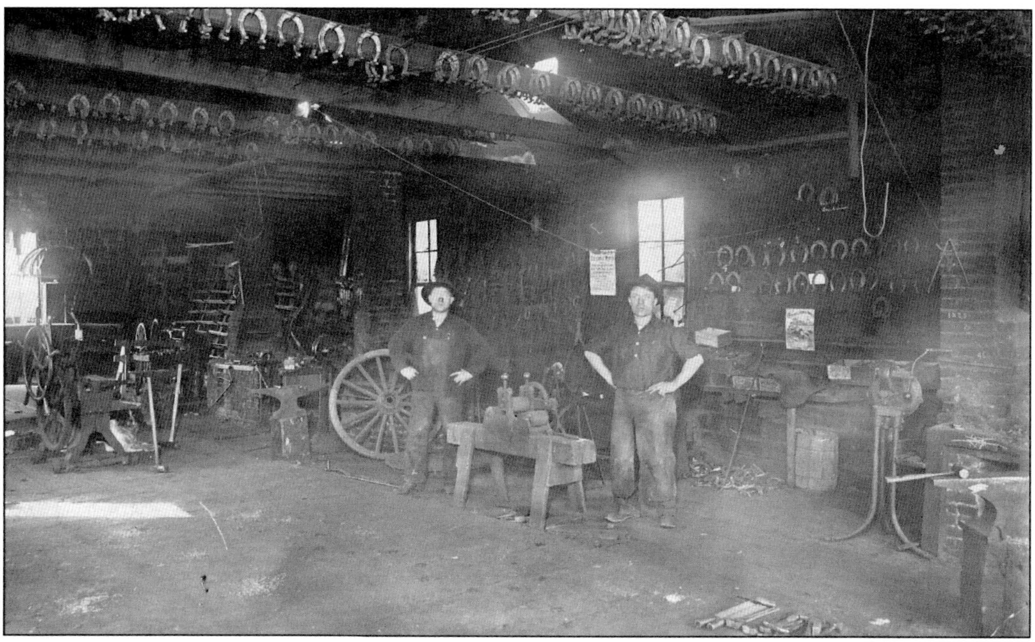

Two blacksmiths are shown standing in the Tennant Blacksmith shop in 1925. The blacksmith fixed everything from big wheels to steam engines. Equipment includes (from left to right) an anvil with an attached press, an anvil, and a ring roller for bending iron. A swage block, a multipurpose tool with holes and depressions for bending or hammering, is on the floor behind the anvil with press (far left).

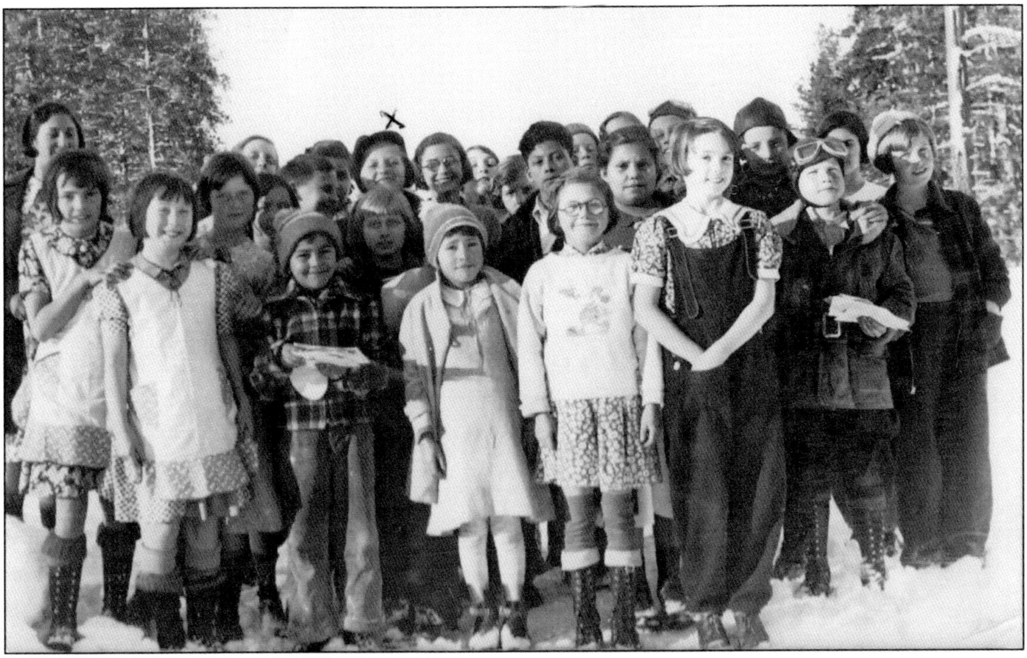

Tennant Elementary School students in 1930 are shown above, and Tennant Elementary School students are shown 11 years later in 1941 in the picture below. (Below photograph by Coffey; both courtesy Donna Steffenson Sartor.)

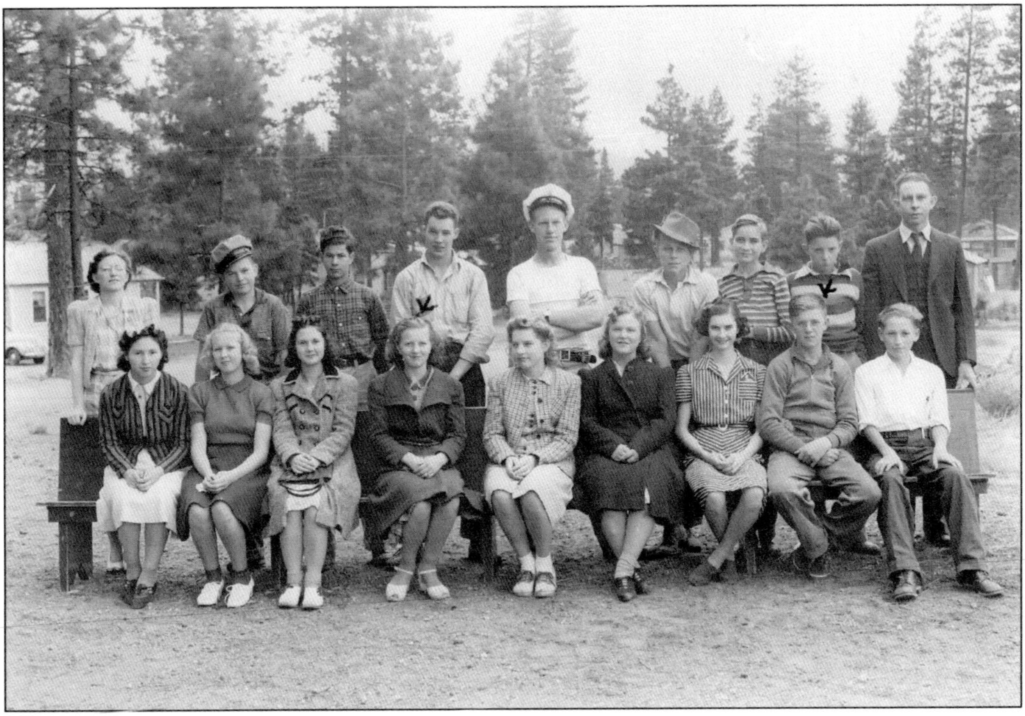

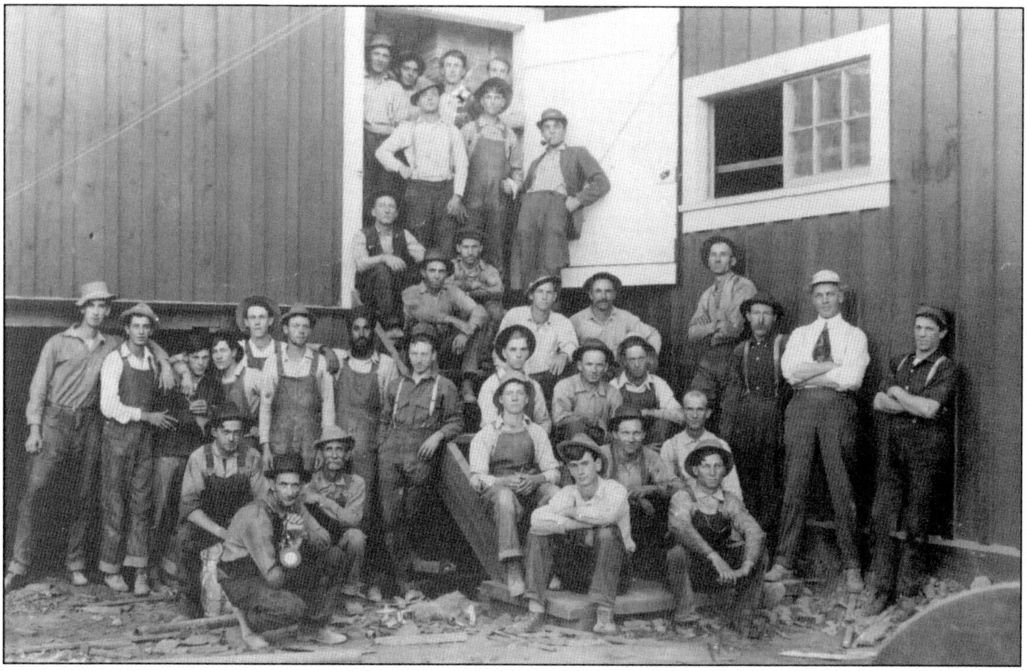

Bray was established by William John "Billy" and Jane "Jennie" (Beck) Bray before the railroad arrived in 1908. He was postmaster, owner of the General Store, a carpenter who built several Victorian homes in Yreka, owner and operator of the Bray Hunting Lodge, and he had an 800-acre ranch. The above photograph shows workers at the nearby Bray Box Factory c. 1916, built by the Bridgeford brothers and George Phenegar around 1910. Known workers include filer Frank Souza (top row), watchman Bee Wilson with lantern (front left), filer Matt Kohn (right bottom step), assistant manager John Hansen (behind Kohn), millwright Bill Gates (in beret at top of steps sitting down), and manager Ed Wright with tie and arms crossed (second from right). Bray Box Factory (below), in the 1920s, is located north of Mount Shasta. (Photograph by Pres Fidler; courtesy Roger Zwanziger.)

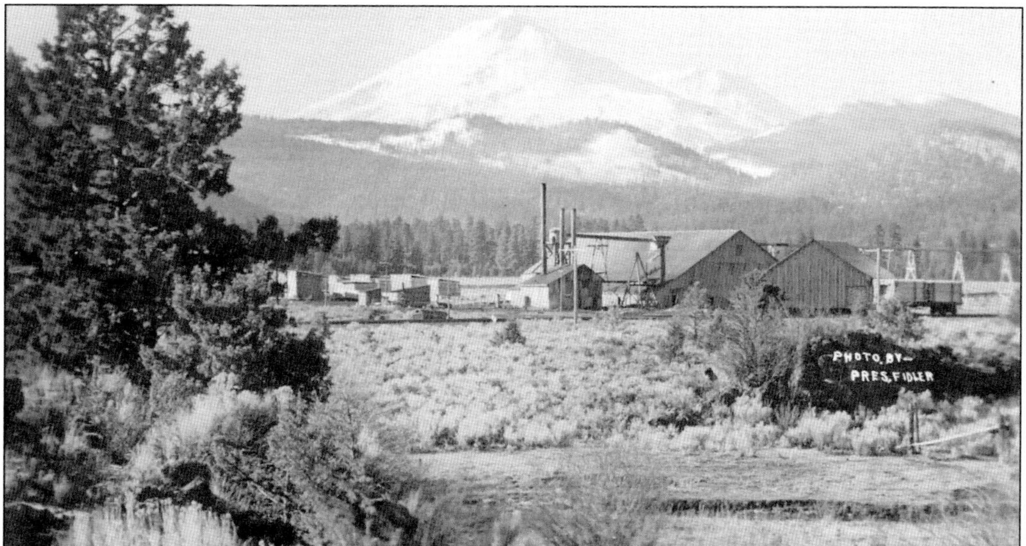

Six

WEED

The town founded by Abner Weed in 1900 was well established before Long-Bell Lumber Company bought out Weed Lumber Company. Rooming House No. 1, complete with a cookhouse on the lower floor, Rooming House No. 2, the justice court, post office, and the Weed Mercantile, which housed the First National Bank of Weed, were built in 1901. Abner's son Horace Weed was the store manager of the Weed Mercantile. A fire system was in place, with an 800,000-gallon cement tank on Reservoir Hill, hydrants around town, and small hose houses around the perimeter of the plant, each holding a two-wheeled cart and a long hose that could be coupled to nearby hydrants. Weed enticed Dr. William "Will" Tebbe to become Weed's first doctor in 1904 by promising to build him a hospital, which he did the next year. Dr. Will, as he was known, built his house in 1905 at 527 Main Street. His brother, Dr. Fred Tebbe, joined the practice soon thereafter and built his house behind the hospital at 458 Main Street in 1906. Both houses are still standing.

Weed was a true company town—providing work, housing, food, and goods from the company store. Part of workers' pay was in coupons or tokens—good only at the Merc. In 1906, Weed Lumber Company built the Florence Hotel, named after the daughter of George X. Wendling. This was also the year the first church was built in Weed, established by the efforts of Phoebe Caulkett. When the school at Igerna, which serviced Weed students, burned down in 1905, the Summit School was moved to Angel Valley. When Weed students outgrew that school, Weed Lumber Company donated land for a new school on Schoolhouse Hill. A four-year high school was established in 1919.

The ethnic make-up of Weed is diverse in comparison to other towns in Northern California and has been since its inception; however, Italians, Greeks, Mexicans, and blacks lived in segregated areas. The company town of Weed provided most of what the workers needed. The rest of their needs were met in Shastina, south of Division Street.

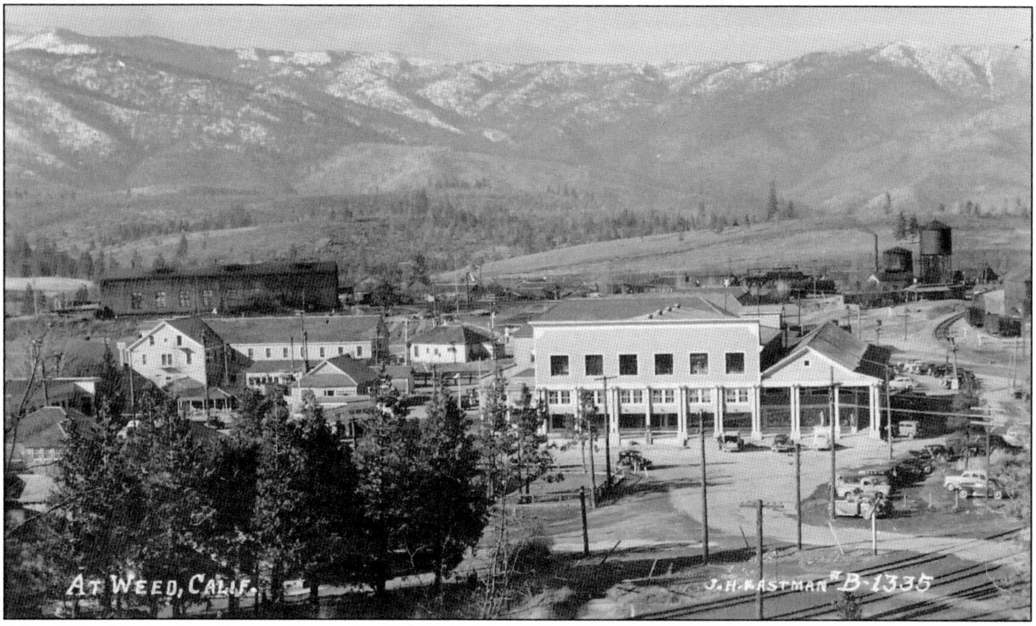

The Weed Mercantile, on the west side of north Main Street, is the large building on the right. Beyond it is the hill near the golf course. The three-story, L-shaped building to the left is the Weed Hotel. Beyond it is the Round House, where the mechanics worked on the steam engines. The small building in the center with the hip roof is the Express Office. (Photograph by J. H. Eastman.)

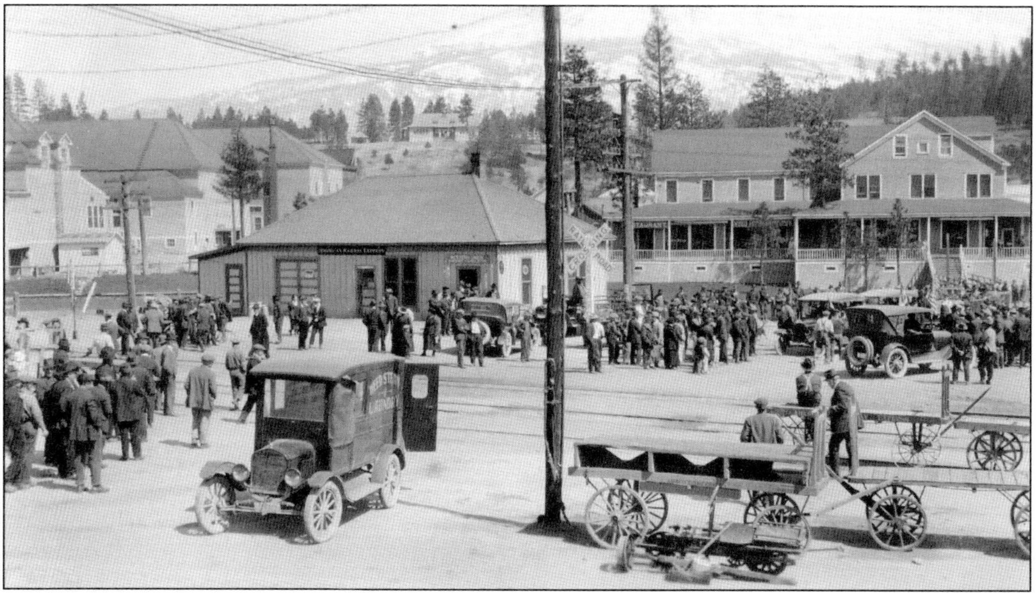

The crowd shown here is waiting for World War I soldiers to return. The Weed Steam Laundry truck (front) was owned by the Heberlies. The Express Office (center) housed the Western Union Telegraph. To its right is the Weed Hotel, built in 1914. To its left is The Club (front) and Florence Hotel (back). The second schoolhouse built in 1910 can be seen on Schoolhouse Hill (back center).

The building on the left in the photograph at right is the First National Bank in 1922, located within the Weed Mercantile building on north Main Street. They had their own money printed, shown below. Some Weed mill employees lived upstairs in the White Pine Inn (center). After the White Pine Inn, originally called the Florence Hotel, was built, it housed the post office, previously located in the Weed Merc. The building on the far right is the Club Theater, which had a barbershop, confectionery, pool hall, and card room. It replaced the old rooming house, which was torn down in 1912. (Photograph by C. E. Yeager.)

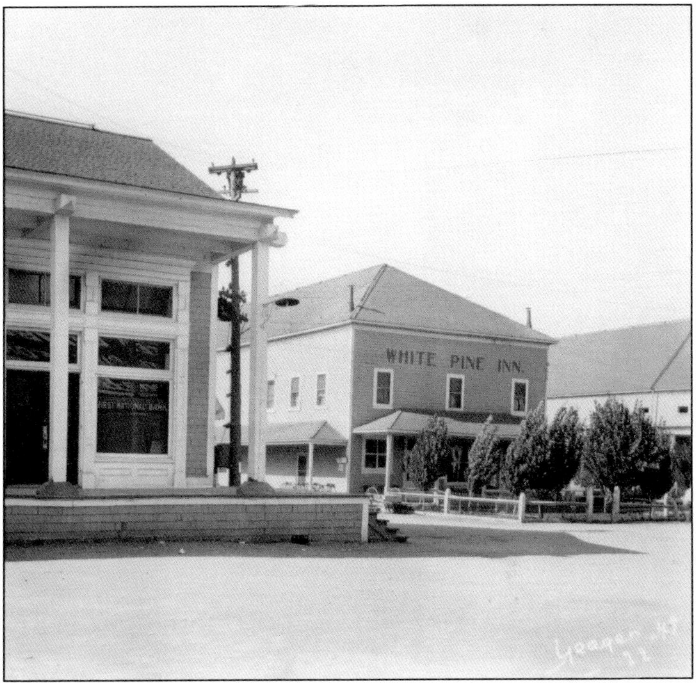

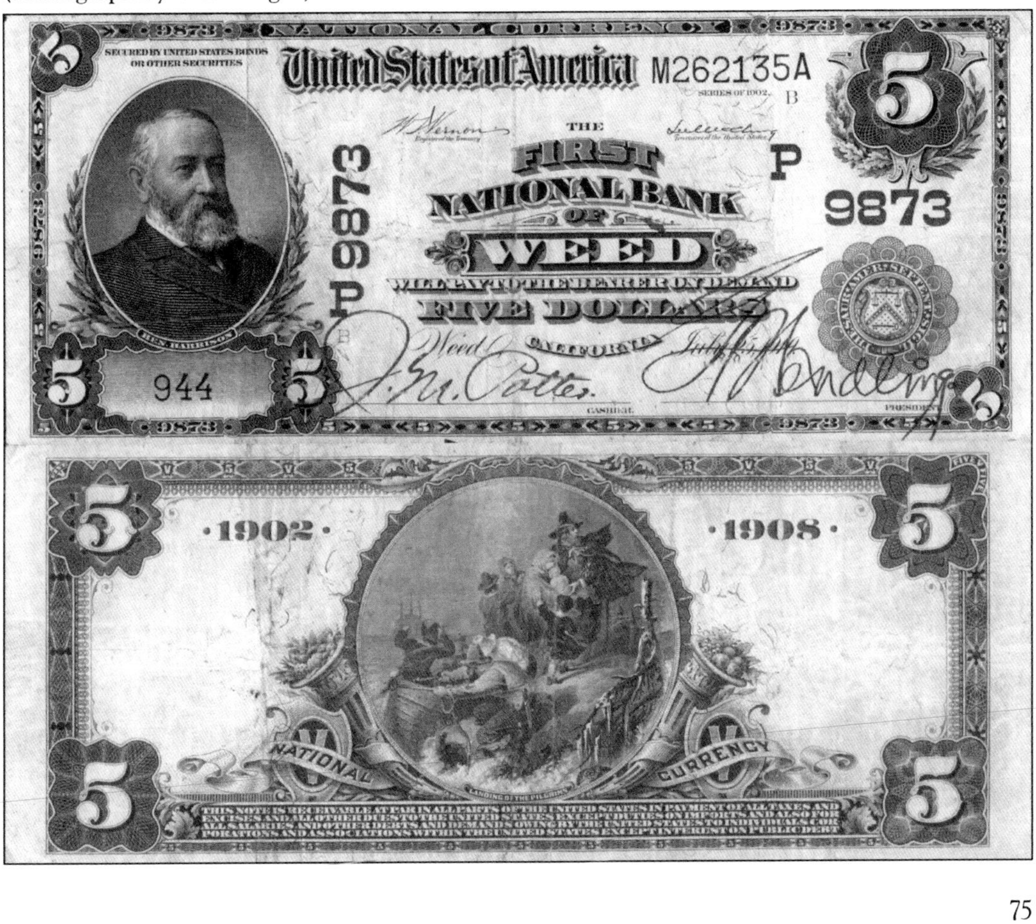

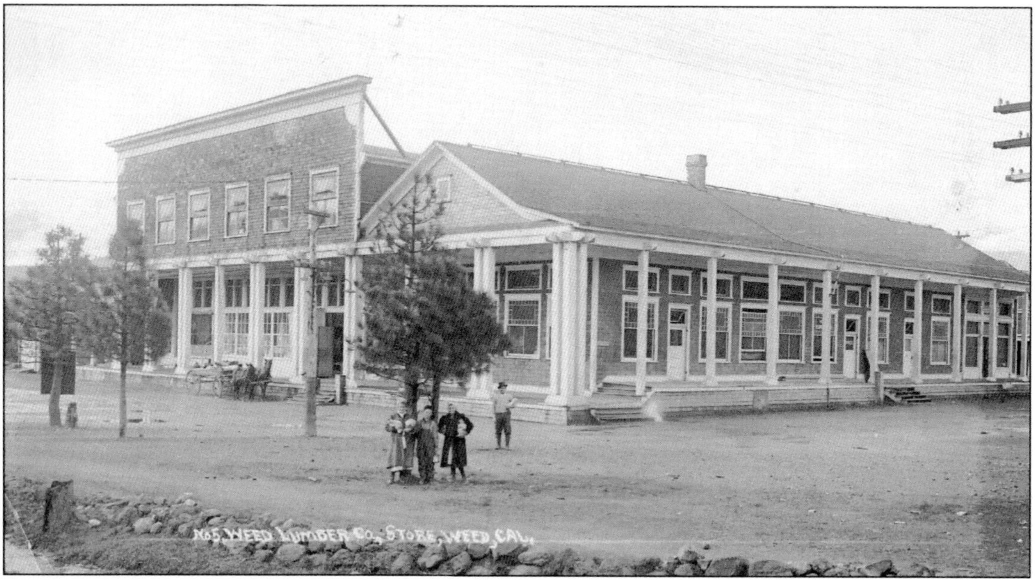

The above image is looking at Weed Mercantile in 1910 from near the railroad tracks. The section of the Weed Merc on the left side was built in 1901 and houses the company store. Weed's son Horace worked here for awhile. The 1908 addition on the right side includes, from left to right, the post office, justice court, and First National Bank. There are two women and a boy under the tree; the woman on the right is holding a live duck in her arms. Employees are standing in front of the Weed Mercantile (below) in 1926. When Long-Bell Lumber Company sold out to International Paper in 1959 the company homes and businesses, including the Weed Mercantile, were sold.

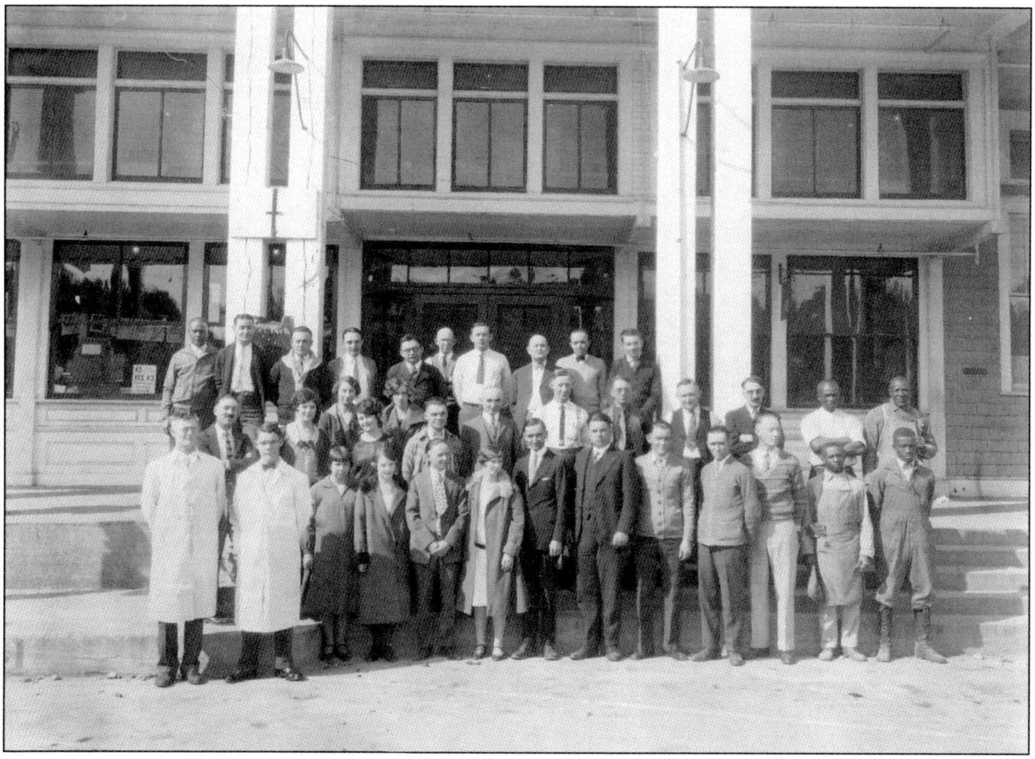

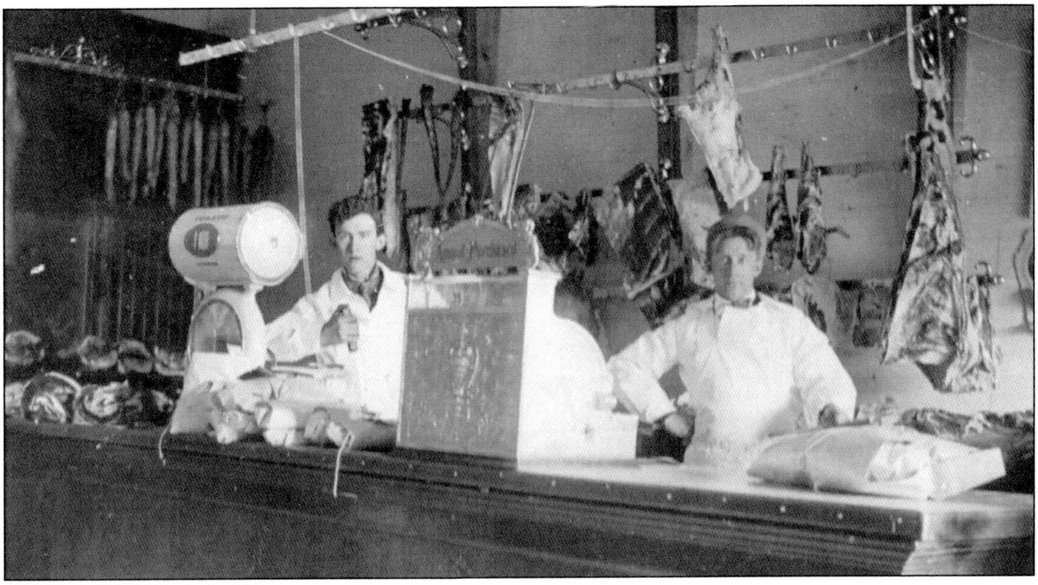

Butchers (above) are shown working at the Weed Mercantile in 1915. Albert Collins is the butcher on the left. Weed residents (below) are at the 50th anniversary of the Weed Mercantile on October 27, 1956. The following from left to right are (first row) Madge Gilliam, Frances DeLuca, Rachel Tallerico Cedros, Irma Acquistapace, Geneva Utley, Louise Lobis, Jackie Samples, Delbert Doehm, Alma Lester, and Carolina Carpine; (second row) Hazel Painter, Margaret Dawson, Bert Arens, Eugene Watkins, Martha Holly, Ernie Pomato, unidentified, David Kersey, and Mr. Langley; (third row) Ralph Study, Dave Johnson, Emelia Kegg, Bill Hanchey, Pete Aiello, Leland Dunlap, Theo Locket, Jim Adams, and Jack Kersey. (Above courtesy Evelyn Collins Graham.)

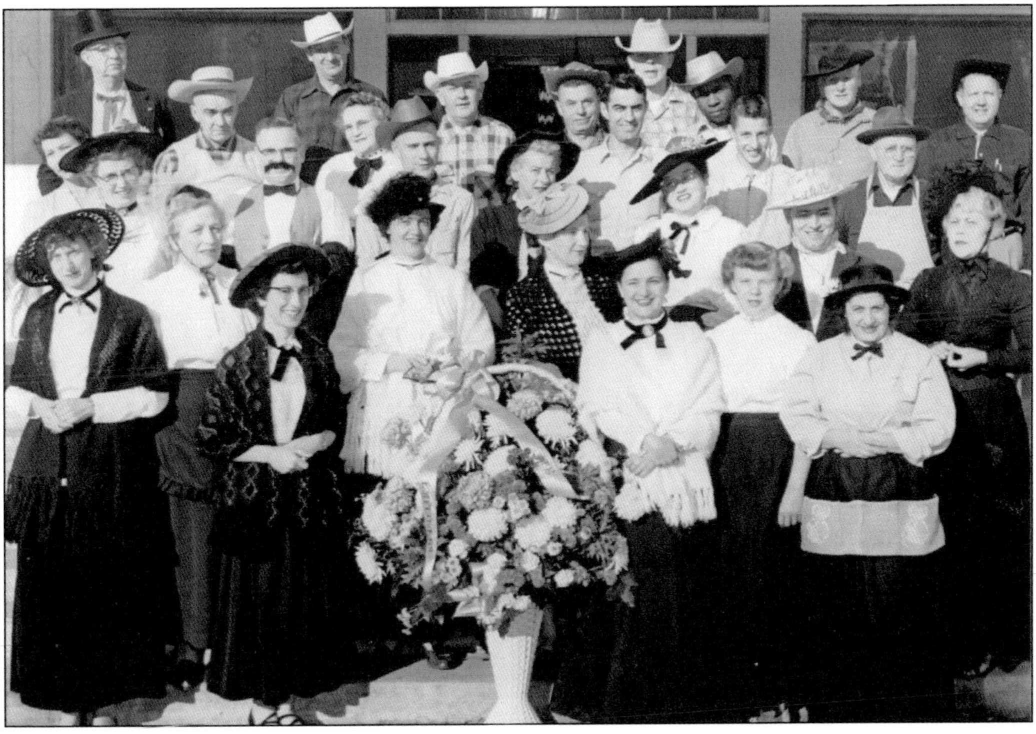

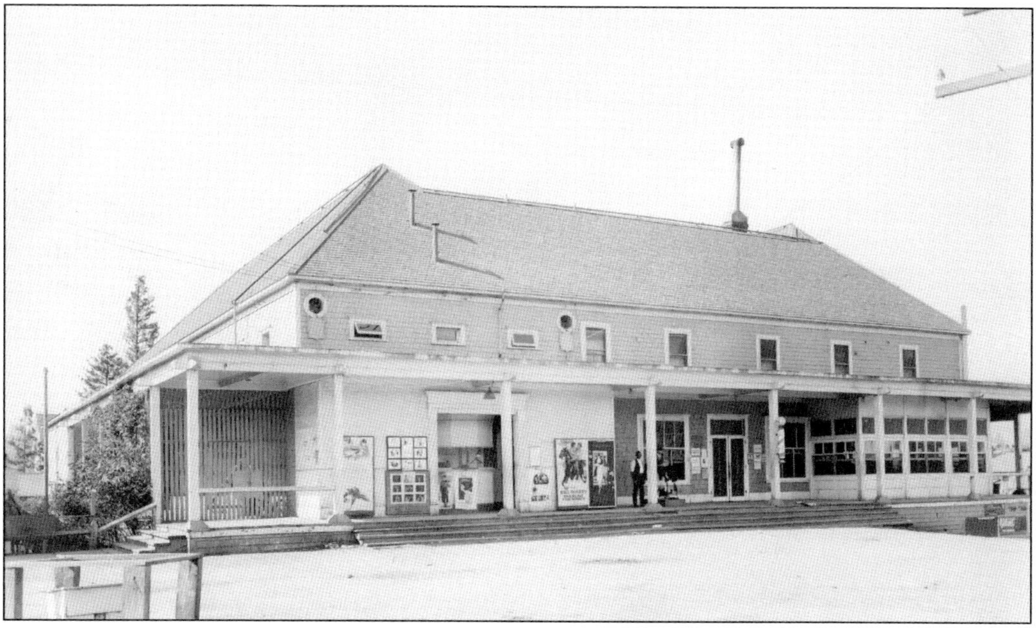

The Club Theater (above) was built in 1913 after the rooming house was dismantled. It had a theater, barbershop, confectionery, pool hall, card room, and a restaurant operated by Wong Louie and his wife, Rose Katherine Jeong. One of the posters on display announces the 1921 film *Doubling for Romeo* starring Will Rogers, a Cherokee-American cowboy, comedian, and actor; and Sylvia Breamer, an Australian actress. Near the center of the porch are a shoe-shine stand and two men. The Club Theater had 200 floor seats, 50 balcony seats, and a 400-square-foot stage (below). When there were no live performances it was used as a movie theater.

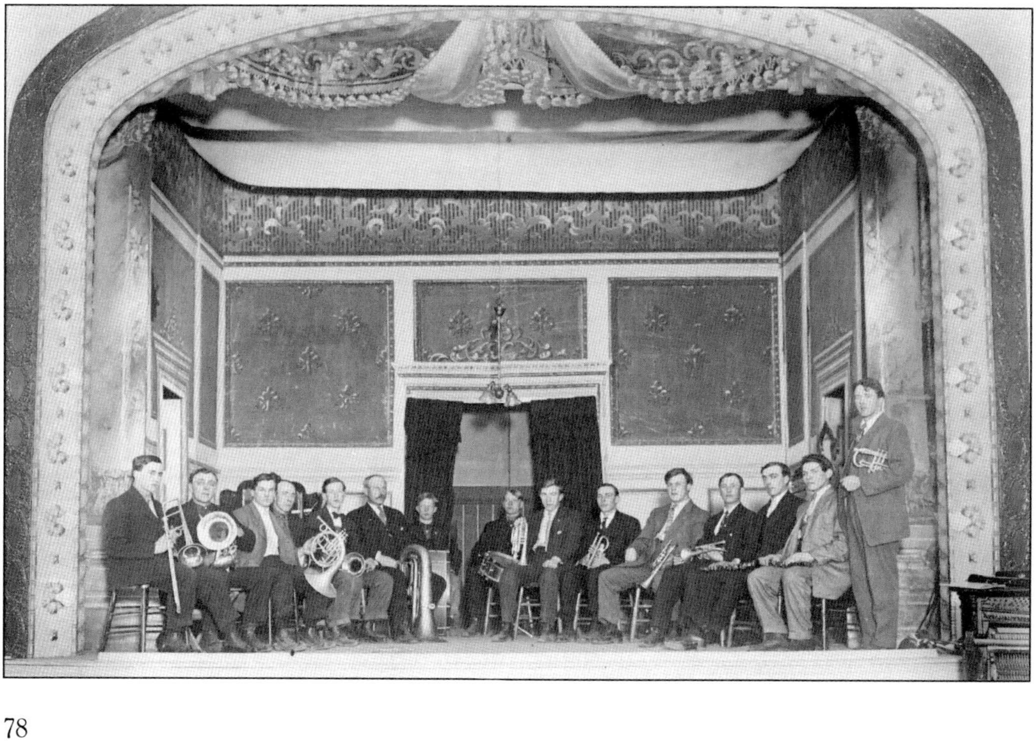

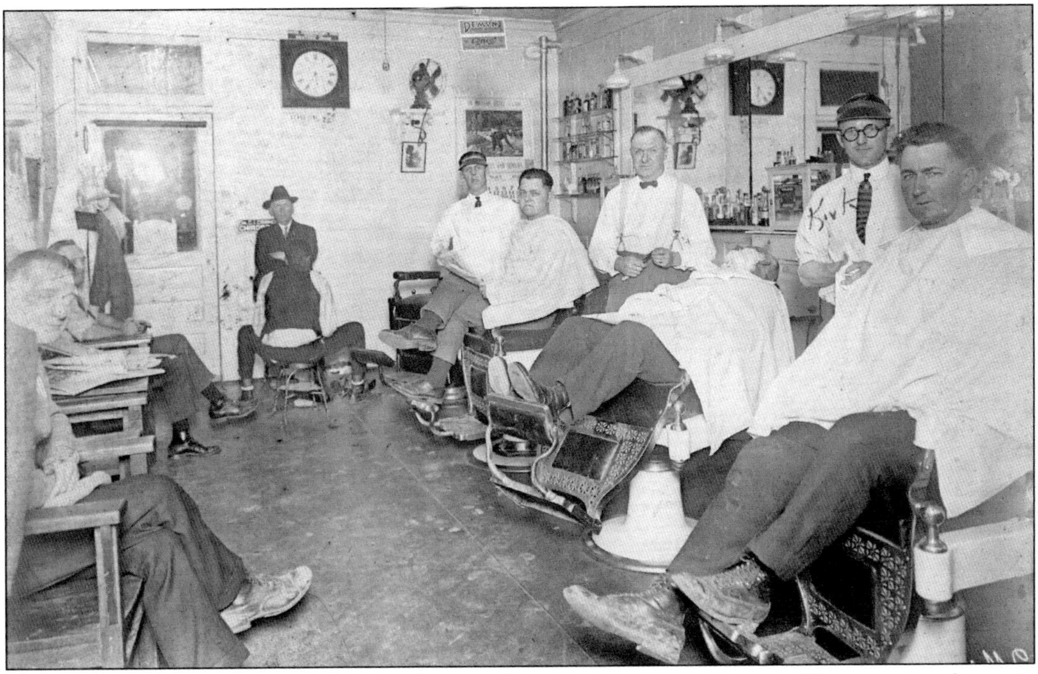

This picture shows inside the barbershop at The Club in 1926 (above). The man in glasses is nicknamed "Kirk the Barber." The barber at the third chair in the back is Lucien E. White, usually called "Whitey the Barber." The door in the back leads into the card room. The lines for the barber were sometimes so long the customers would take a number then go play cards. The Weed Hotel (below) was built in 1914, nine years before this photograph was taken. The hotel rooms were on the second and third floors. Roomers on the top floor had to share a bathroom. The restaurant, bakery, saloon, and lobby were located on the ground floor. The bakery was known among locals for making "really good" French bread. The Weed Lumber Company store baseball team had showers and lockers in the basement.

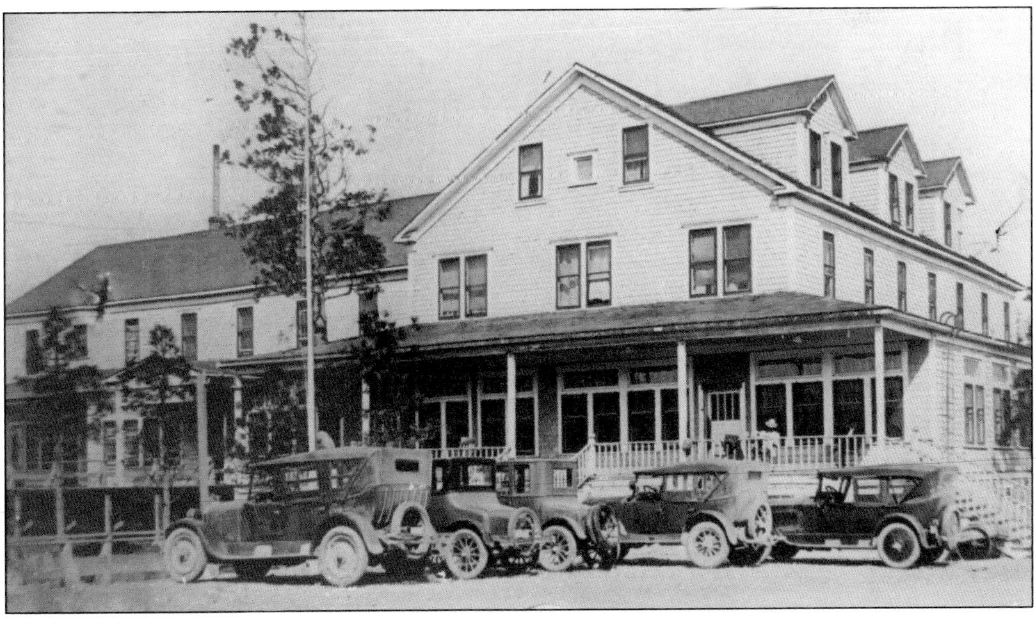

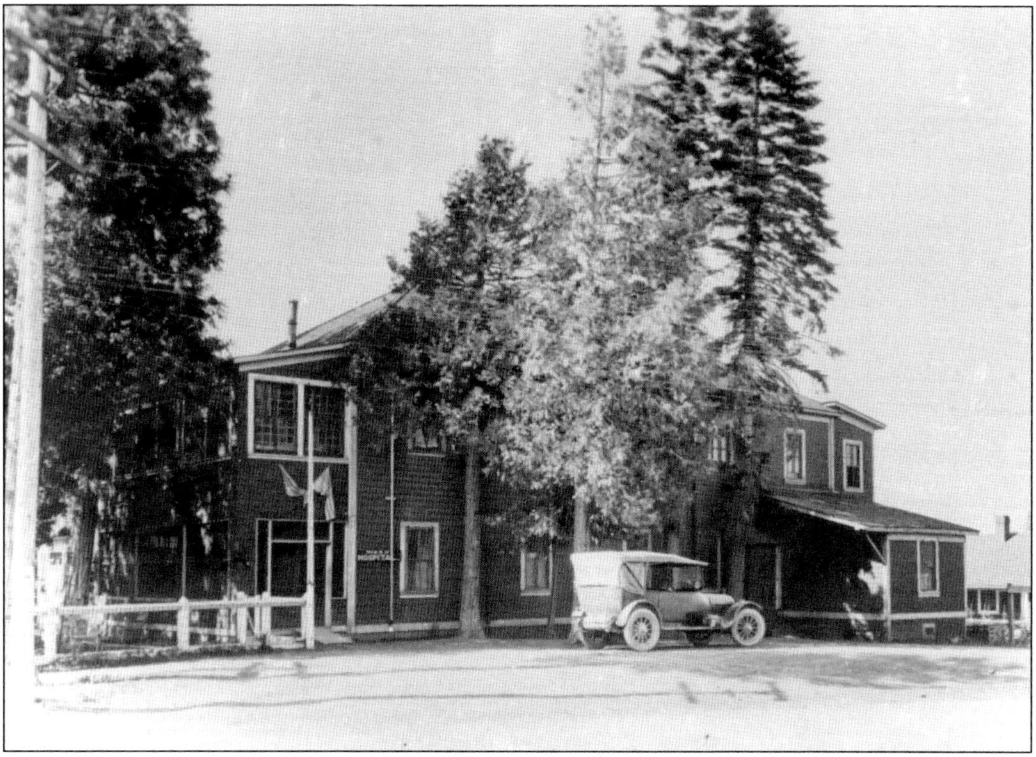

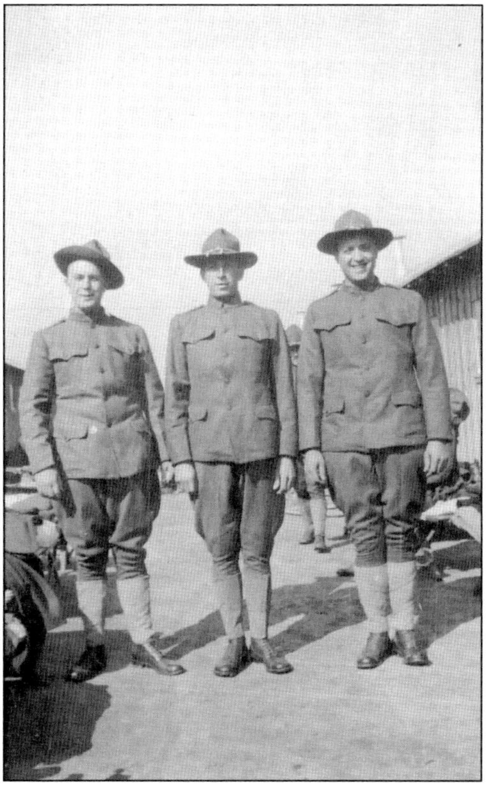

In 1904, Abner Weed hired Dr. William "Will" Tebbe to be the doctor at Weed with the promise that he would build a hospital, which he did in 1905. Will started his career as a teacher in Etna in 1889, and his brother Fred joined him in 1895. After their father's death in 1897, they quit teaching and went to medical school. Will joined Dr. George W. Dwinnell's practice in Montague. Dr. Dwinnell was instrumental in the establishment of Dwinnell Reservoir, now known as Lake Shastina. In 1905, Will married Katherine "Katie" Mugler. Fred worked with Dr. Charles Nutting Sr. from 1902 to 1906 then joined his brother's practice in Weed from 1906 to 1920.

Three World War I veterans pose proudly in 1918 (at left). Dr. Will served at a naval base in Scotland. Several Weed men served, including Alfred "Buck" Cremer, Al Collins, Tom Kundert, George Schuler, and George Zwanziger, many of them in Company D, 2nd Battalion, 20th Engineers in northeastern France.

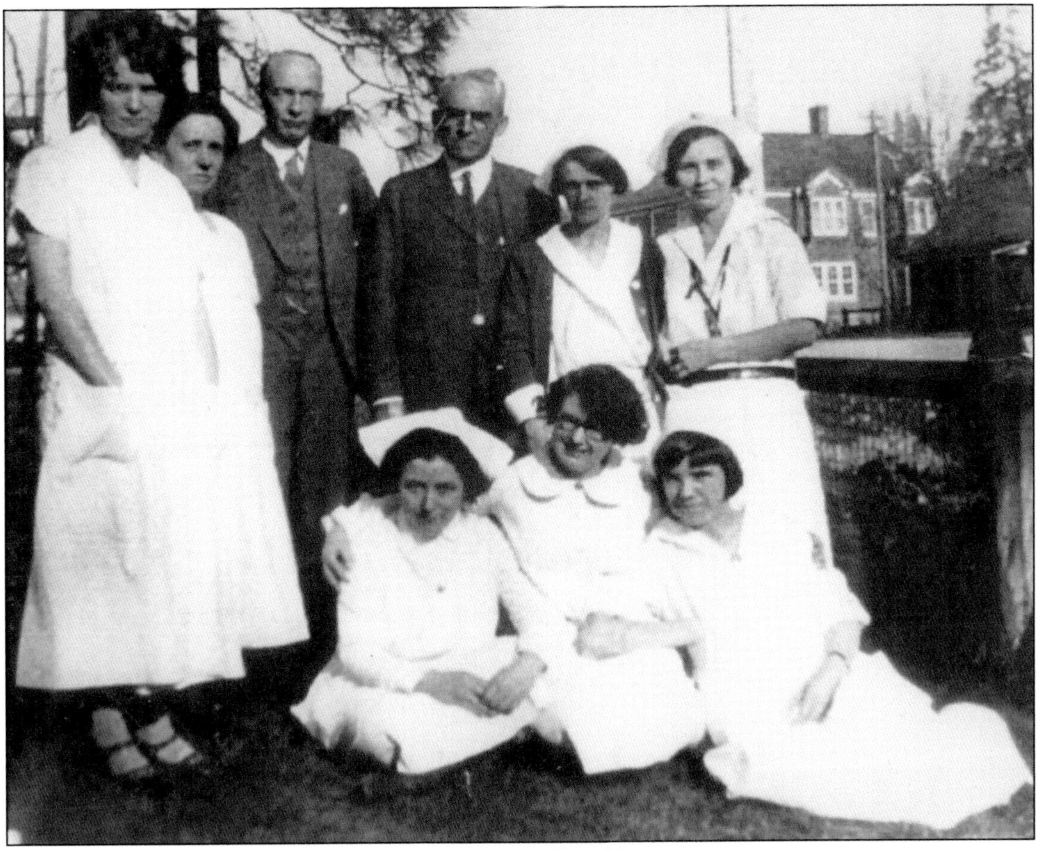

Dr. Charles Nutting Jr., third from left, and Dr. Will Tebbe are pictured with nurses in front of Weed Hospital. Dr. Will and Katie (Mugler) Tebbe had three children who grew up at 527 Main Street (far right). Herbert Hoover was a friend of Dr. Tebbe. For several years they went camping together on the Salmon River; after Hoover was elected president, he and Dr. Will celebrated by going to the Klamath River in 1928.

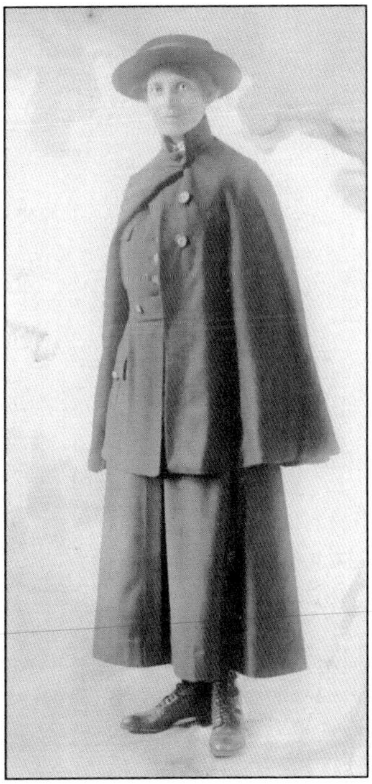

Nurse Gertrude (Horn) Condrey, right, was born around 1882 and graduated from Stanford in 1905. She was one of the nurses at the 20-bed Weed Hospital. She served in France in World War I and earned an FOE (Fraternal Order of Eagles) medal. She married George E. Condrey. Her 17-year-old son David H. Johnson and 23-year-old nephew Chester K. Horn were living with them during the 1930 census.

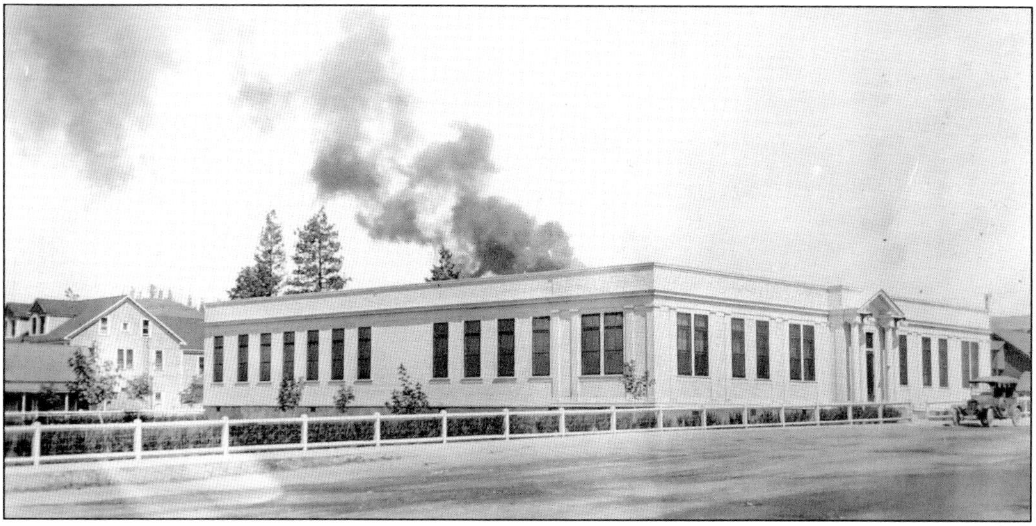

Long-Bell Lumber Company slowly gained control of Weed Lumber Company. When Weed Lumber Company went public in 1903, R. A. Long, whose company had been looking for a site on the West Coast, purchased stock. By 1916, Long-Bell Lumber Company owned the majority of the stock and by 1922 had complete ownership. The company office (above and below) was built in 1920. The carpenter crew from the mill built it. Today this building houses the courthouse, police station, and city offices, which had previously been located in the old Weed High School structure behind the elementary school. (Photograph by Harold Frodsham; courtesy Carole Steele.)

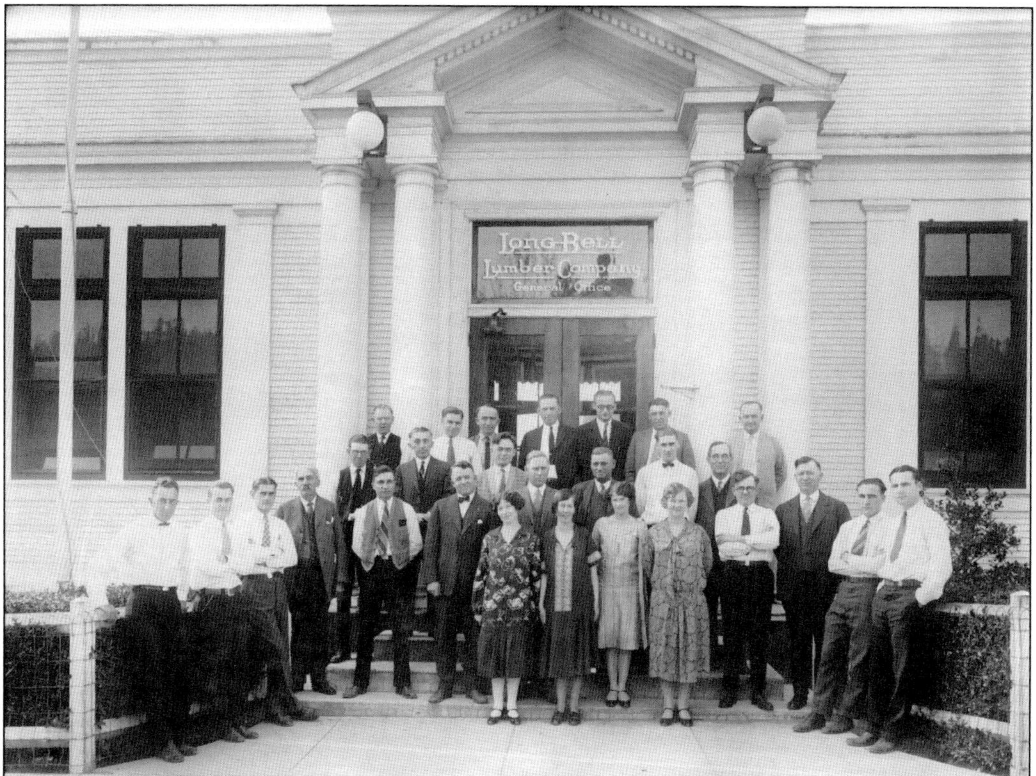

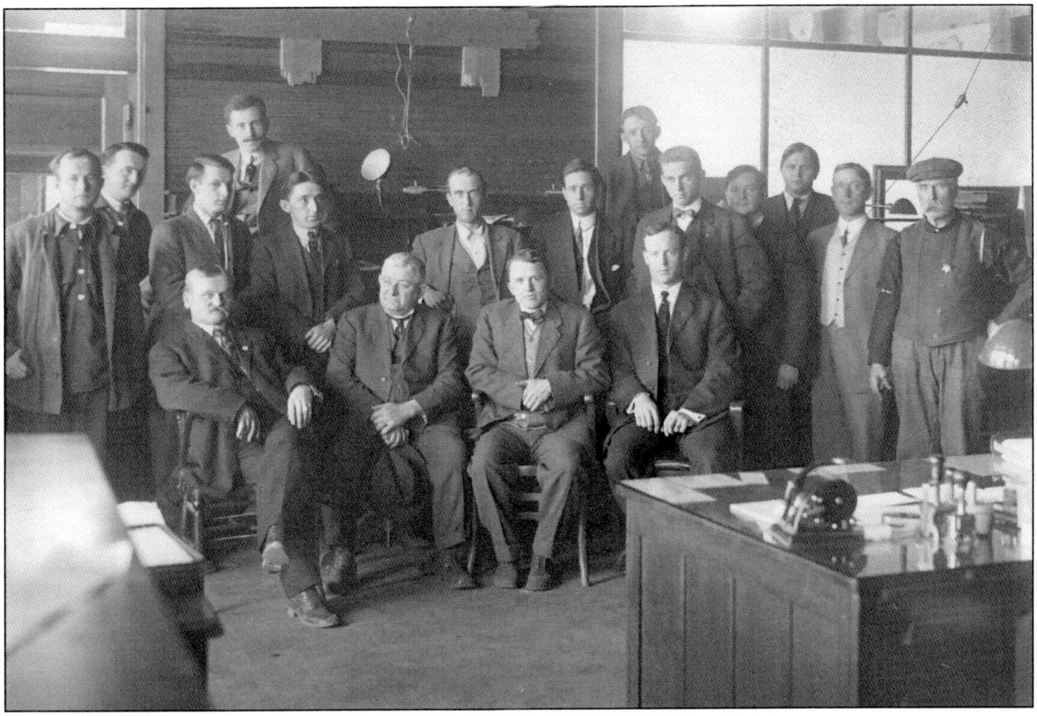

Julian M. "Jude" White Sr. and his son Julian (above, seated second and third from left) take central stage in this 1920s photograph. Jude came to Weed with his parents and five siblings in 1906. Jude worked on the green chain at Mill No. 1 when he was in high school. He became the company cashier in 1910, was appointed plant manager from 1919 to 1948, and was president of Long-Bell Lumber Company from 1948 to 1964. Constable Joseph "Joe" Lockyear (far right) was also a local artist.

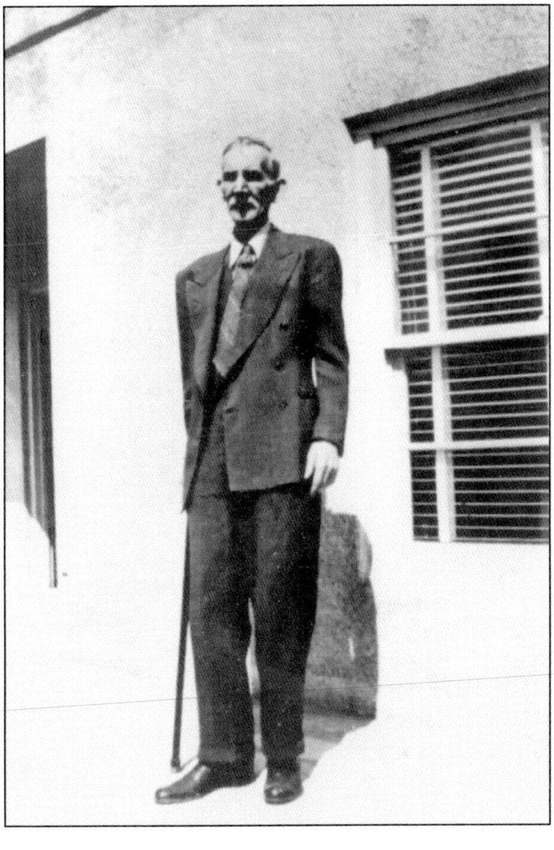

Judge J. P. Bradley (right), pictured in 1947 or 1948, was born in Roseburg, Oregon, in 1869. He was a policeman and sheriff before he moved to Weed in 1912 with his wife, Hattie (Payton) Bradley. Their oldest daughter, Goldie, and her husband, H. H. Oller, ran the Bradley Ranch near Hornbrook, caring for 500 milk goats. (Courtesy Roger Zwanziger.)

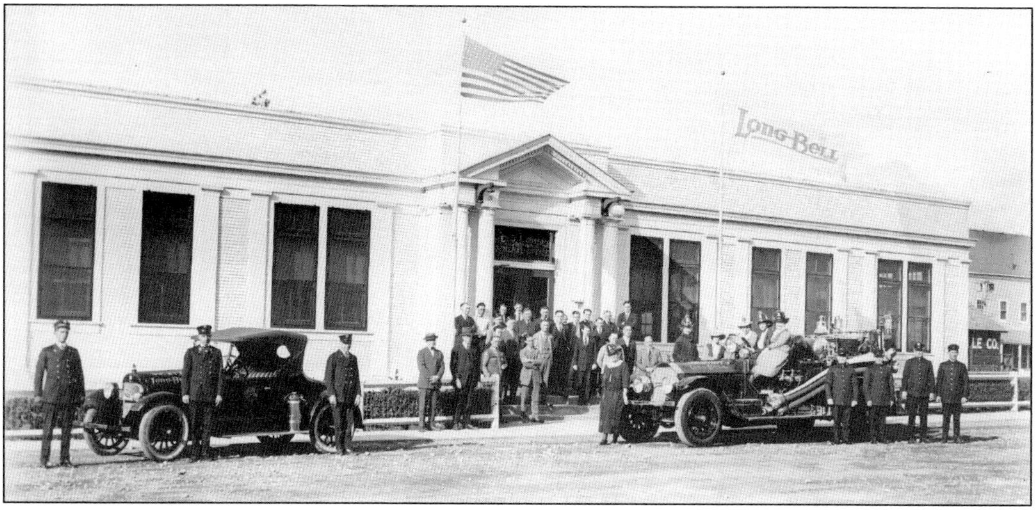

The Weed Fire Department (above) is showing off its new 1922 American-La France fire engine in front of the Long-Bell Lumber Company office building in 1923. Dorian Small was the fire chief from 1923 to 1942. Capt. George Oeschgar became the next fire chief until he retired in the 1970s. The famous 1915 Yard No. 3 fire (below) was set by a teenager who wanted money to go to the Panama-Pacific International Exposition, better known as the 1915 San Francisco World's Fair. After the fire, he wrote a letter to Weed Lumber Company demanding $500 and threatened to start another fire if he did not get the money. He was apprehended when he picked up the empty money bag and sent to reform school for two years.

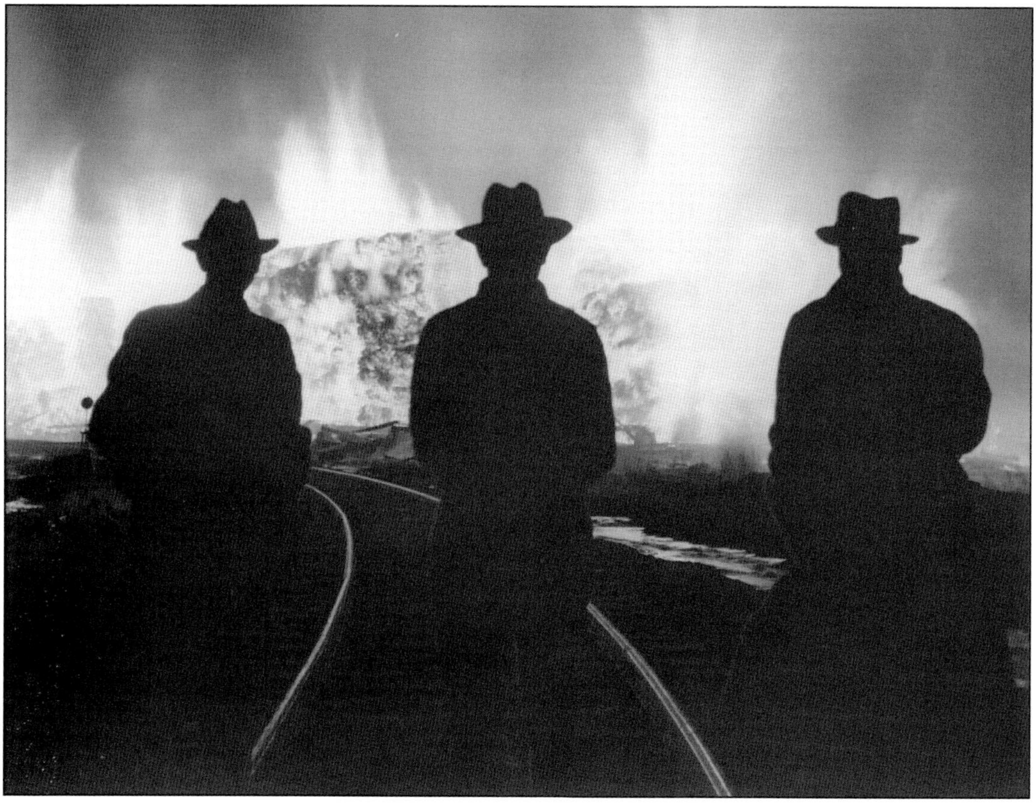

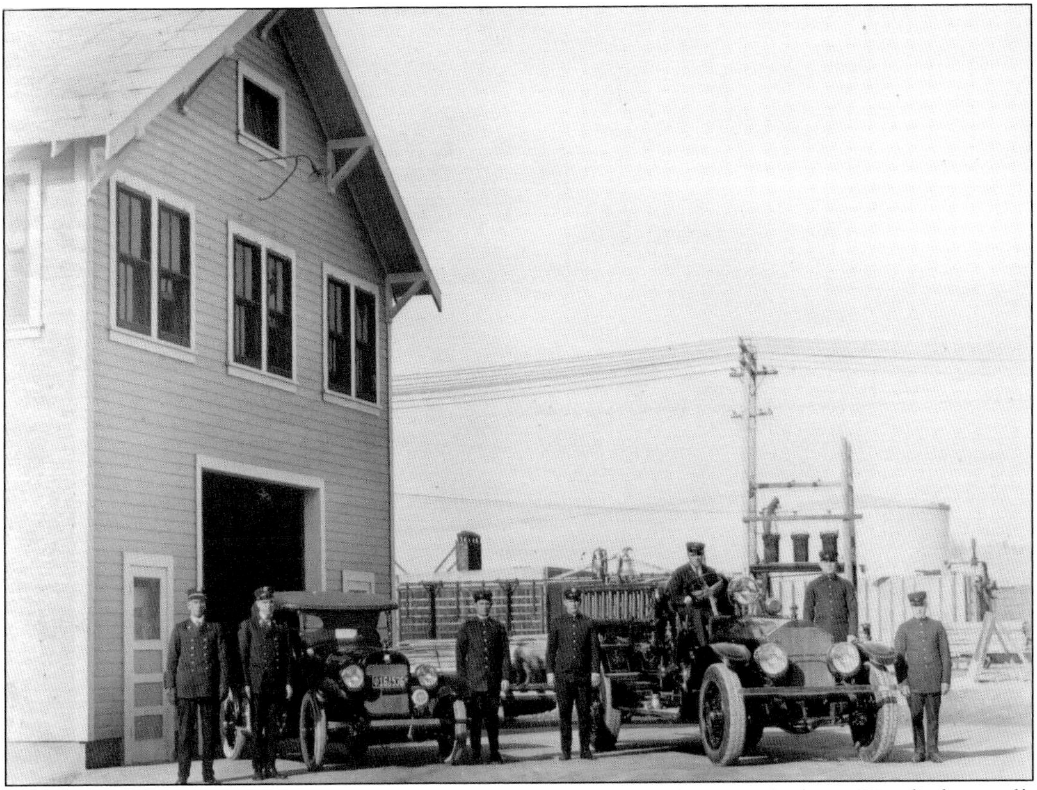

The new Weed Fire Department (above) was built in 1923 at the site of Abner Weed's first mill. Chief Small is second from left, Jim Small is fourth from left, and Mike Hogan is behind the wheel. The two 1922 American-La France fire engines are housed in the Weed Historic Lumber Town Museum and are still operational. Standing on the side of the fire engine around 1947 (below) are, from left to right, Chief Oeschgar, Junior Parker, and Claude Samples. Wood construction was highly susceptible to fires. A July 15, 1920, headline in the *Sisson Headlight* claims, "Weed Suffers Six Fires in Past Thirty Days—Company Barn Burns Last Night." The Shastina Volunteer Fire Department was organized in 1928 after two major fires broke out in Shastina.

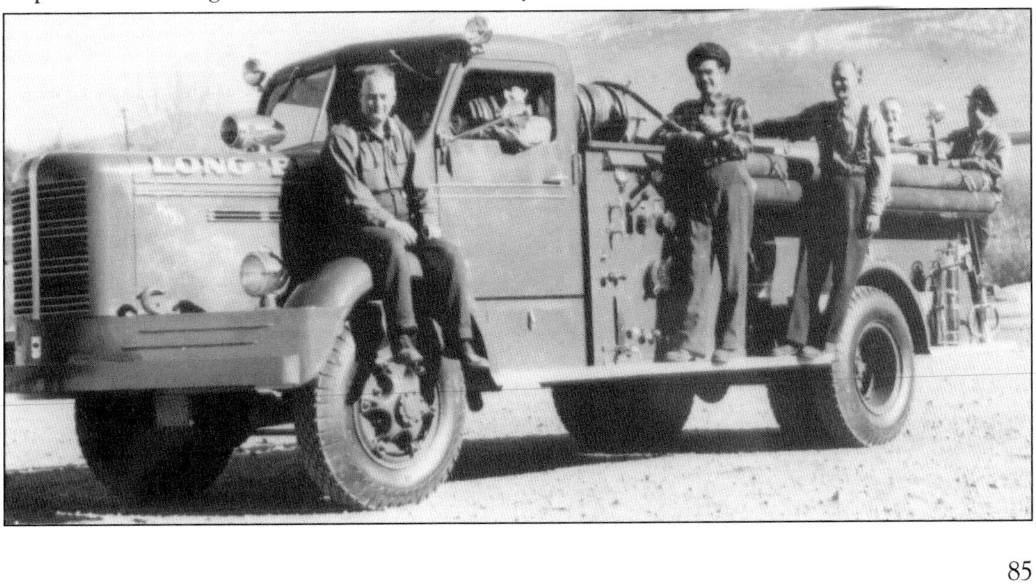

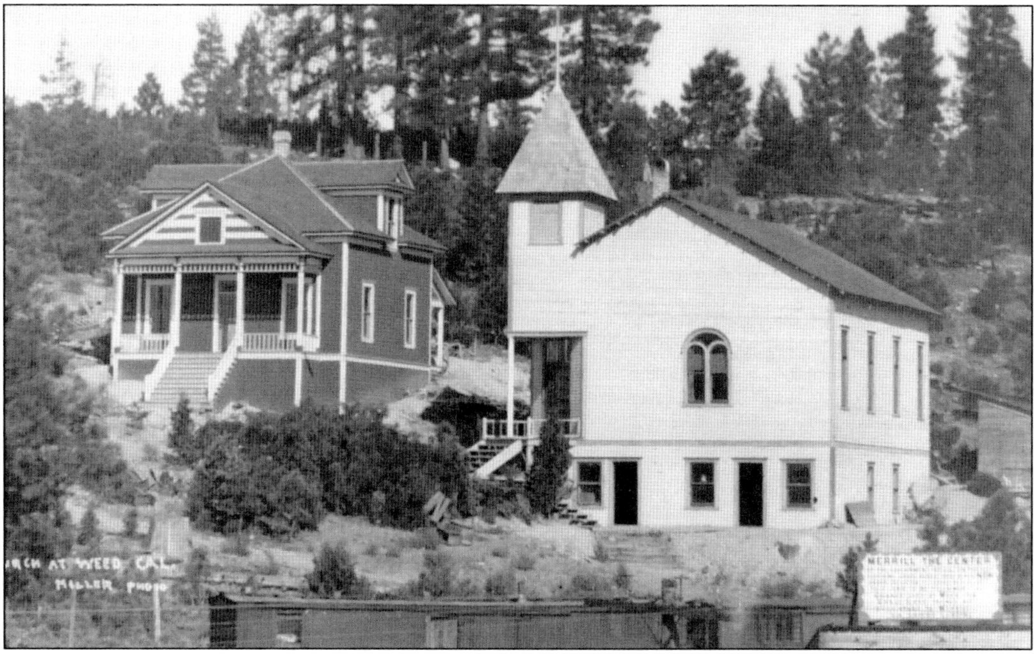

Prior to 1907, when the first church in Weed was built (above, right), townspeople gathered together on Sunday evenings in the area between the present-day Catholic and Presbyterian churches. In 1904, Phoebe Caulkett started a Presbyterian Sunday school in Moffett's Hall. In 1906, Reverend McCullagh from Sacramento organized the church in Weed, and Weed Lumber Company donated the land near what is now White Avenue. Weed Lumber Company also made the pews for the new Mount Shasta Church. The dedication service on September 1, 1907, was titled the "Greatest Day in the History of Weed and Vicinity." The parsonage is to the left of the church. The church was well-attended, as shown in the photograph below. (Above photograph by Charles R. Miller; below courtesy College of the Siskiyous Library Mount Shasta Collection.)

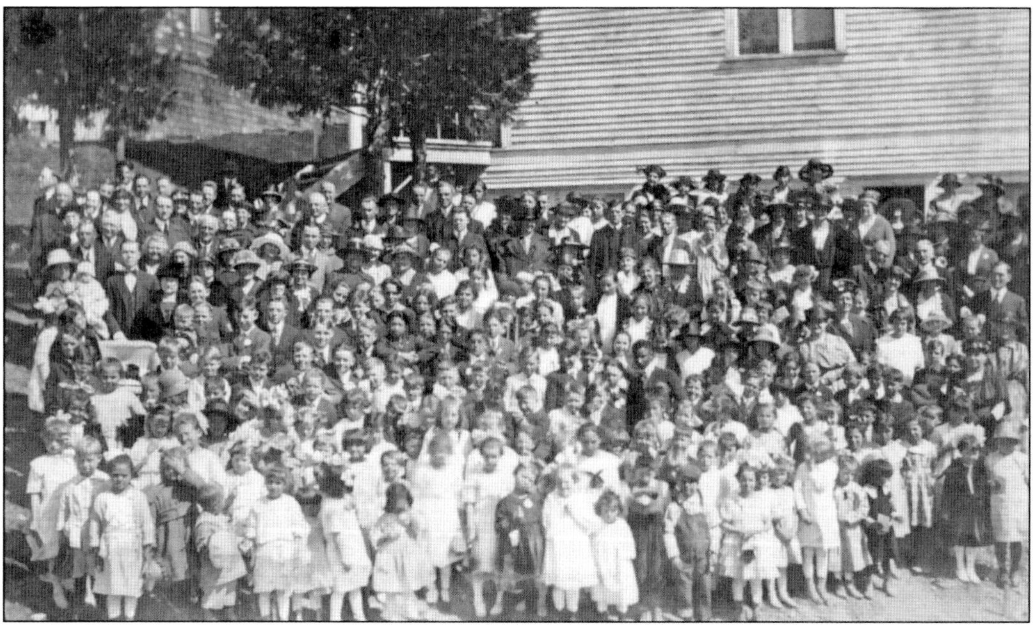

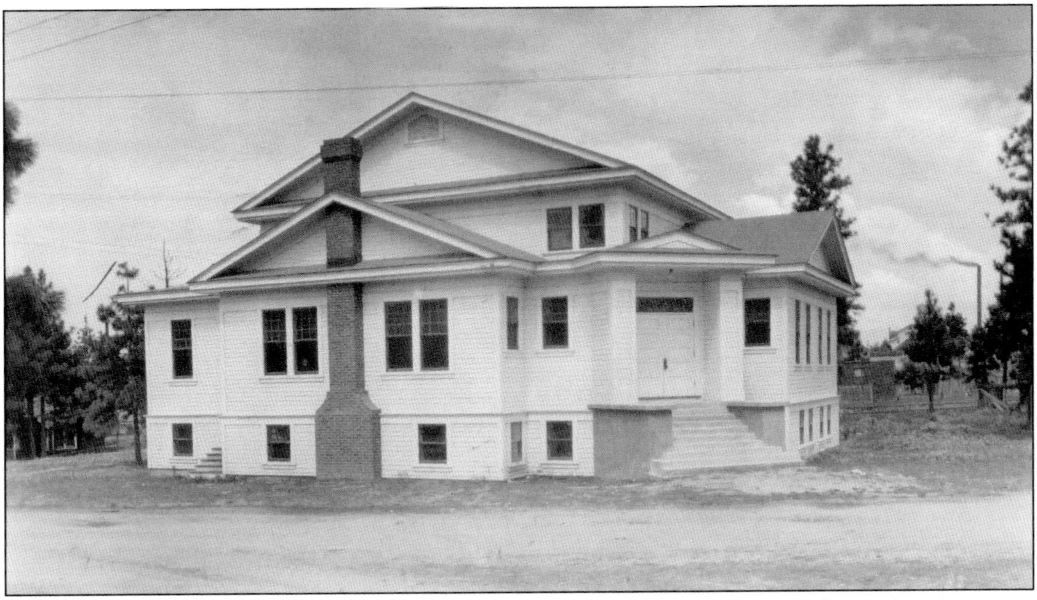

In 1920, the Mount Shasta Church decided it needed a new home. Long-Bell Lumber Company said it would provide matching funds, and, in November 1921, the new church was dedicated. In 1938, the name of the church was changed to the Weed Community Church because the nearby town of Sisson had changed its name to Mount Shasta City, causing confusion as to the location of the Mount Shasta Church. (Photograph by C. E. Yeager.)

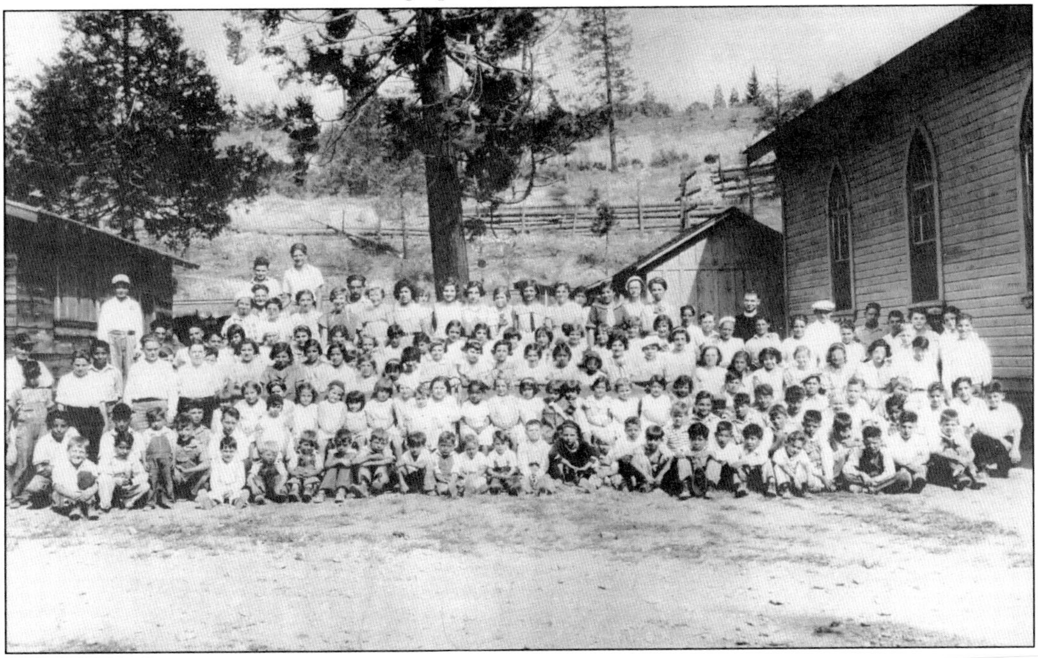

The first Catholic Church in Weed, St. Catherine's Catholic Church, was built in 1913 between Gilman Avenue and the railroad tracks. Fr. Michael Carr was the first priest. Fr. Michael Lucid (back right) was the priest when this photograph was taken in 1937. He helped establish the new Holy Family Catholic Church at 1051 North Davis Avenue, which was completed in 1937. (Courtesy Holy Family Catholic Church.)

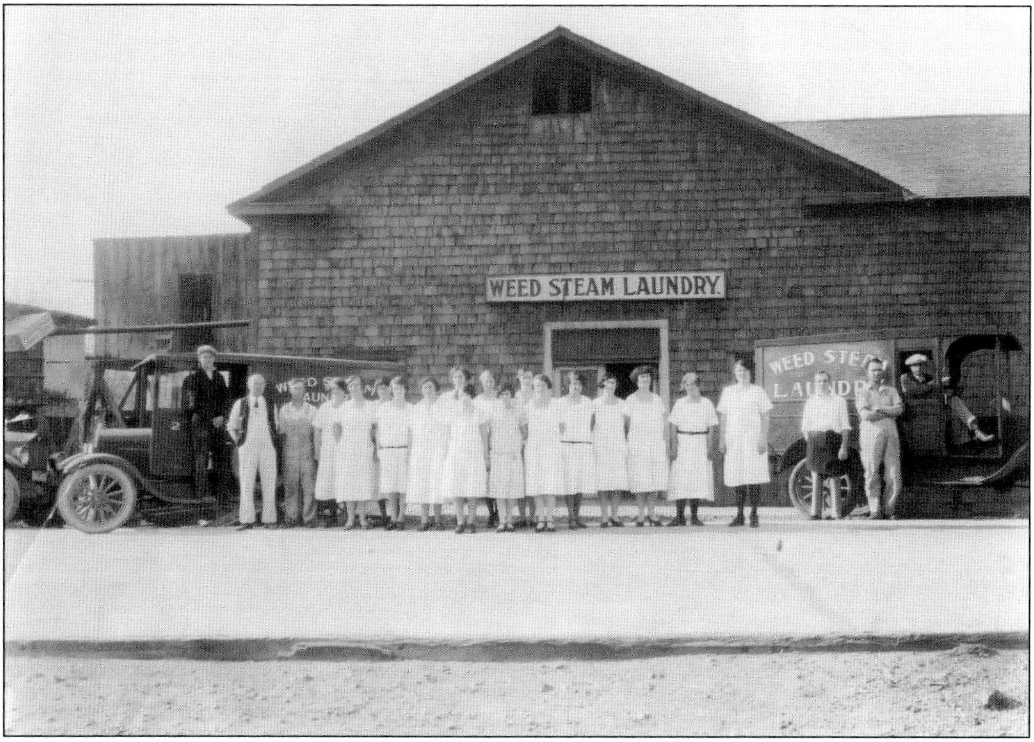

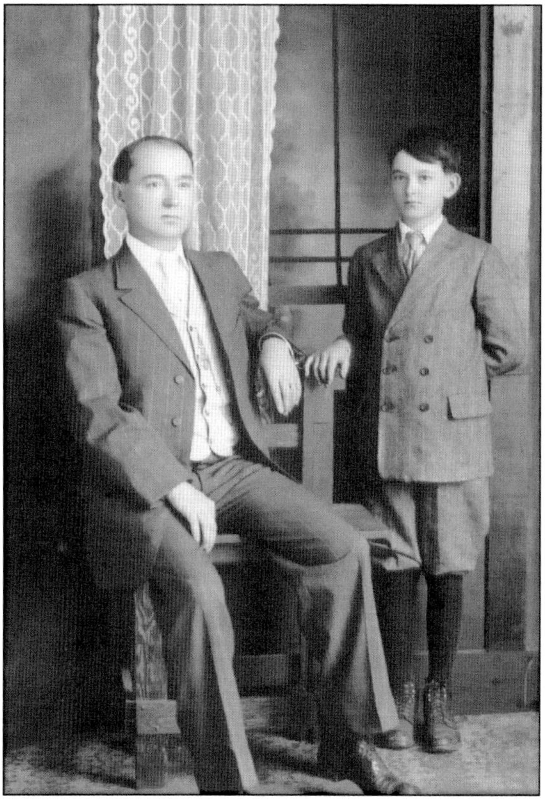

The Weed Steam Laundry (above) was established by Frank Heberlie at the request of the lumber management to serve the growing needs of the company and community. Frank was the owner and operator of a laundry in Ashland, Oregon, and the management made a trip to Ashland to ask him to establish a laundry service in Weed, which he did in 1910. The laundry was a success from the beginning with Frank Heberlie making his son Bernard Heberlie (left) a partner when he reached his majority. Their success continued until 1945. The business was eventually acquired by Jim and Katie (Barbieri) Fruzza who ran the laundry from 1946 to 1977 without any vacation days except holidays. (Information courtesy Elinor Heberlie Shelton and Katie Barbieri Fruzza.)

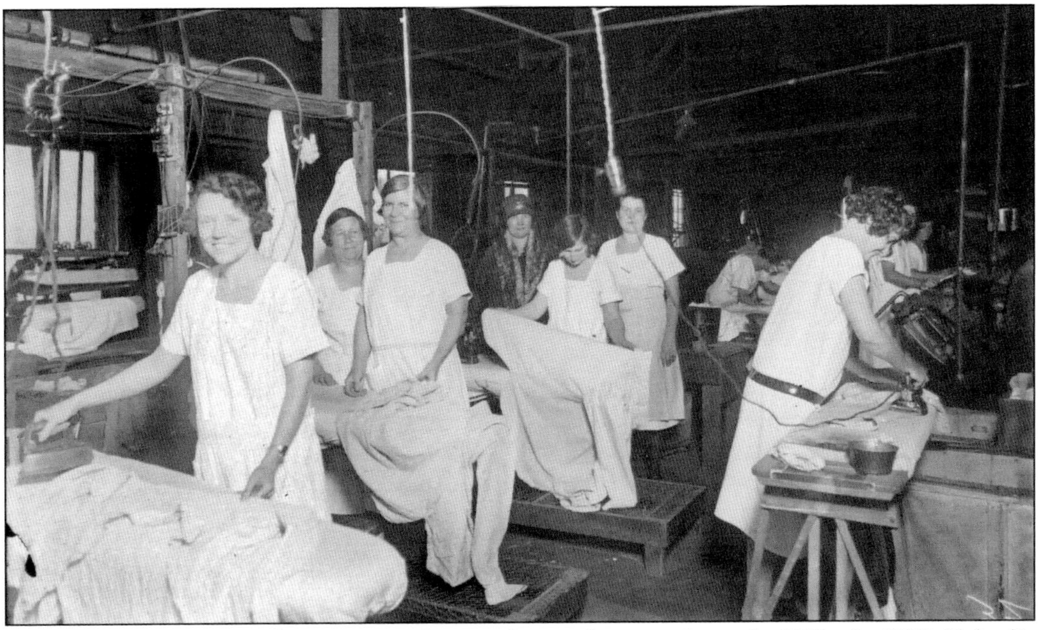

Laundry workers at Weed Steam Laundry are shown above in the early 1920s. In 1930, Heberlie employed 18 workers. Wong Louie (below, right) is shown with his wife, Rose Katherine Jeong, holding their two children, Jing and May. Rose's sister Yeen "Bessie" Jeong, who came to live with them in 1911, is standing in the front. When she was in the seventh grade, Wong decided to sell her, so Rose helped her run away to San Francisco, where she eventually became a doctor. The Wongs originally operated a laundry near the hospital. After Rose died during the 1918 influenza pandemic, Wong married Aking, who was 34 years younger than him. Together with the children, they operated the restaurant in the El Monte Hotel. Wong Louie, his wife Aking, and his two children are listed along with 10 other Chinese workers in the 1920 U.S. Census. They worked in the laundry, restaurant, hotel, and dry kilns.

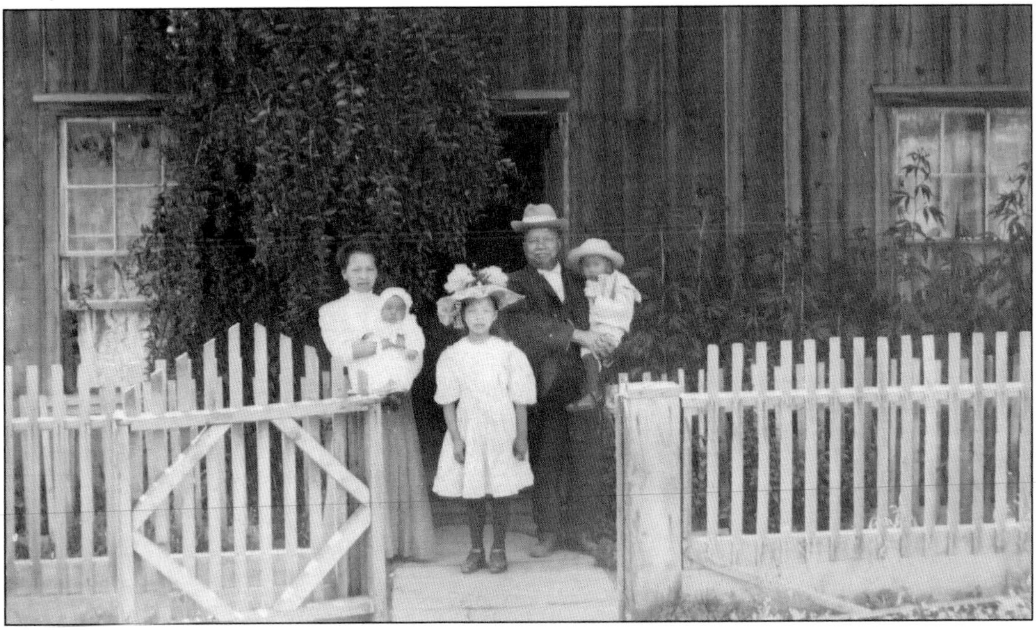

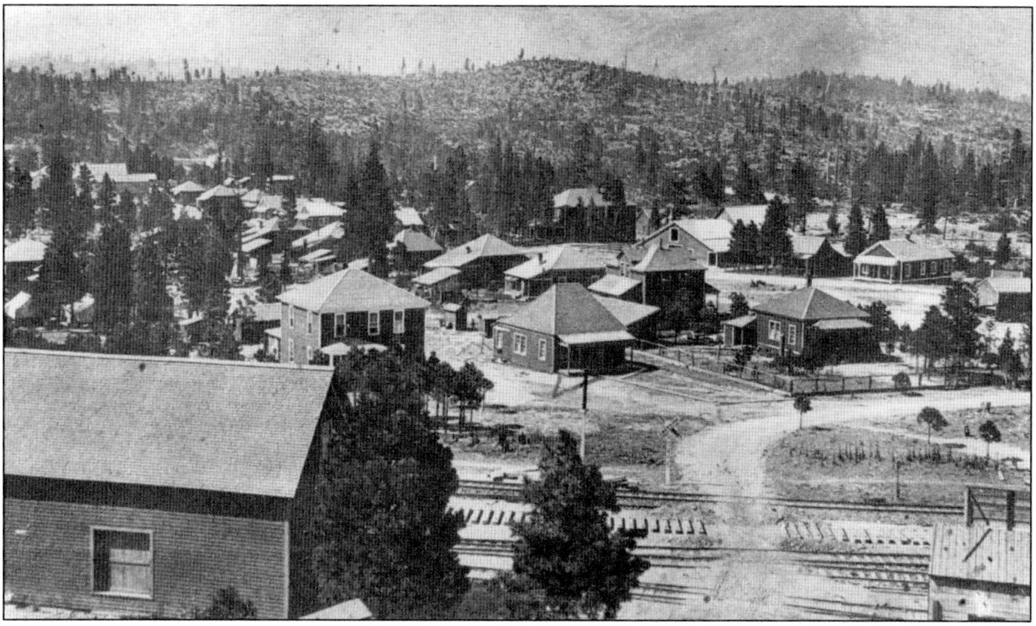

The view overlooking north Main Street (above) was taken from Schoolhouse Hill in 1915. Don Montgomery's livery barn (right center) is where the city hall is now located. To its right are the Don Montgomery and Lu Hobson homes. The two-story building to the left of the barn is the Weed Hospital, built in 1905. Weed Lumber Company collected $1 per month from each employee for hospital services. Doctors associated with Weed include Dr. Will Tebbe (1904–1929), Dr. Fred Tebbe (1906–1920), Dr. J. Roy Jones (1920–1922), Dr. Charles Nutting Jr. (1922–1929), Dr. Harold L. Vidricksen (1929–1970), Dr. McVicker (1936–1942), Dr. Victor Thompson (1952–1983), and Dr. William Schnack (1960–1977). Dr. Thompson's son-in-law, Dr. Sam Williams, has been a doctor in Weed since the 1970s. The 1905 view of Main Street (below) is to the south. (Below photograph by Charles R. Miller.)

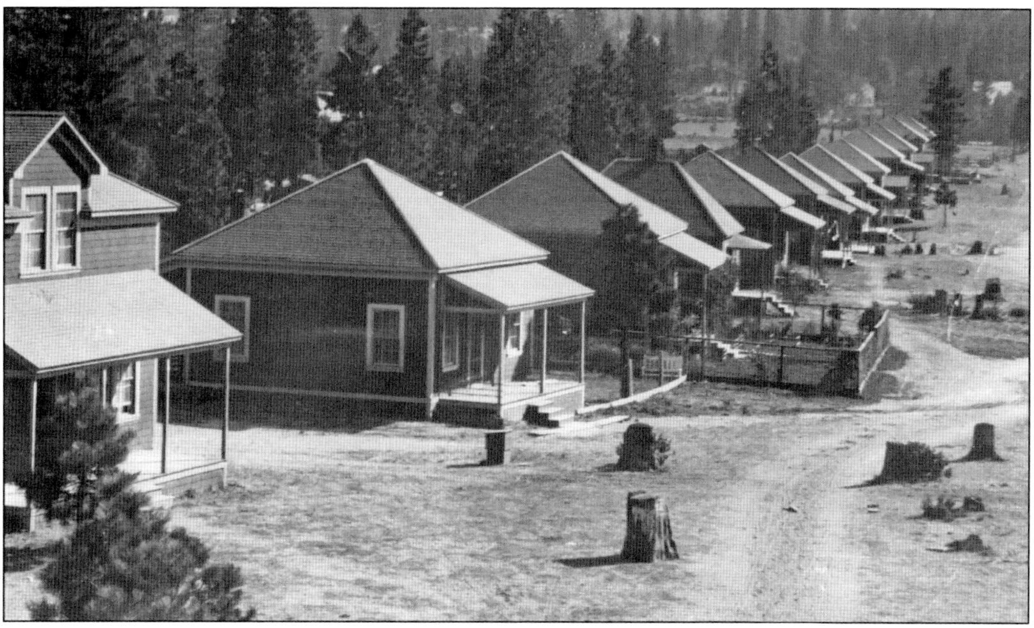

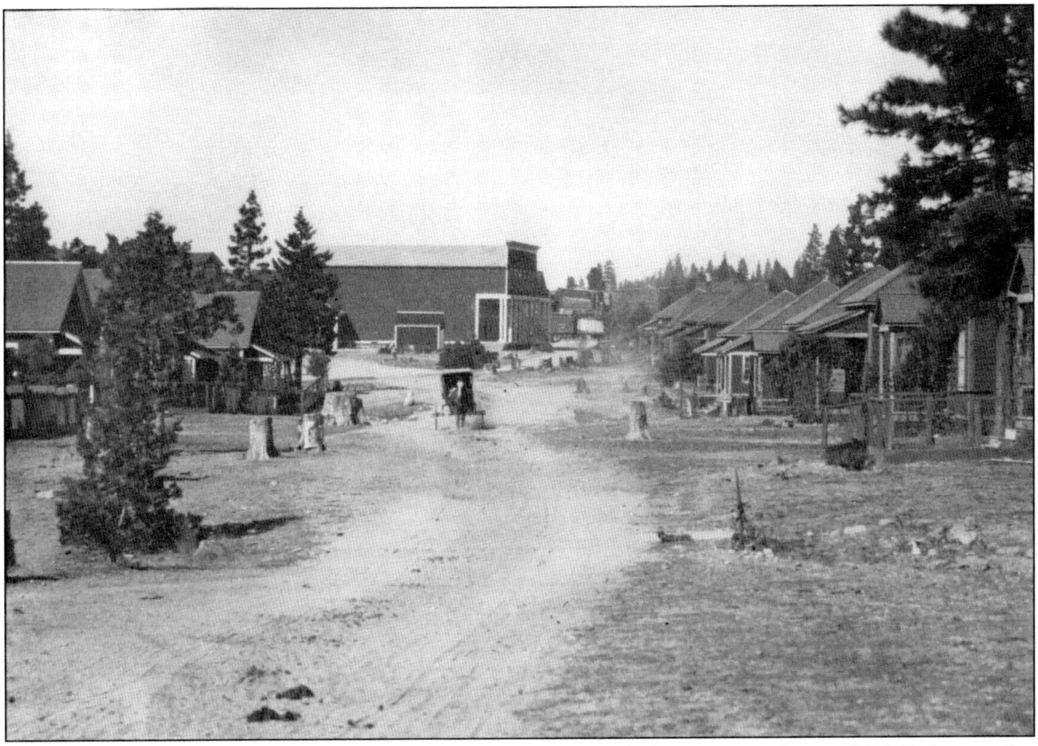

The image above is of Main Street looking north toward the mercantile in 1907. Below is the same view of Main Street about 10 years later. Each company house was painted barn red with a white trim. The box on the telephone poles (front right) is a fire alarm. Every block had one, and each block had its own alarm code. To ring the alarm, the glass had to be broken and the lever pulled. The alarm on this pole was two rings followed by a pause and two more rings. All alarms were repeated two times, so everyone would know where to go to help. The alarm up the street by the mercantile had two rings, pause, then one ring. All company houses had a fire alarm list with the codes.

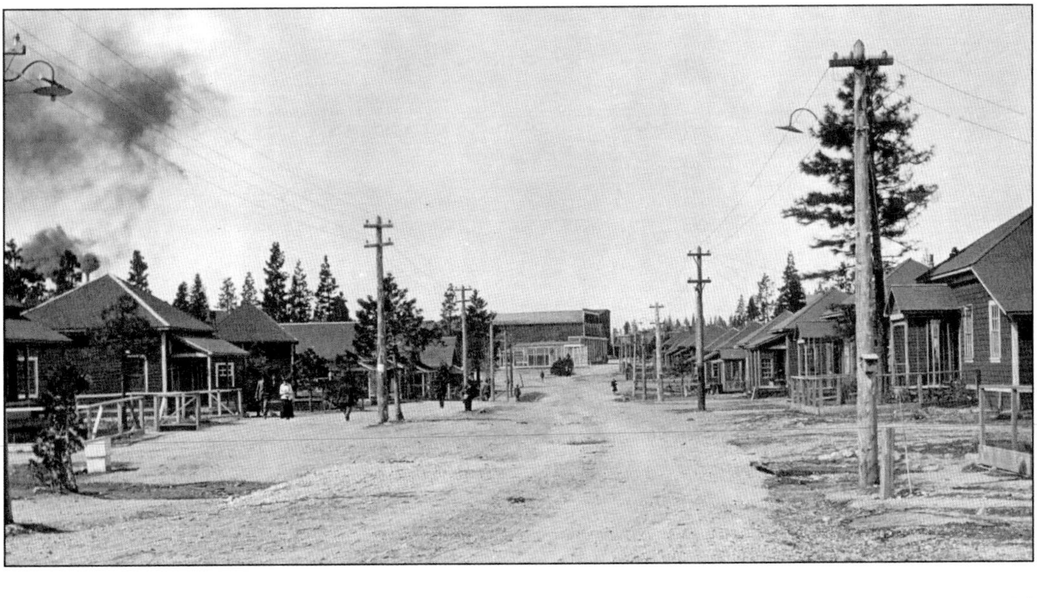

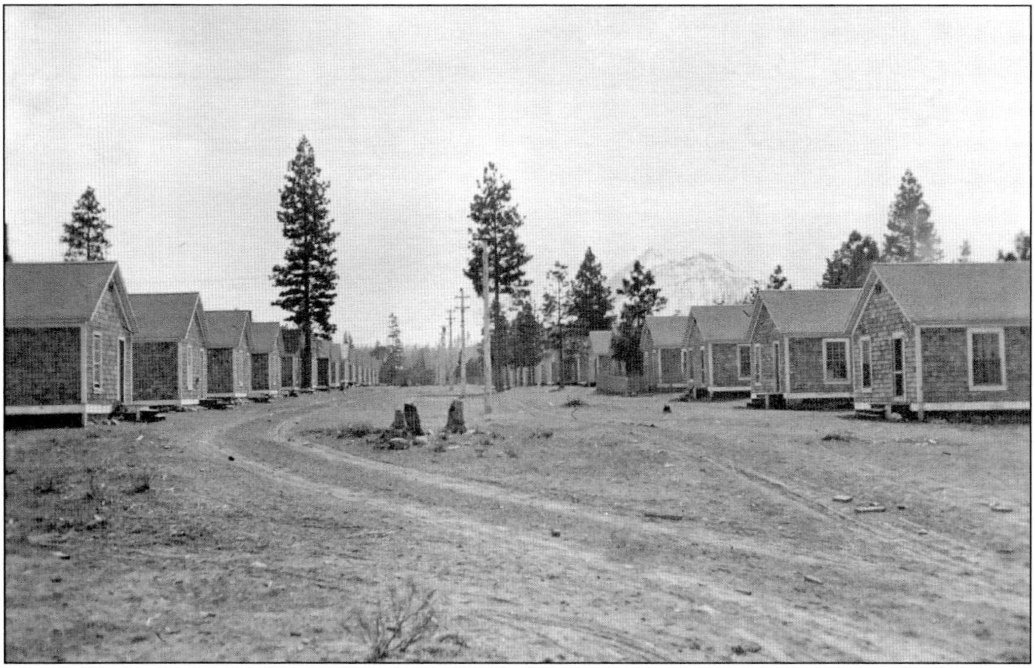

Houses at Rabbit Flat (above), shown in 1913, were not as elaborate as houses on Main Street. Black Butte can be seen in the distance. A decade later, yards and fences were added to the company houses, as seen on Liberty Avenue (below) looking north in 1922. The houses on Liberty had porches because they were for the higher class workers with jobs such as sawyers, filers, and millwrights. Workers who became foremen were moved to the upper-class areas, such as Main Street, Gilman Avenue, and Shasta Avenue. The homes from Rabbit Flat, Liberty Avenue, and Stringtown were relocated to Oak and Morris Streets in Angel Valley. (Photograph by C. E. Yeager; courtesy Ellen Barnum Martin.)

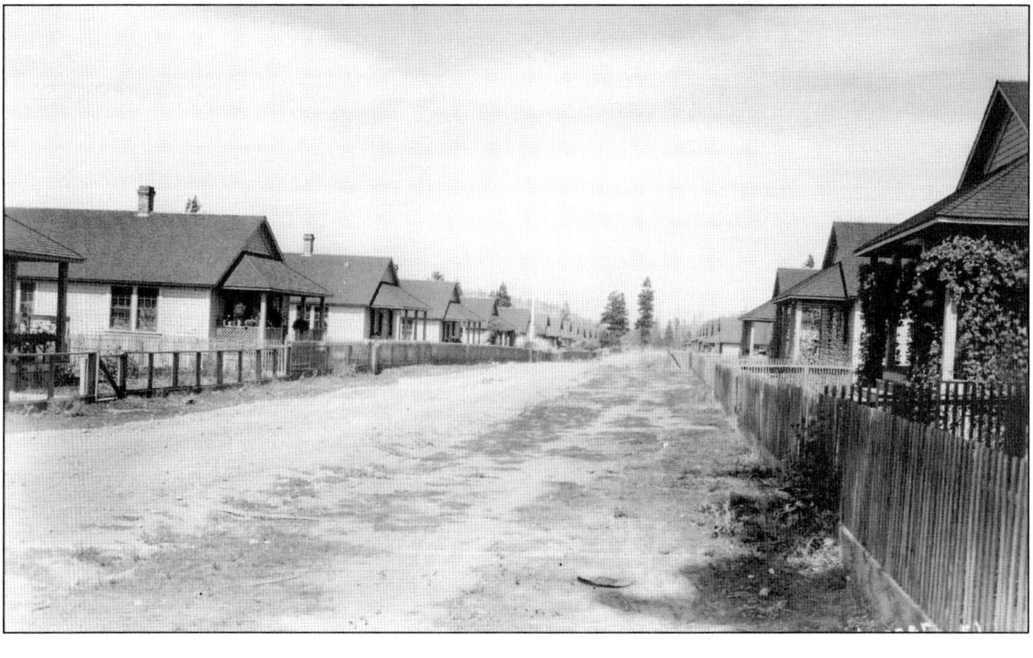

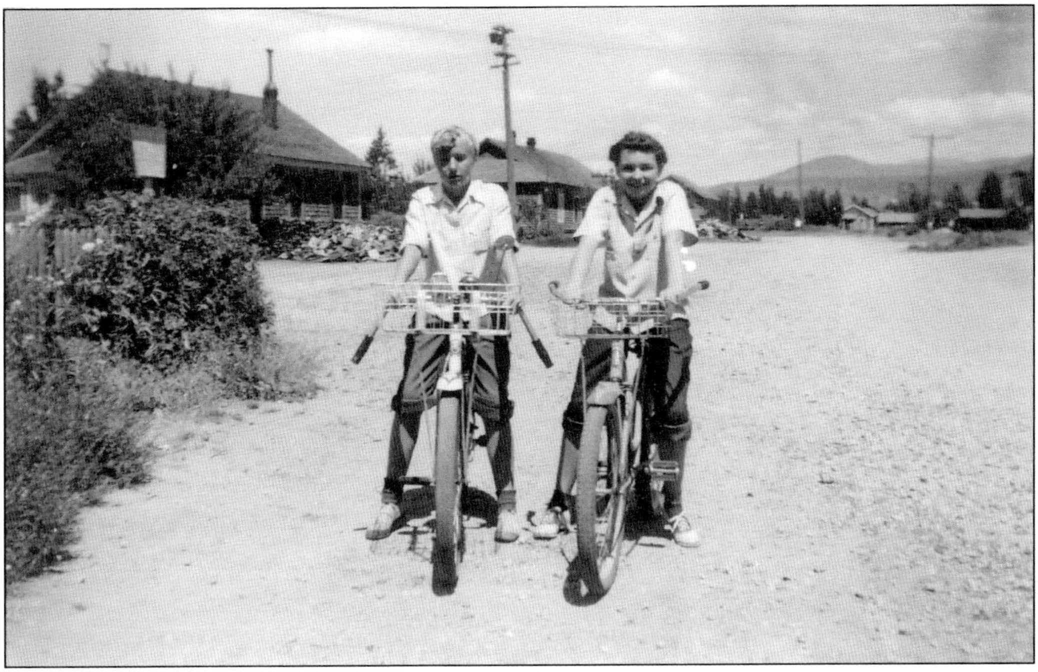

Best friends (then and now) Vivian Welborn (above, left) and Eleanor Rippon are shown riding bicycles in Rabbit Flat in 1944. They would ride their bikes all the way to Edgewood. Eleanor was the daughter of Cy and Sally (Kouts) Rippon, owners of the local newspaper who contributed greatly to the preservation of Weed and Siskiyou County history. (Courtesy Vivian "Vi" Welborn Mauden.)

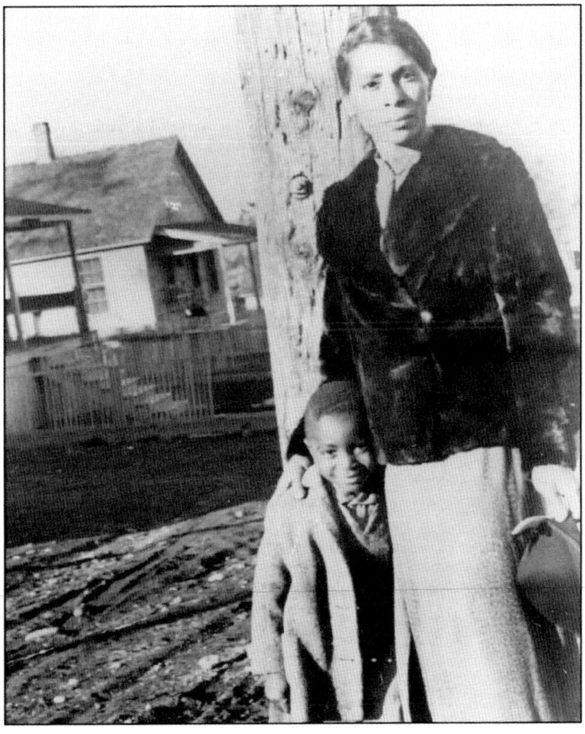

Aplis with son Dave Cameaux Jr., shown around 1928, lived in "the Quarters," now known as Lincoln Heights. Aplis Camble was born in Louisiana. In 1926, her husband transferred to Weed, where he worked for Long-Bell Lumber Company as a wholesale stocker. Aplis earned an operator's license at a Los Angeles beauty school then opened her own salon at her home in Weed. (Courtesy College of the Siskiyous Library Mount Shasta Collection.)

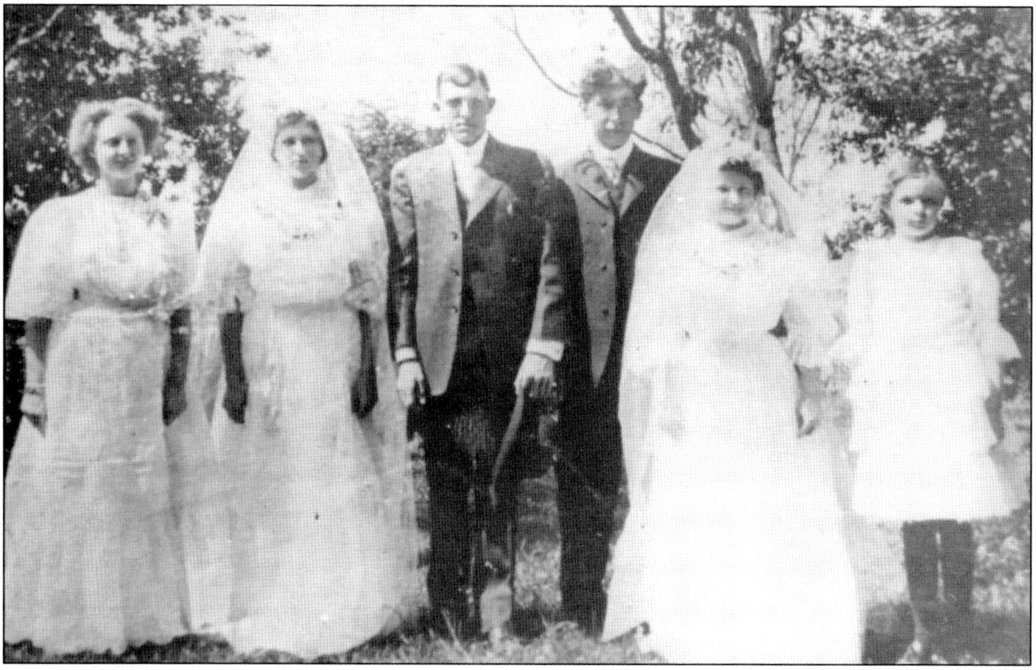

The July 4, 1907, *Sisson Headlight* featured what it called a "Double Wedding at Edgewood" (above). This was the first wedding at the Methodist church in Edgewood. The bridesmaids are Claire McCombe and Bernice Stone. The wedding couple on the left is Maud Kundert and Henry D. Bagley. The couple on the right is Thomas W. "Dick" Linville and Golda M. Schuler. "Both couples boarded the 4:25 p.m. southbound train for a brief honeymoon," according to the article. The Linville house (below) in Angel Valley, shown in 1920, had three bedrooms, a kitchen, a living area, and a bathroom. The water tank on left was for this house only. The Linville family includes, from left to right, grandfather Henry Schuler, mother Goldie (Schuler) Linville, and children Alford, Edna, Jack, Rachel, and George Linville, who still lives in the house today. (Photograph by Dick Linville; courtesy Alford Linville.)

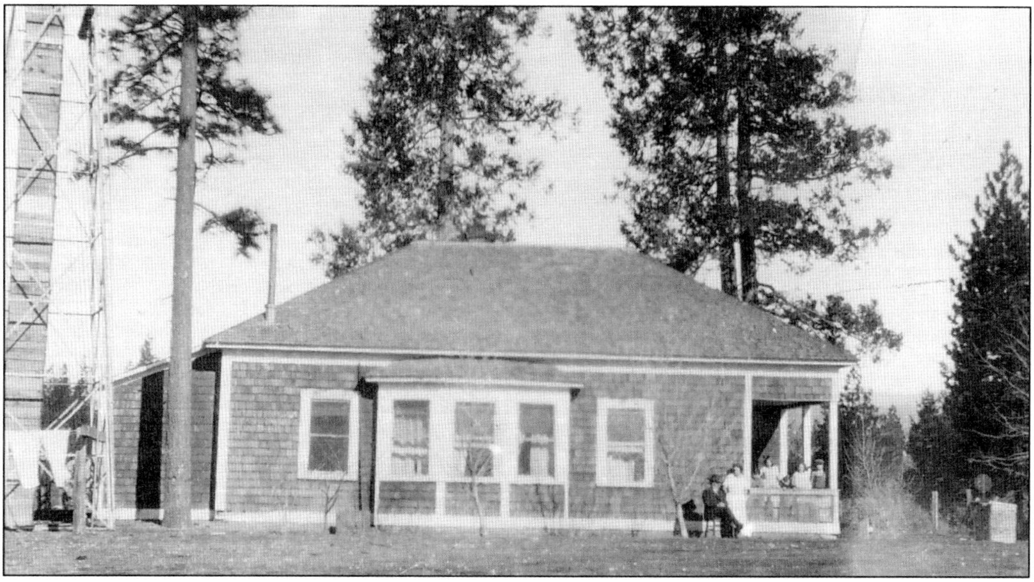

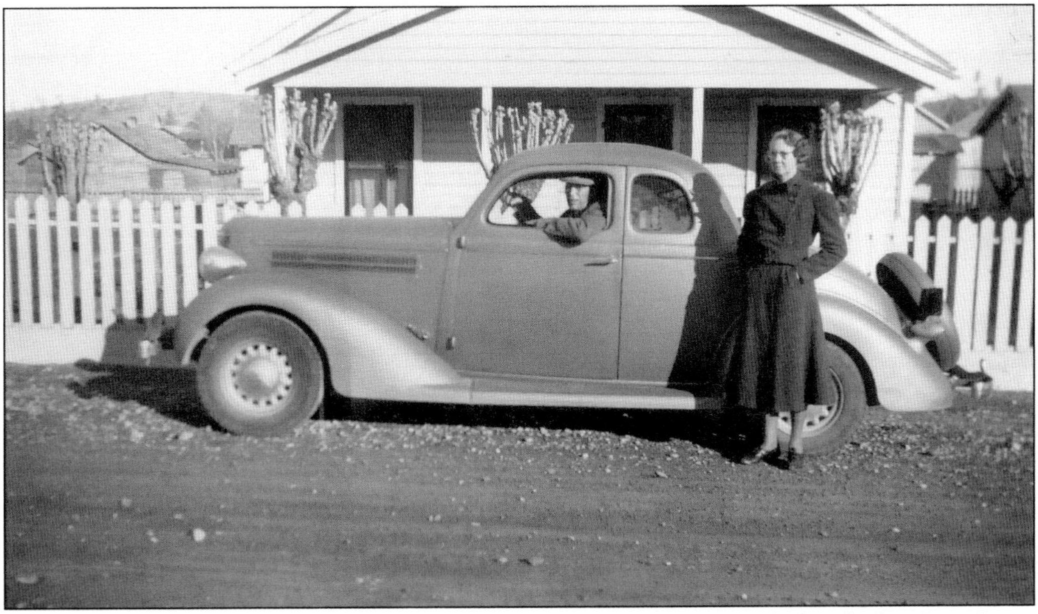

Vern (left) and Angie (Courtney) Norris are pictured on Pine Street in 1936 beside their brand-new Chevy coupe. Vern was a jack-of-all-trades, ranging from tree-topper to log roller to rumrunner to sheriff. They once owned a restaurant in Dorris. Angie was a fantastic cook and seamstress. (Courtesy Vivian "Vi" Welborn Mauden.)

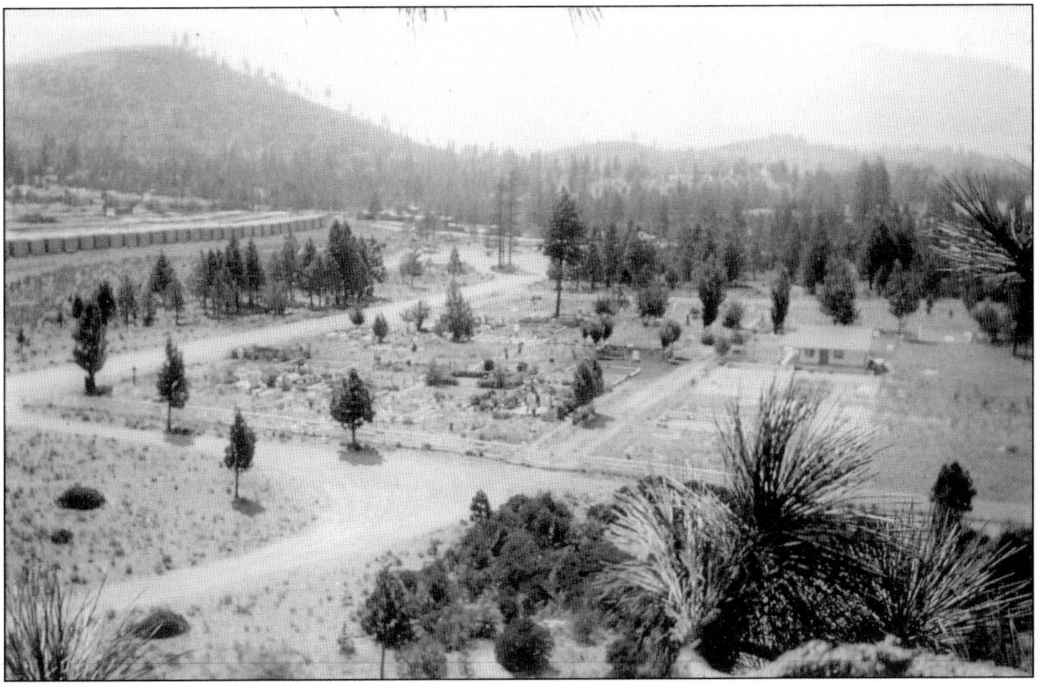

Winema Cemetery is located on the north side of Weed next to Highway 97 near Angel Valley. The oldest surviving headstone dates back to 1901. This photograph was taken from a "crow's nest" in a nearby tree in 1937. Lincoln Heights Cemetery is located across the highway; Long-Bell Lumber Company segregated blacks and whites in life and in death. (Photograph by Alford Linville.)

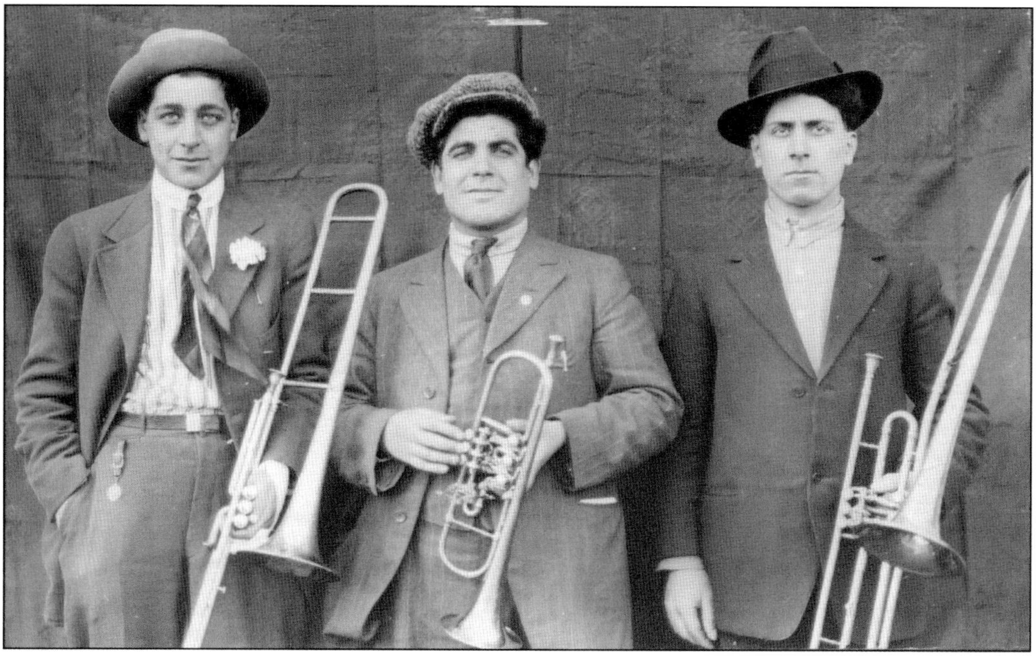

Pictured above are Frank Girimonte (left) and Mike Paletta (right) with their music teacher Mr. DeMarco (center). Paletta came from Italy to Weed in 1913 at age 19. His two older brothers already lived in Weed. He worked for Long-Bell Lumber Company until 1923 when he started his own shoe shop in Dunsmuir. He moved his store, Mike Paletta's Shoe Shop, to Weed's Main Street in 1926 and worked there until he retired in 1968. Paletta joined the Weed Italian Band (below), led by DeMarco (center), soon after he came to Weed. He played the trombone and baritone. When the troop trains came through Weed during World War I, the band would play for them. At the start of the war there were 25 band members but 10 died during the war.

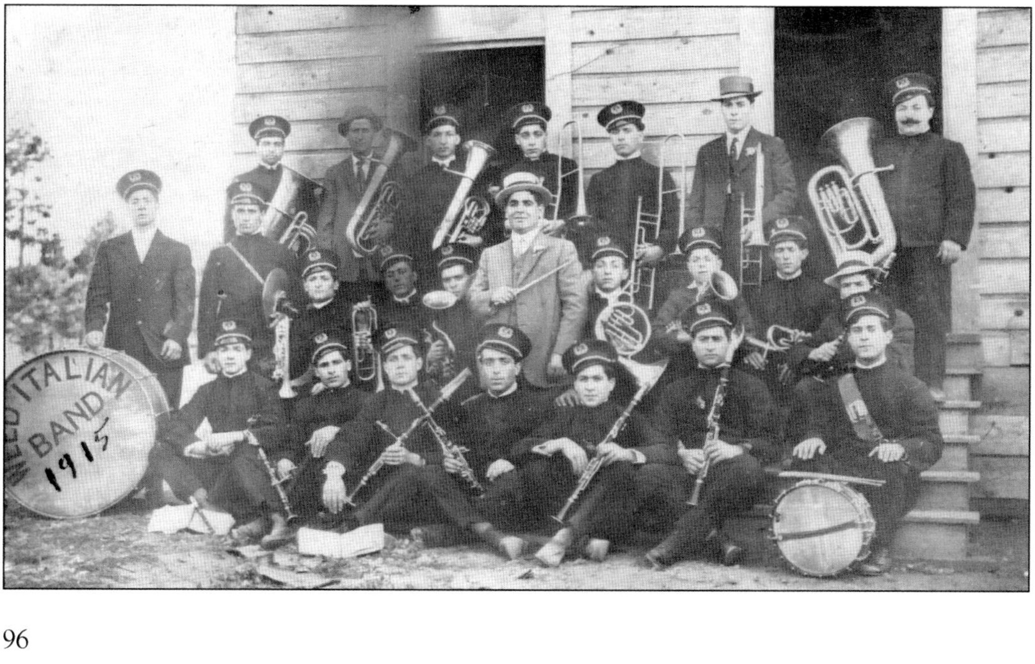

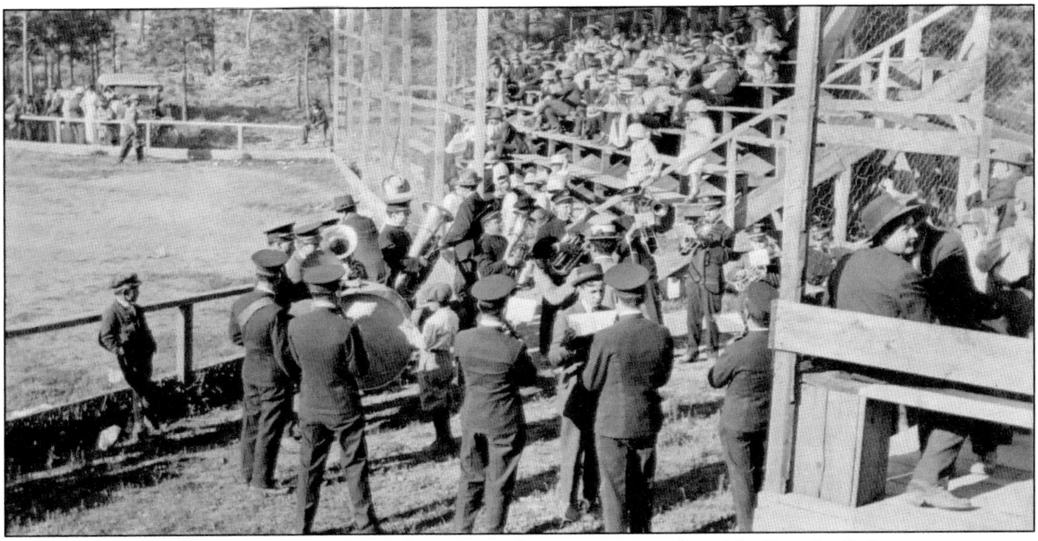

The Weed Italian Band (above) is playing at the grammar school ballpark. Below, two young musicians, including Bill Barni (front left), are playing for a bachelor's party, shown on the steps of the Weed Community Presbyterian Church in Weed in 1929. The following are, from left to right, (first row, behind standing boys) Secondo Chiment (seated), Euginio Bailo, Primo Bastiznon, Giovanni Duchi, Agostino Bece Peruzzi, Erminio Boito, and Paul Brunello (seated); (second row) Domenico Andregetto, John Sartor, Cesare Peruzzi, Ci Borio (in bow tie), and Atillio Pozzabon; (third row) Louie Filipen, Lorenzo Benato, Bruno Zandona, Francesco Boffa, and unidentified; (fourth row) Luigi Ducin (standing), Guiseppe "Joe" DePaoli, Lorenzo Belinoanta, Guiseppe Scarabello, Innocente Gardin, Albino Zambonin, and Pete Gasparivi (with hand on hip). (Courtesy Jill Colombana.)

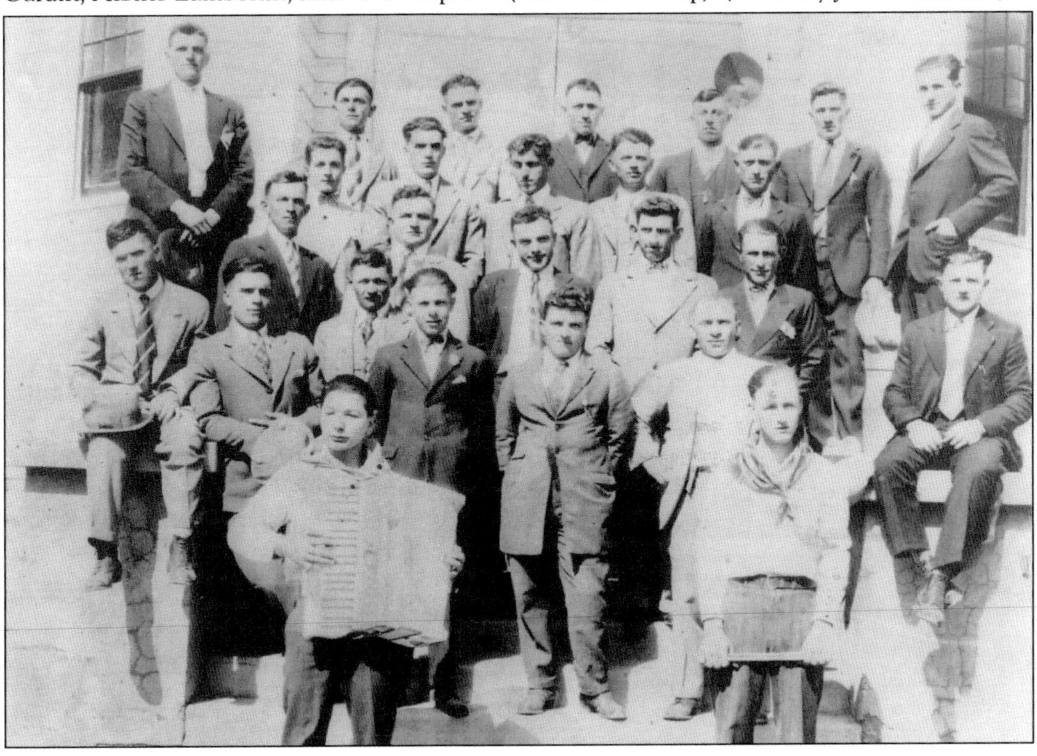

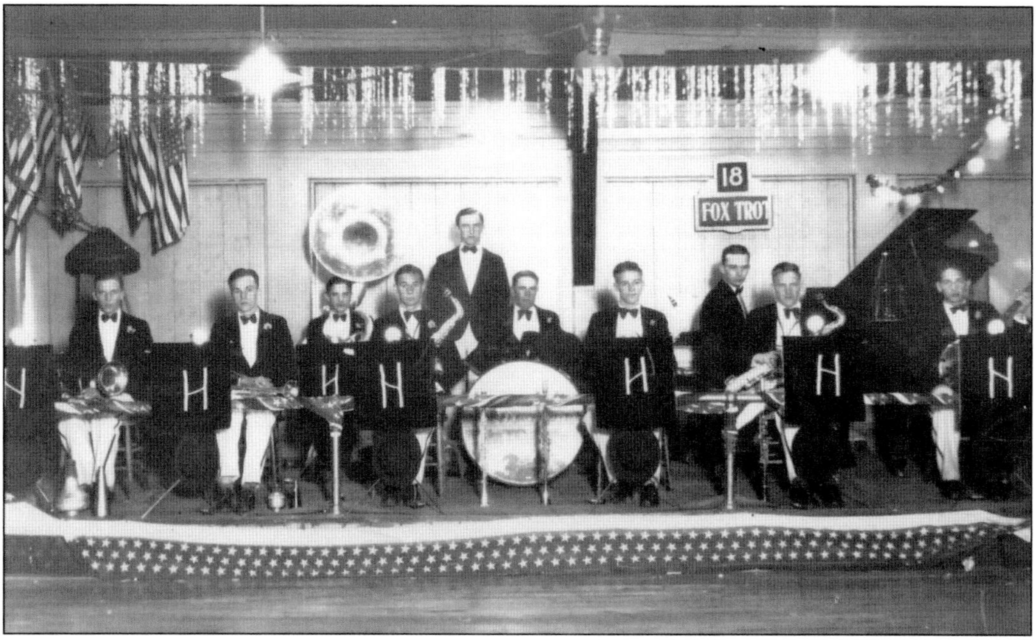

The famous Hottentots played in the Hippodrome from 1930 to 1958. The band manager is Lawrence Tolosano (standing), pictured with band members, from left to right, Joe Mazzei (trombone), Melvin Martin (trumpet), Doug Dragos (bass), Doug Thorpe (saxophone), Bud Cook (drums), unidentified, Dick Hyland (piano), Dan Fenno (saxophone), and Sam M. Mazzei (banjo). Tolosano organized the band when he was 17 years old, taught the band how to read music, and arranged the music.

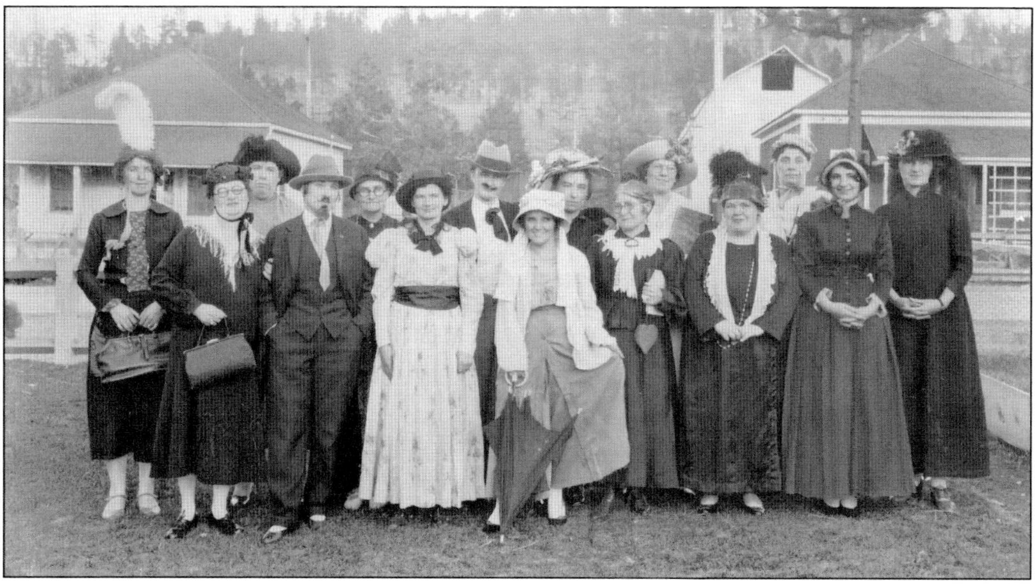

The drama club in Weed, around 1927, included from left to right: two unidentified, Mary Jaine Kegg, two unidentified, Mable Jones, two unidentified, Edna Reed, Dora Lynch, Myra Angel, Thelma (Caulkett) Betts, Irene Mallory, Mary (Engemyer) Scott, and two unidentified. The Long-Bell horse barn in the background is the site of the Weed Historic Lumber Town Museum. The houses were later relocated to 367 Main Street (left) and 363 Gilman Avenue (right).

Joe Lockyear moved to Edgewood in 1900 and became the constable in Weed in 1912. He was a well-known artist with a studio at 210 Main Street. He painted large murals on the walls of Black Butte Saloon and El Monte Hotel. The Weed Museum has one of Lockyear's paintings of Crater Lake, which was painted for Dick Linville in the 1920s. (Courtesy Glenna Pittock.)

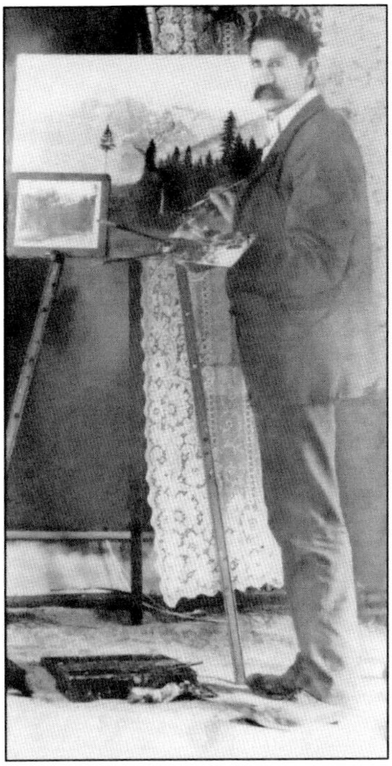

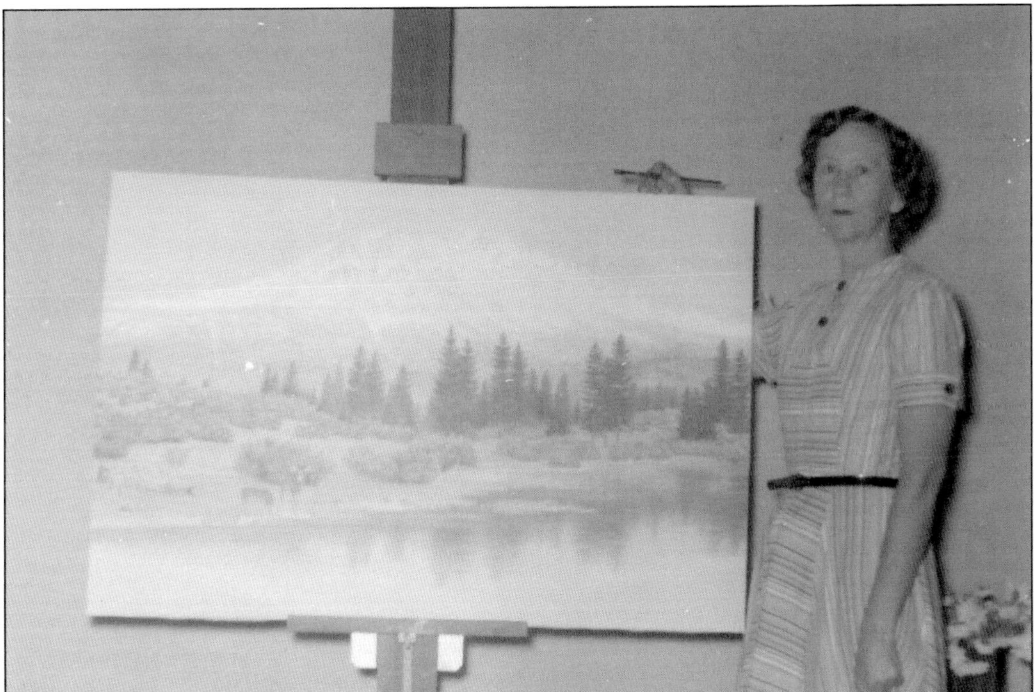

Verna (Norris) Welborn, shown in 1956, began painting at the age of 10 and took lessons from Joe Lockyear. Three of her paintings of Mount Shasta were at Hotel Weed in Dunsmuir but were stolen during the hotel's renovation. When Lockyear died in 1924, Verna was given his easel and paint box. Verna finished her last painting at age 94, just before she died in December 2000. (Courtesy Vivian "Vi" Welborn Mauden.)

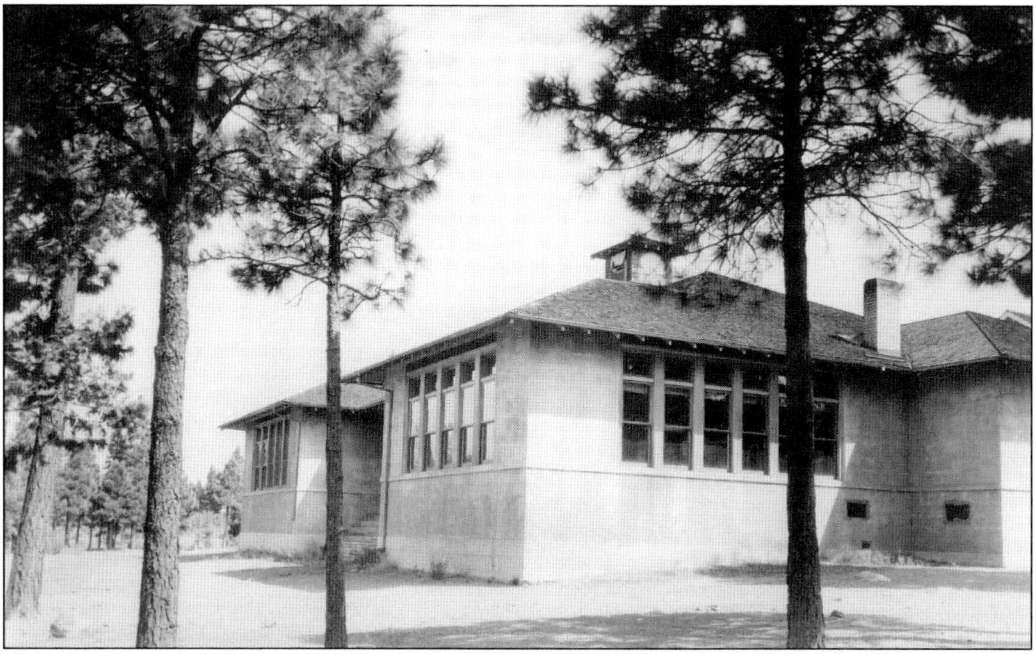

Summit School was originally located near Black Butte and served Igerna and Weed. It burned down in December 1905, so it was temporarily relocated to Angel Valley. In May 1906, Weed Lumber Company donated some land on a nearby hill, later known as Schoolhouse Hill. George E. Luttrell, the new principal hired in July 1908, built a schoolroom on the donated land. In 1910, a new four-room cement-block school was built (above), which housed the entire school. The old bell from this schoolhouse is located at the Weed Historic Lumber Town Museum. Pearl Sullaway (below, right) began teaching in 1915. At that time, the cement-block schoolhouse was overflowing, so she taught at the Mount Shasta Church. Below are Miss Sullaway's third-grade students around 1918. (Courtesy Joe Girimonte.)

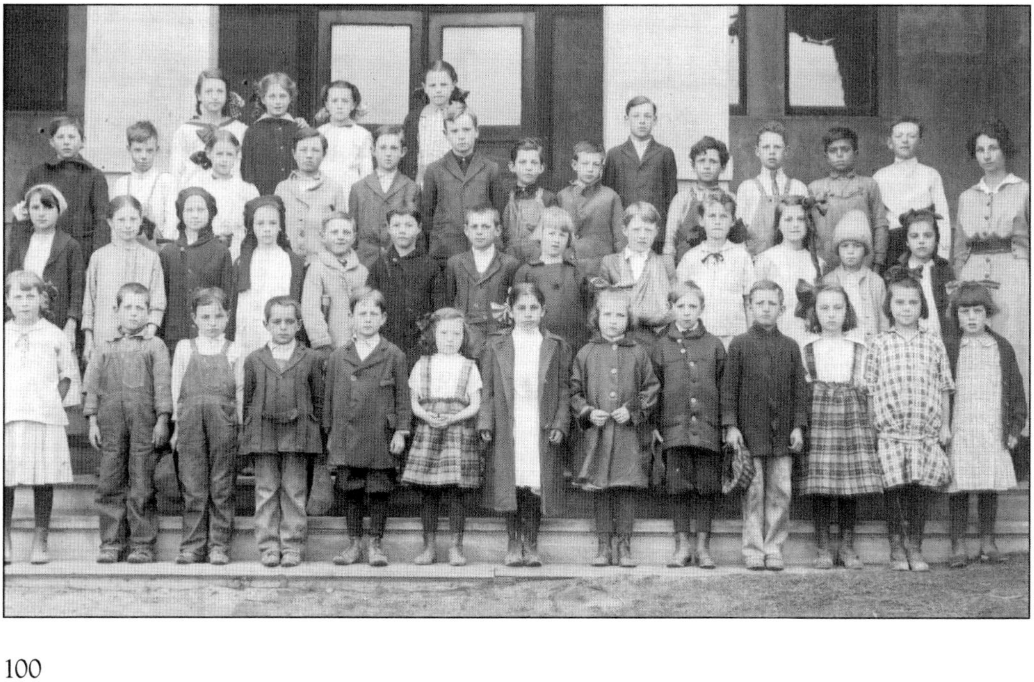

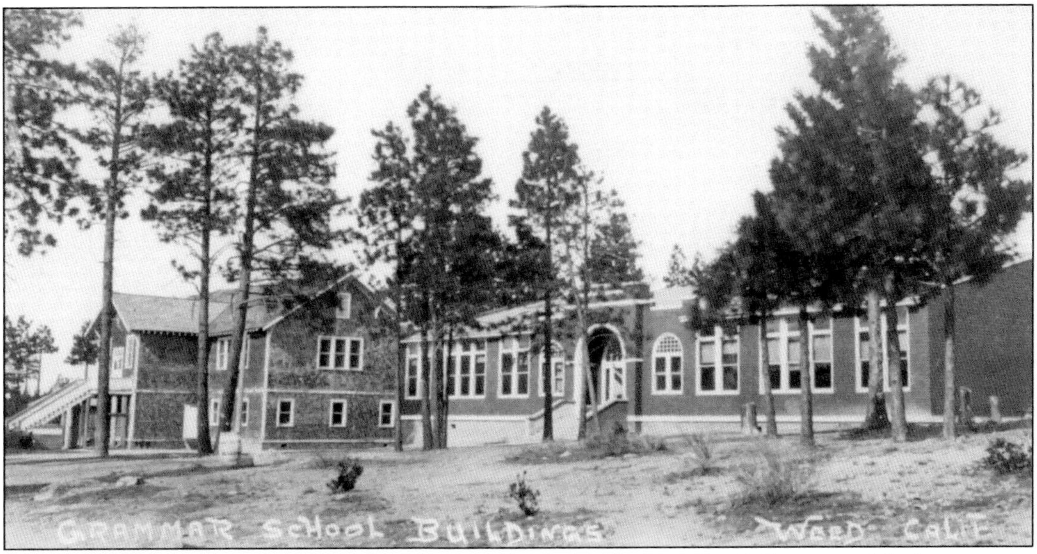

In 1915, a new two-story wooden building (left) was built near the 1910 cement-block grammar school. The first school built on Schoolhouse Hill became the band room. Continued expansion due to the prosperity of Weed resulted in the construction of the fourth building (right) in 1920 and a fifth building in 1925 (attached to the back of fourth building). The Summit School District was renamed Weed Union School District in 1921.

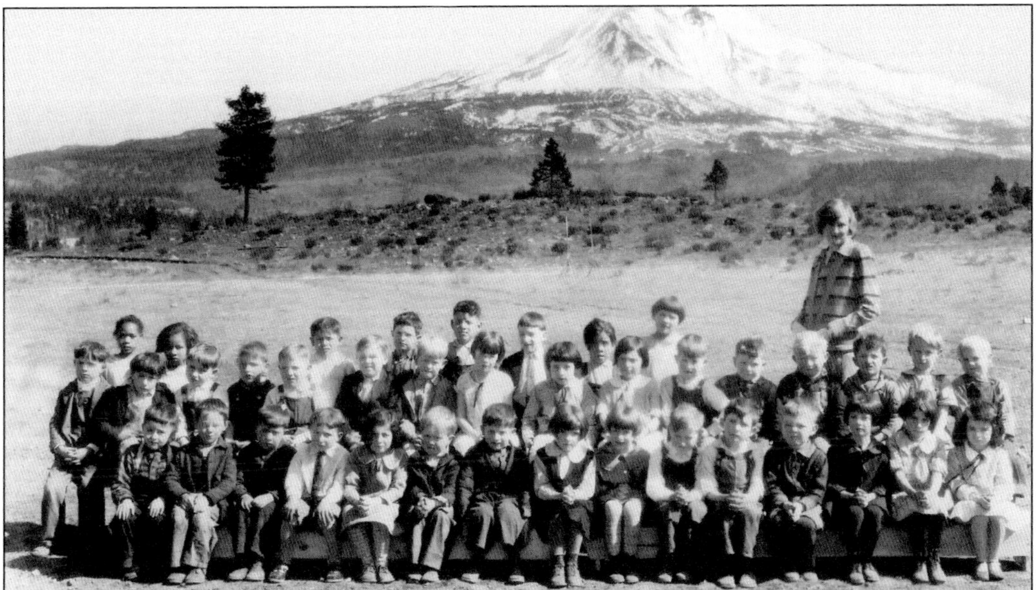

Evelyn Womble's first-grade class of 1927–1928 included the following, from left to right, (first row) Sam Durante, unidentified, Joe Cortez, three unidentified, Joe Aquila, unidentified, Camile Cremer, unidentified, Fred Bertoli, George Kent, Josephine Fontana, Carolina Bianco, and unidentified; (second row) Louis Piva, unidentified, Joe "Jake" Barcaglia, two unidentified, Ned Goss, Cedro Serna, George Meline, Sam Catalano, David Dumble, Joe Delgado, June Clark, Tony Esposito, Severina Cortese, Meltshore ? (father worked for Southern Pacific), unidentified, LeVern Bisoff, Joe Millard, two unidentified, Guido Cunial, and two unidentified. Evelyn Wambold later married Floyd Barnum. (Courtesy Terry and Larry Dalin and Caroline Carpine.)

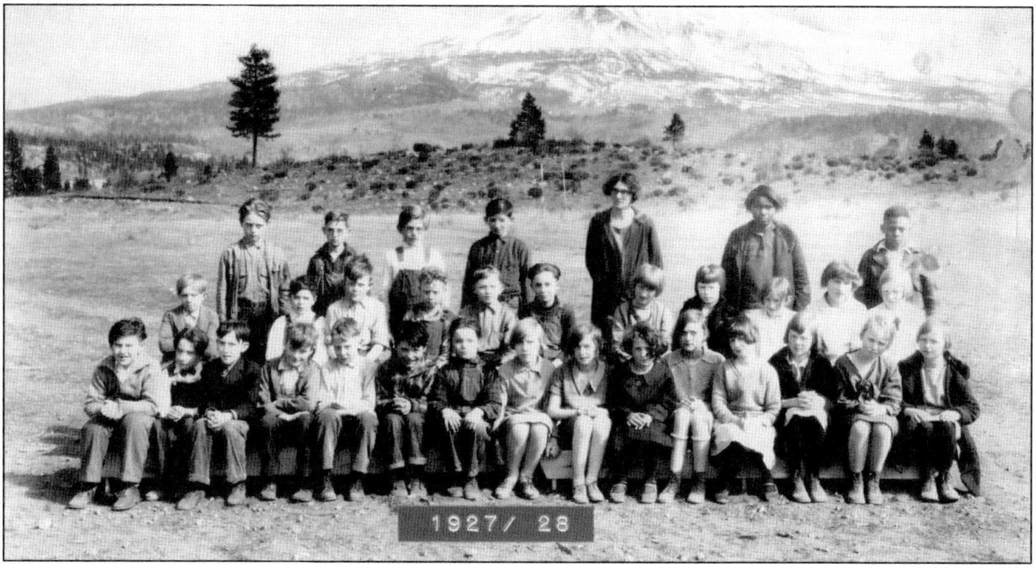

Miss Edson's 1927–1928 fourth-grade class included, from left to right, (first row) Frank Leonetti, Tony Wilson, Charles Welch, Hiram Cheney, Edwin Kersey, Alford Linville, Etalo Barbieri, Bernice Angers, Anita Sbarbaro, Lia Cavarzan, Medreth Jones, Lorraine Melin, Juanita Melin, Mary Maxwell, and Marie Sexton; (second row) Russell Riley, George Tallah, Robert Coleman, Leo Angers, David Mealiffe, Leo Francisco Cavarzan, Clella Mokler, Dorothy ?, Helen Hecker, Wilhelmena Bisoff, and Margie Welch; (third row) Louie Welch, Louis Perry, Woodrow Speer, Enrico Nani, teacher Miss Edson, Roberta Smith, and Arthur Smith. (Courtesy Alford Linville.)

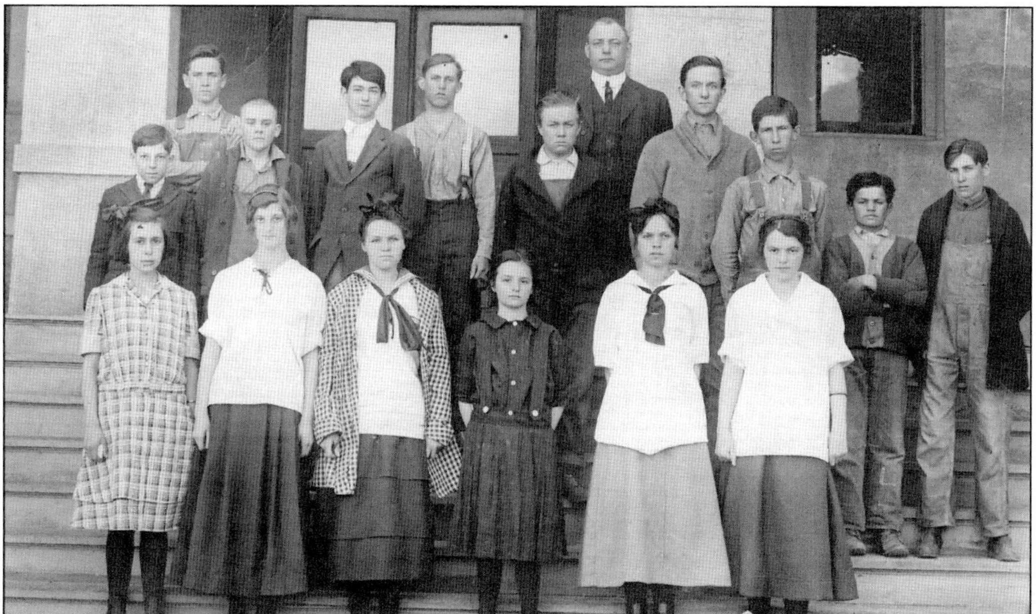

George E. Townes was hired in 1911 as the Summit School principal. He taught at Weed until he retired in 1935. Word has it that "you wouldn't want to go to his office or you'd be looking for a good whippin' with a cat o' nine tails." Melvin Carpenter (second row, far right) and Lea Acquistapace (second row, second from right) are in this 1925 photograph.

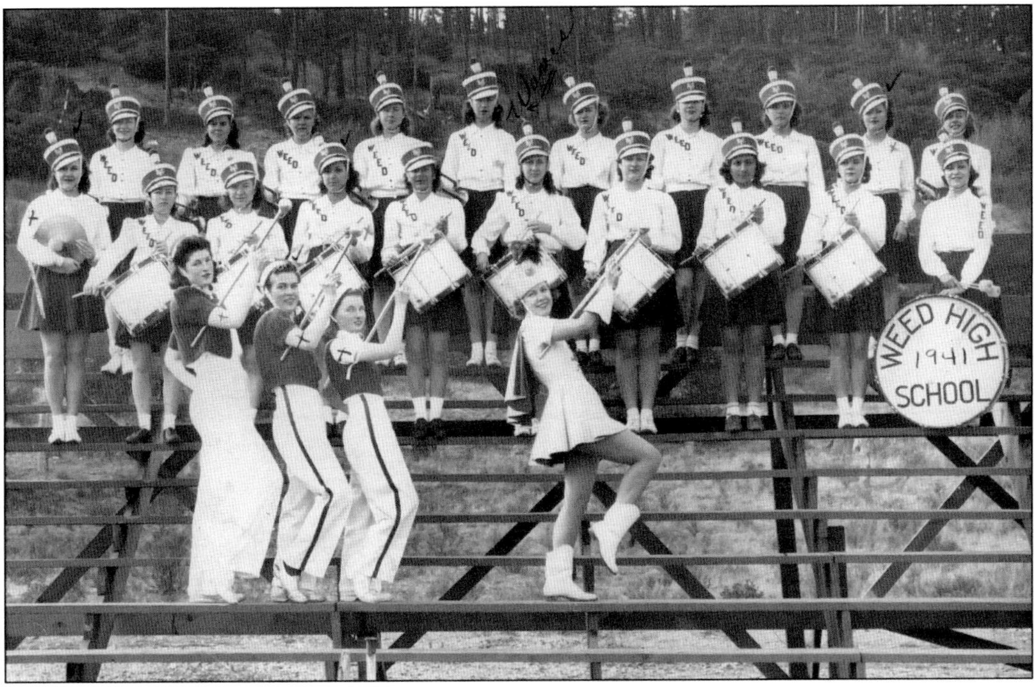

The Weed High Steppers all-female marching band was organized in 1940. The band was directed by Don Colvig. Majorette Nayda Costen and twirlers Ann Kegg, Peggy Clark, and Peggy Yost led the steppers at ball games and school assemblies. Ann Kegg married Hank Dorrel during her senior year; the school wanted to kick her out, but she went on to become valedictorian. (Courtesy Lou Caulket and Pauline Caulket Toms.)

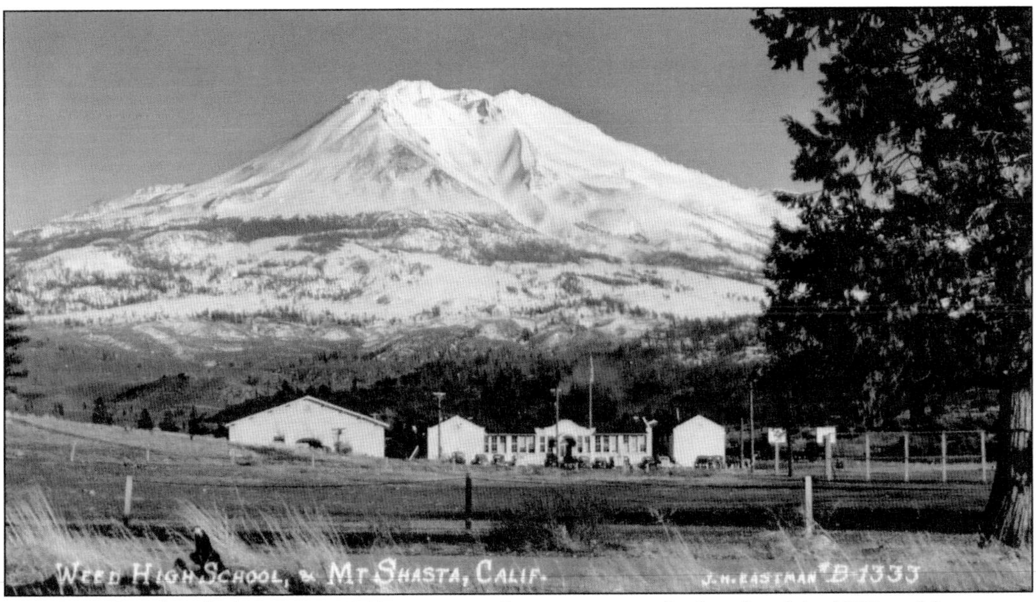

Weed High School, shown in 1941, originated as a two-year high school in 1917 and became a four-year high school in 1919. In 1923, a new high school was built, which is still standing behind the present Weed Elementary School. It housed Weed City Hall until it was moved to the old Long-Bell Lumber Company office. (Photograph by J. H. Eastman.)

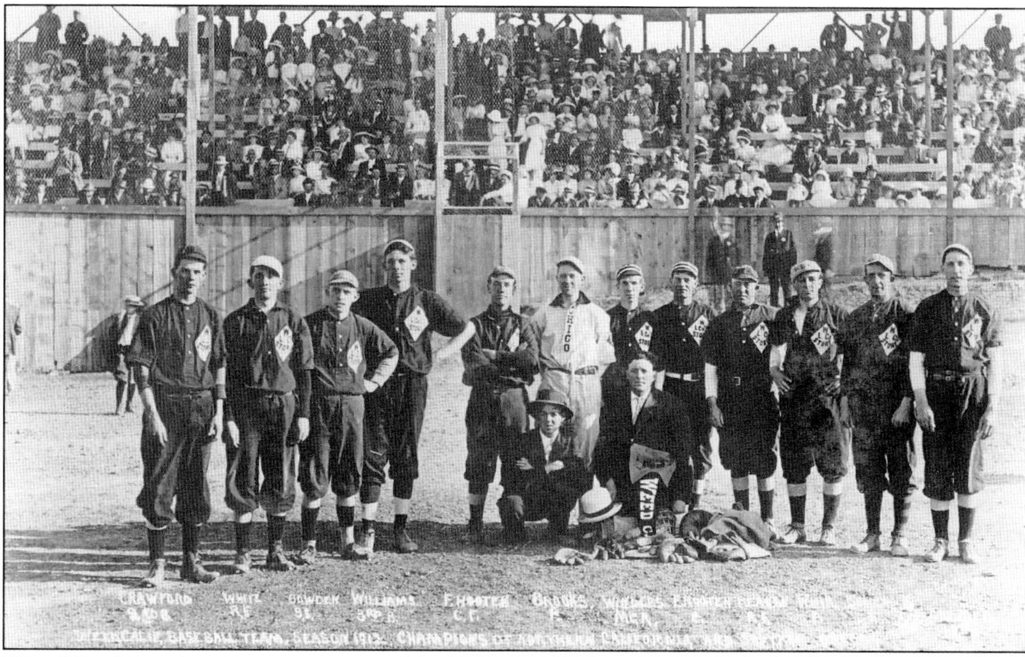

The Weed Lumber Company store baseball team (above) was the Northern California and Southern Oregon champion team in 1912. The ball field is located where Weed Elementary School's playground is today. From left to right are Crawford, Allen White (brother of Jude White), Bowden, Ken "Dink" Williams, F. Hooten, Brooks, Winders, E. Hooten, Reagan, Wihr, Souza, and Alfred "Buck" Cremer. Williams later played outfielder for the Cincinnati Reds, St. Louis Browns, and the Boston Red Soxs. In 1922, he scored 39 home runs and 155 runs batted in for the St. Louis Browns, both records in the American League that year. The Weed baseball team (below) is playing Sisson on June 19, 1915. Buck Cremer ran the carpenter crew at the mill and married Alta, the sister of Julian "Jude" White Sr., who was the general manager at Long-Bell's Weed operation from 1918 to 1948. (Courtesy Roger Zwanziger.)

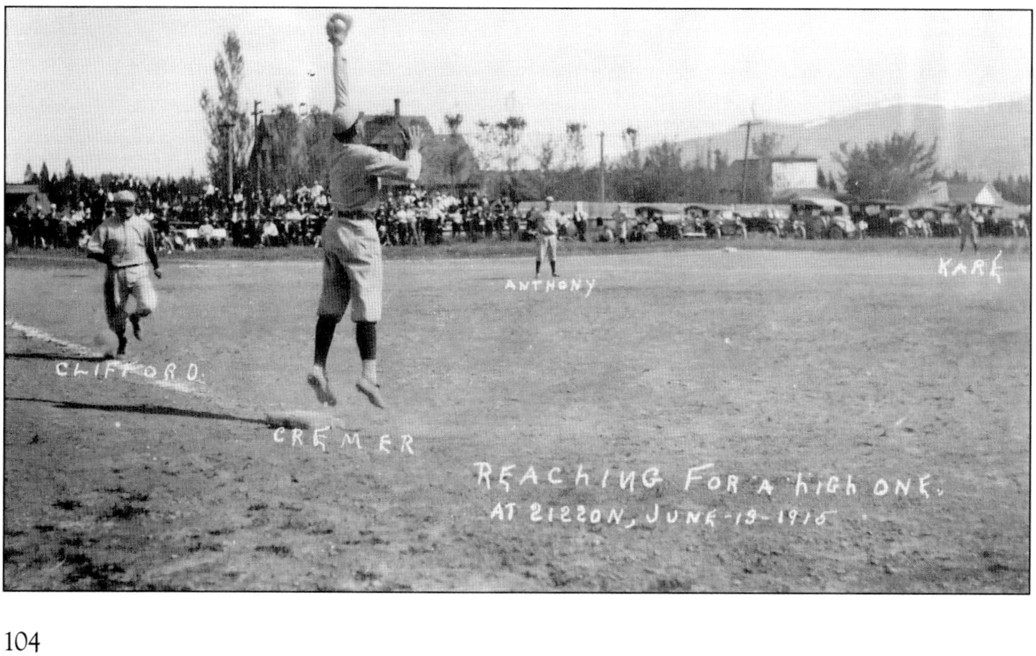

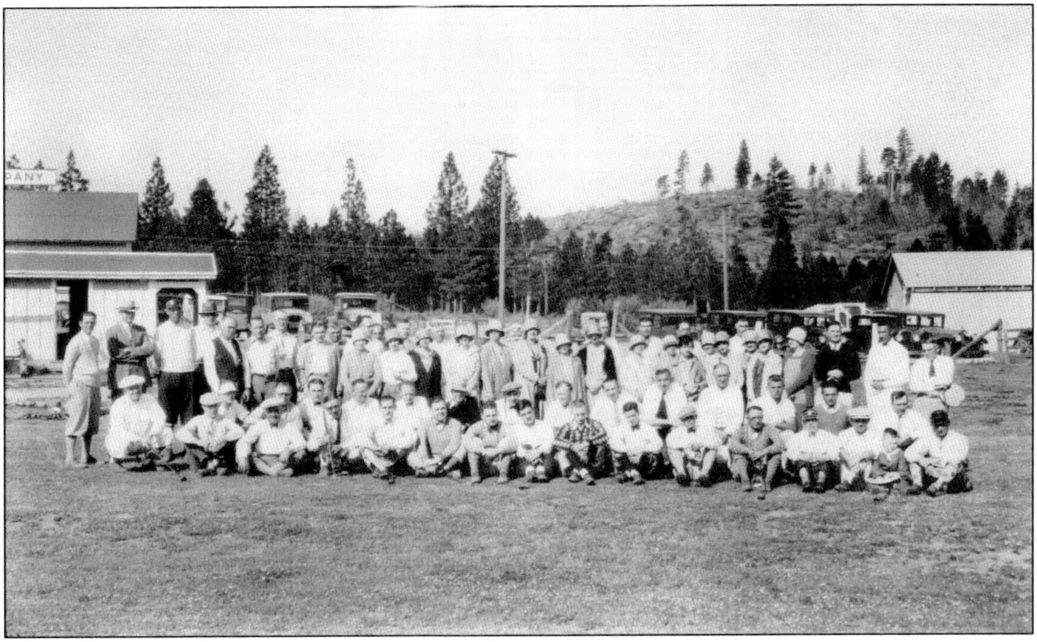

Weed golfers are shown above in the late 1920s or early 1930s. Known golfers include the following, all seated in the first row: Mr. Neimeyer, purchasing agent for Long-Bell, fourth from left (holding club); banker Ray Grase, sixth from left; superintendent Willy Runyon, seventh from left (in bow tie with knees up), who married Florence, the sister of Julian M. White Jr., assistant general manager of Long-Bell from 1947 to 1954; and Dr. Harold L. Vidricksen "Doc Vid," fifth from right (wearing glasses, with matching socks and sweater). Golfing tended to be a game for the elites. Three golfers are shown at the Weed Golf Course tee box (below) around 1940.

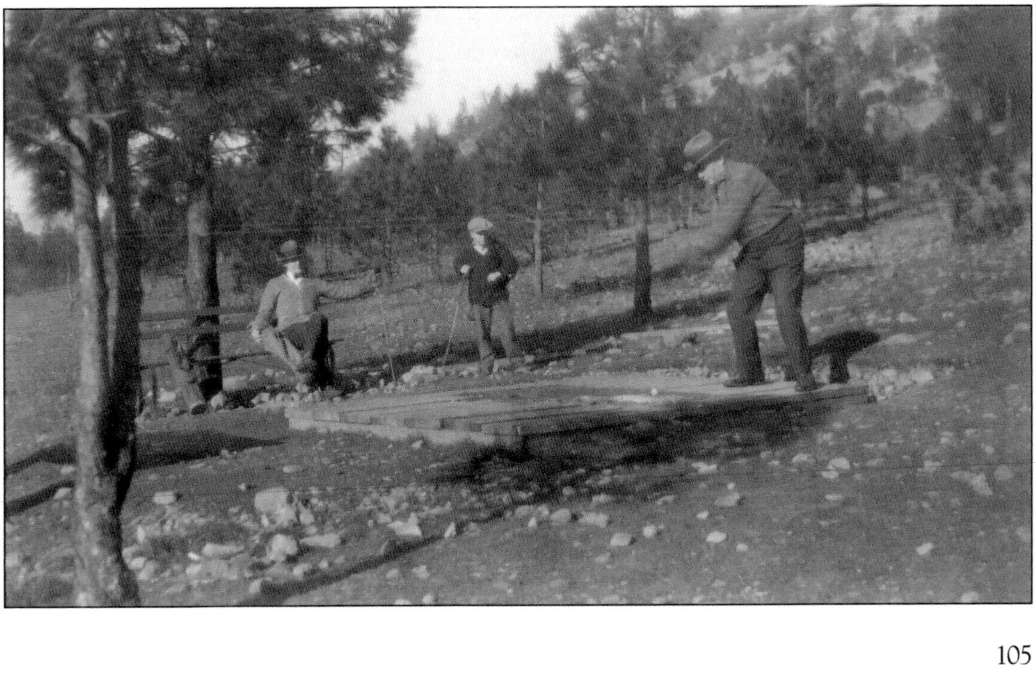

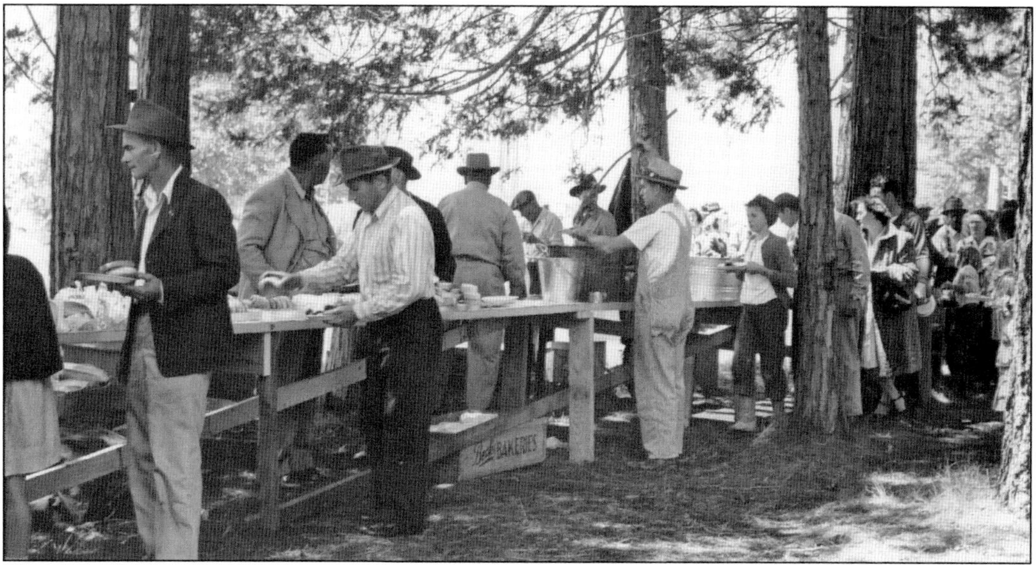

Charles William Murphy was the logging superintendant for Weed Lumber Company from 1911 to 1932. The annual picnic at Murphy's Grove was a highly popular event. This property was previously owned by Frank and Lury Alvina (Stone) Griffin. When Abner Weed proposed to buy their land, they agreed only under the condition that they could live on the property the rest of their lives and that the woods surrounding their home would not be logged. When Murphy became the logging superintendent, this forested area became known as Murphy's Grove. The water for the millpond came from a spring near the grove.

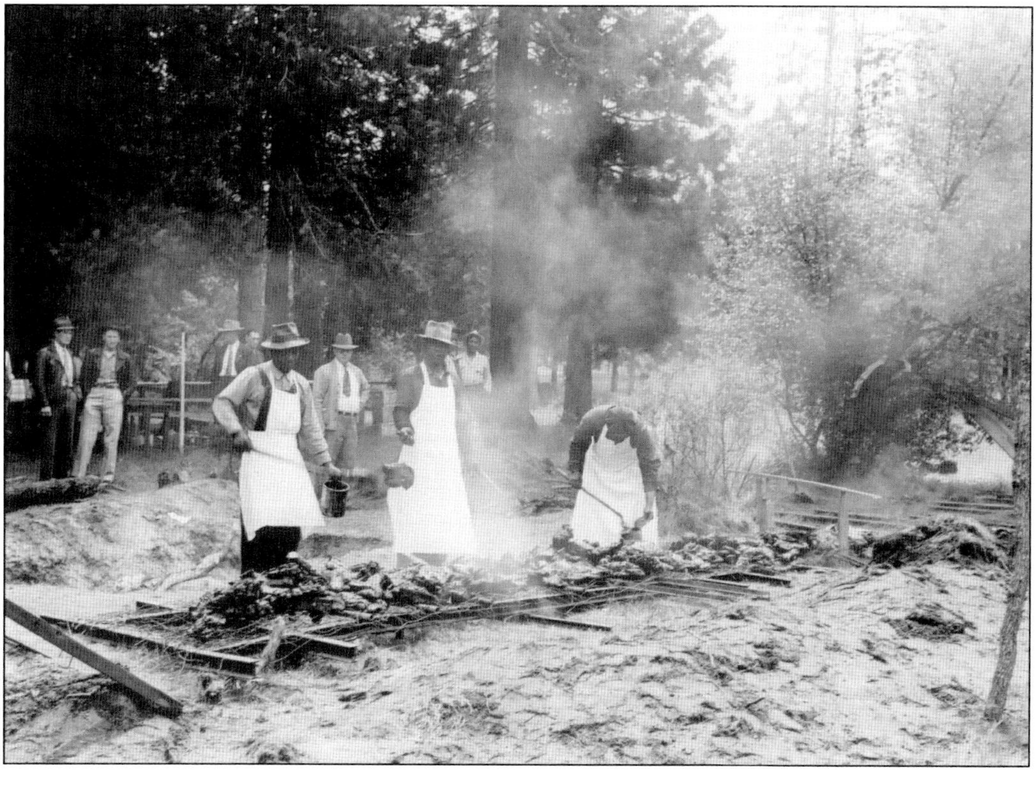

Seven

SHASTINA

Division Street originally divided the company town of Weed from the rowdy town of Shastina, which was taxed separately until Weed became incorporated in 1961. Some people along Division Street had to pay taxes twice. James M. and Eva (Decker) Preston first squatted on the land that is now known as Shastina in 1893. A few years later, in 1898, they sold their property to Thomas and Georgeanna "Anna" (Sullaway) Sullivan. They established a ranch and dairy, selling their products to the people in Igerna.

In 1905, the Sullivans began selling lots and built the second home in Shastina for their sons Lawrence and Myrtle "Myrt" (Taylor) Sullivan. The Sullivans built a saloon in 1906, the first of many to sprout up in Shastina. By 1910, there were several more saloons, including the Pastime Saloon, the Old Oaken Bucket, and Mugler's Saloon. Shastina was also an important business district, boasting a confectionery, men's clothing store, Chinese laundry, pool hall, dry goods store, bakery, grocery store, and several rooming houses and hotels, including the Neimeyer Apartments, El Monte Hotel, Mount Shasta Hotel, the Western, and Savoy Hotel. Shastina was also famous for its red-light district located near the Y Café until the 1918 influenza pandemic. The women turned their rooms into a 20-bed hospital, but the county closed them down after the epidemic ended.

On a windy day in October 1917, after a long, hot summer, a devastating fire broke out in Shastina, which destroyed all but seven buildings. The fire began in the Weed Bakery, built in 1906 by the Alfier brothers, one of whom died in the fire. Soon after the fire, numerous businesses were built, many made of cement block, including Joe A. Leonetti's Quality Store, Black Butte Saloon, Weed Bakery, Log Cabin Hotel, Little's Barber Shop, Upton Mortuary, the People's Store, Mock's Drug Store, the Weed Arch, Carl Phelps Motors, Wright and Morris Garage, Royal Hotel, Neimeyer Hotel, Pastega Shoes, and Eastman's Photo Studio. In the 1920s, the Sullivans divided their property to the southwest forming the Sullivan Addition, now known as Bel Air subdivision.

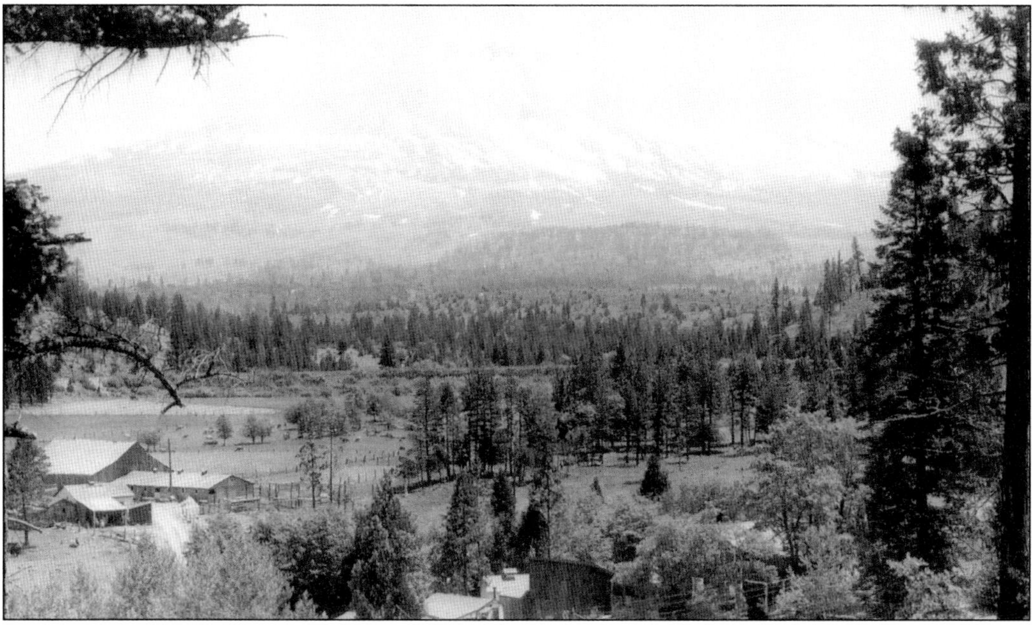

The Sullivan farm is shown above in 1900 with Mount Shasta and Shastina in the distance. George Decker originally owned the land north of Division Street, which he sold to Abner Weed. James and Eva (Decker) Preston homesteaded 200 acres south of Division Street in 1893. Five years later the Prestons sold their ranch to Thomas and Anna Sullivan, who had previously homesteaded Rainbow Ranch near Sisson (now under Siskiyou Lake). Thomas and Anna Sullivan had four children: Lawrence E., George, Rita, and Inez. Their son Lawrence Sullivan (below, left) and Will Tonkin are in the milk wagon in front of the Sullivan farmhouse in 1905. Will Tonkin, who died in 1921, was a Southern Pacific Railroad station manager and telegraph operator. Inez Street in Shastina is named after their youngest daughter.

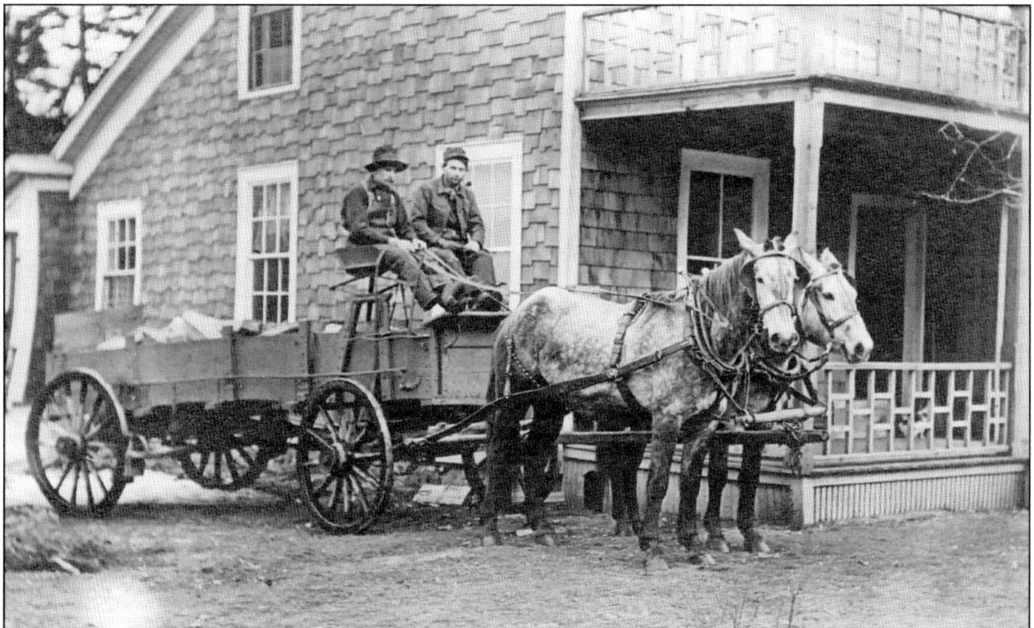

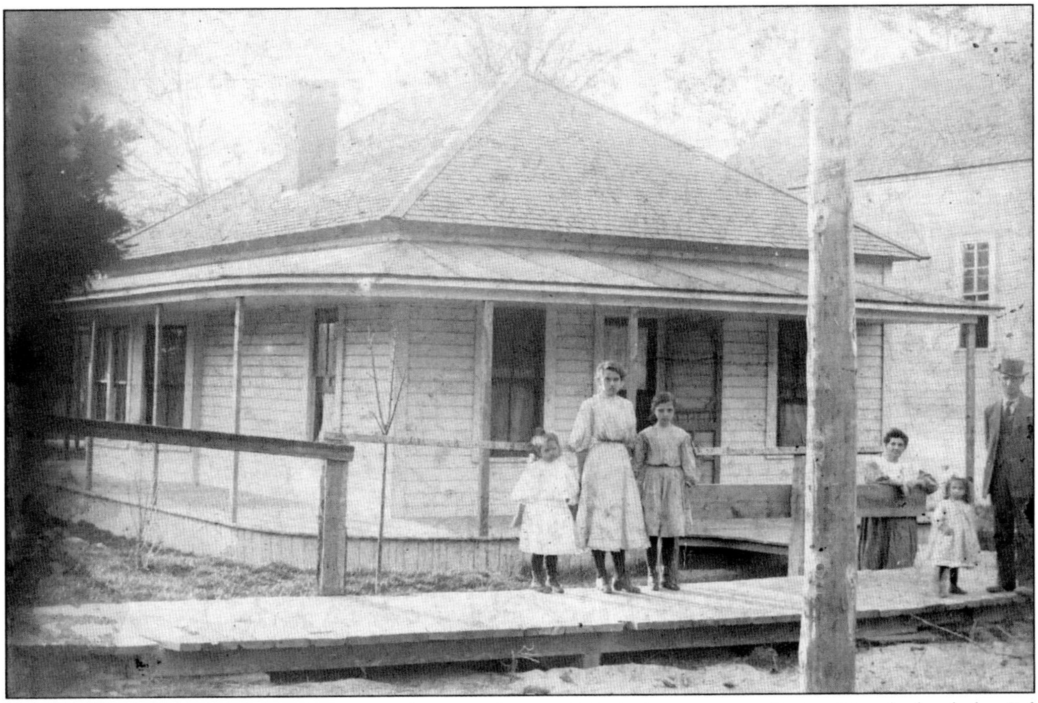

The Edward Anthony family is standing in front of their house near Boles Creek, built by Ed Wright. The Anthony house later became the Upton Mortuary. The wooden sidewalks in Shastina were still in place when Weed incorporated in 1961. The city's first project after incorporation was to have them removed.

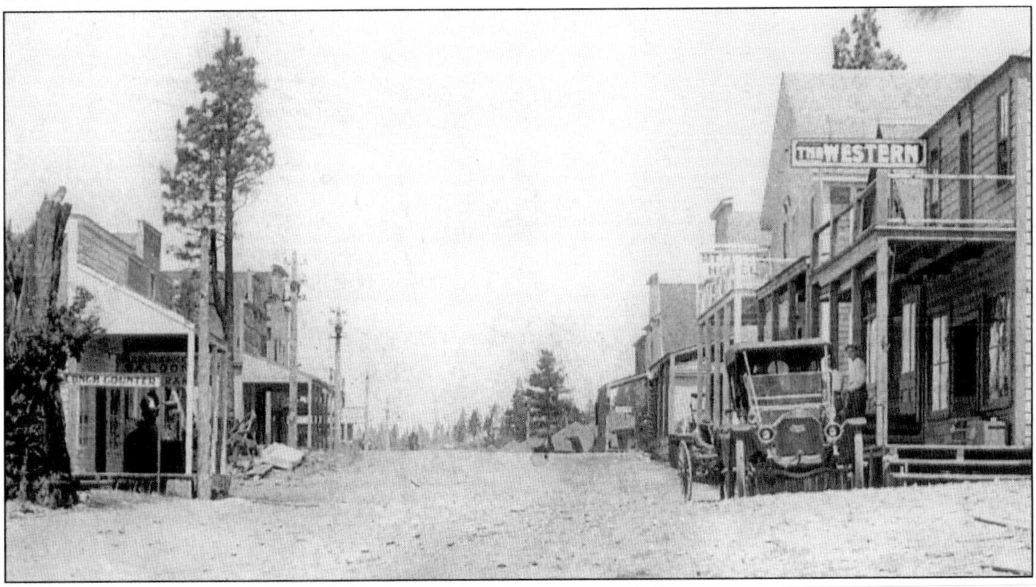

This is the oldest known photograph showing the town of Shastina, looking north in 1907. On the right side of Main Street is the Western hotel, Weed Bakery, the Mount Shasta Hotel built by Red McCoy, and George Romley's Dry Goods Store. The Leonetti store was later built at this site. On the left is the Old Oaken Bucket Saloon, Mugler's Saloon, and C. H. Kirk's men's clothing store. (Courtesy Mary Ewing.)

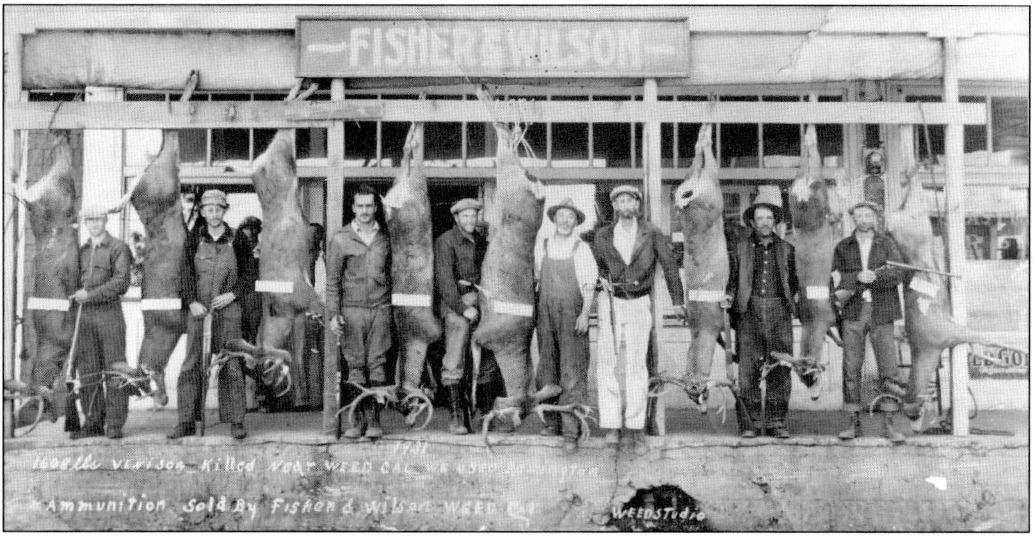

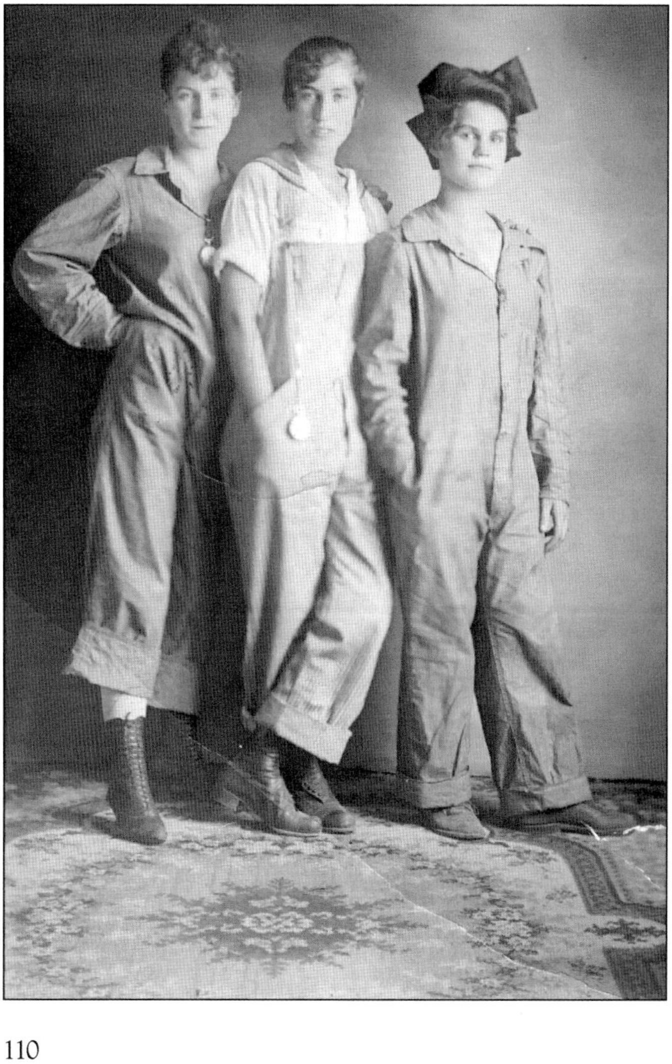

Proud hunters (above) in front of Fisher and Wilson sporting goods include, from left to right, A. C. Borgnis, Virgil Fisher, Stanley Tebbe, Bob Collins, Frank Wilson, Pete Minoletti, Bill Falkner, and John Fisher. Virgil Fisher moved to Weed in 1920 and opened the store with R. N. Wilson, Frank Wilson, and John Fisher.

Lewis reports that the area between the Y Café and Mallory's Garage consisted of four houses of ill repute. Violet Leslie, a schoolteacher, and Georgie Clark were madams. They operated a makeshift hospital during the 1918 influenza epidemic. After these operations were shut down they moved to Sullivan's Field. In the 1930 U.S. Census, six Weed women from Oregon, Indiana, Missouri, Lithuania, Scotland, and California are listed as harlots. The photograph of three Weed women (left) was taken in 1916. (Courtesy Donna Kohn Brooks.)

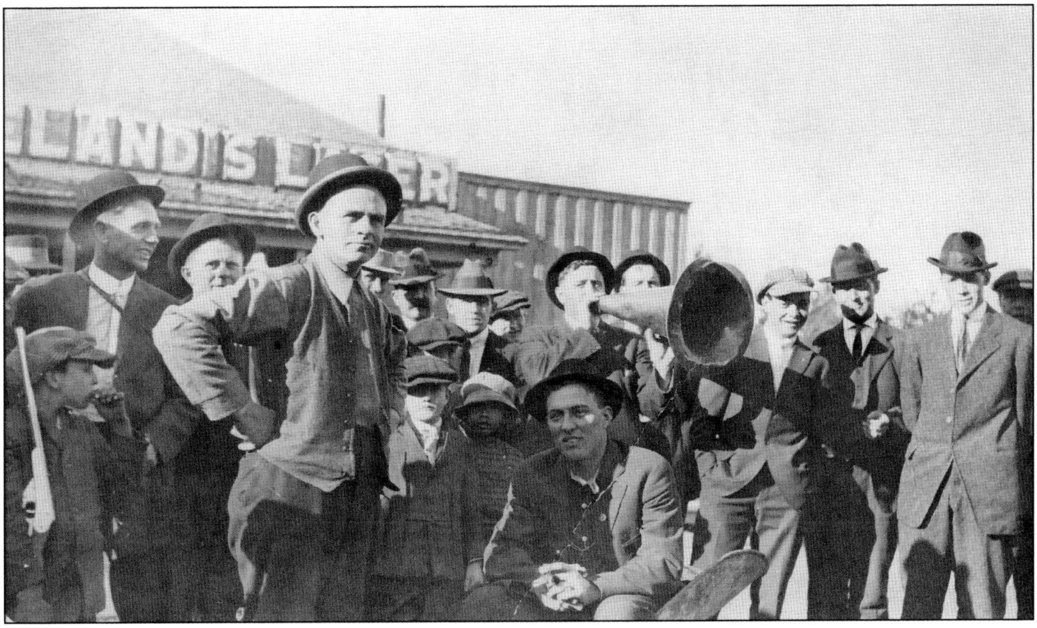

Don Montgomery, pictured above with megaphone, owned and operated the Montgomery Livery Stable, which was originally located where the Long-Bell company office was built. Before Montgomery, Johnnie Beard, son of Siskiyou County superior judge John Samuel Beard of Yreka, operated the livery. Don Montgomery also ran the Weed Hotel after it was constructed in 1914. The two boys in the center are Morris Hobson (left), born in 1907, and Jing Louie, born in 1908. Because Jing's father, Wong Louie, went by his Chinese name with surname given first, Jing was sometimes called Jing Louie instead of Jing Wong. The tailor shop (below) was located in C. H. Kirk's first clothing store across the street from the El Monte.

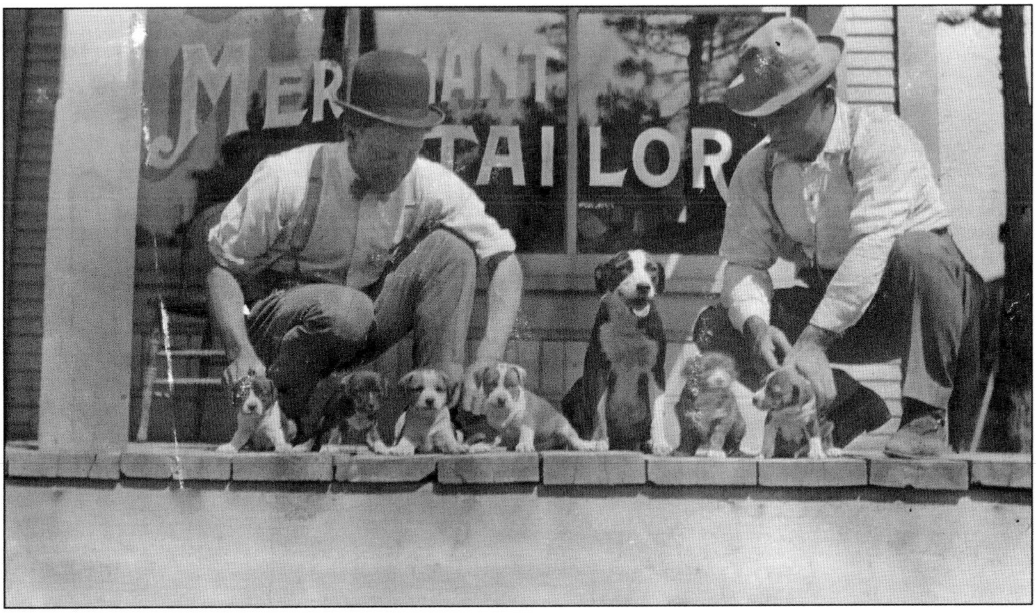

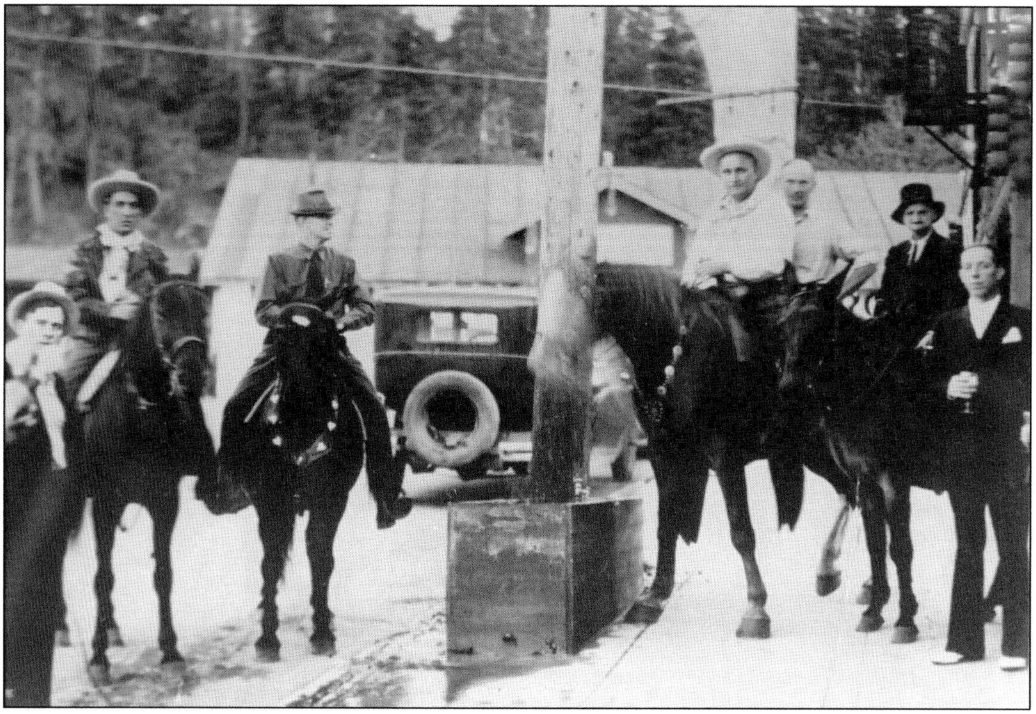

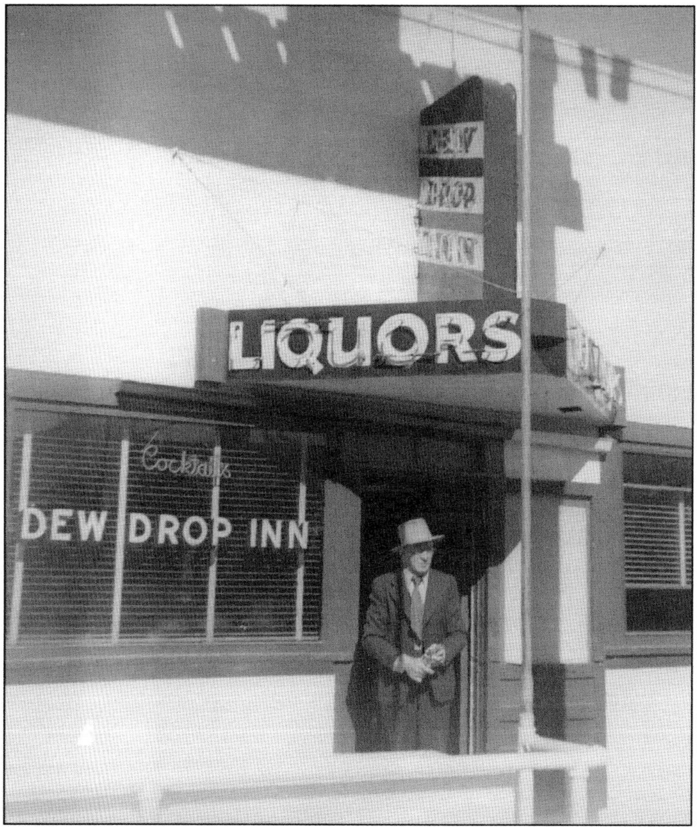

Horses and riders are shown above standing beside the water trough in front of the Dew Drop Inn in 1936. The men on horses are, from left to right, John Cordero, Louie Paroletti, Bud Mazzini, and Bill Douglas. The Dew Drop Inn was located on Main Street near the Weed Arch and Log Cabin Hotel. In the 1930s, James Floratos and Spiro Toskas, both from Greece, were the proprietors of the Dew Drop Inn. When Floratos came to America in 1920, he worked at the McCloud Lumber Company for three years then moved to Weed. He married an Italian woman, Louise, in the 1920s. Prior to running the Dew Drop Inn, he worked at the box factory. By 1945, Gus George (at left) was the proprietor of the Dew Drop Inn.

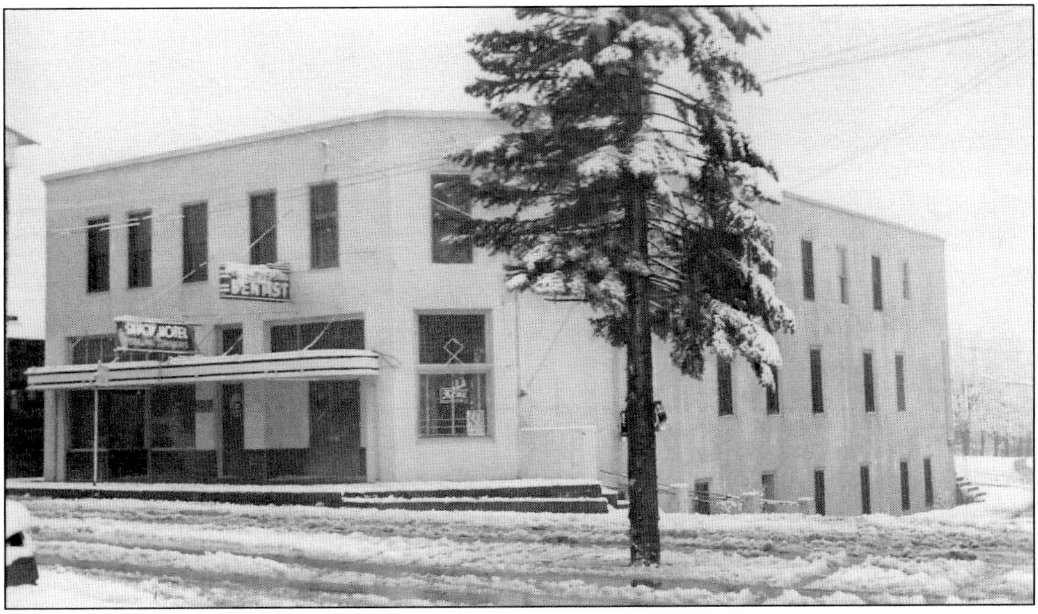

The Sbarbaro family emigrated from Genoa (Genova in Italian), Italy, to McCloud in 1900. Giovanni "John," Antonio, and Luigi were brothers, and Camillo was their cousin. After working in McCloud for several years, Antonio, followed by the others, came to Weed in 1914. Together they built several businesses. Antonio and Luigi built the Weed Theater and the first swimming pool in Weed. Antonio Sbarbaro and Efisio A. Rosa built the Savoy Hotel and the People's Store. Antonio also built the Pine Tree Saloon and the Genova Hotel, which served as a boardinghouse. The Savoy Hotel is still standing at 298 Main Street. Many people fondly remember Peter Patella, who operated Center Pharmacy in this building until his unfortunate death in 1993. (Courtesy Donna Steffenson Sartor.)

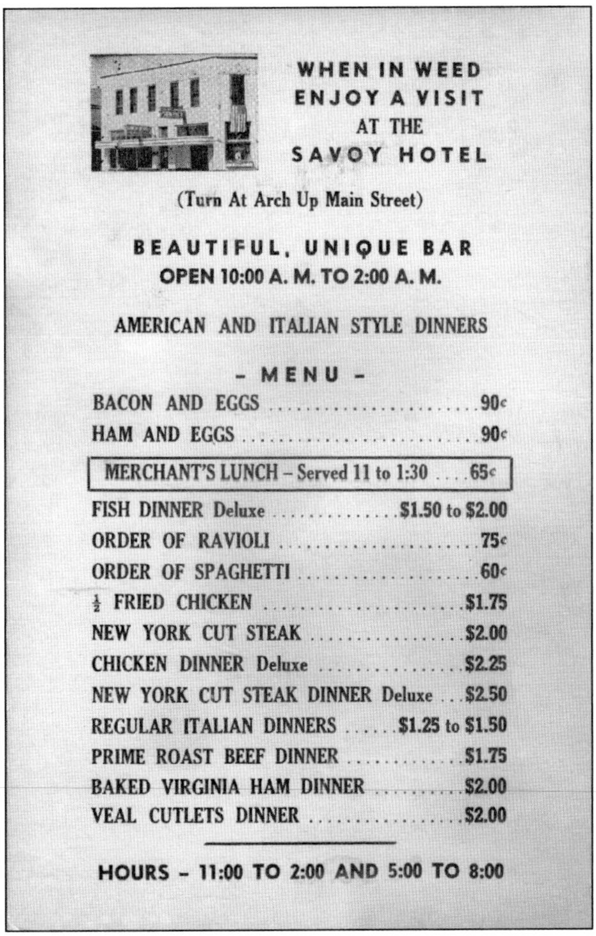

WHEN IN WEED
ENJOY A VISIT
AT THE
SAVOY HOTEL

(Turn At Arch Up Main Street)

BEAUTIFUL, UNIQUE BAR
OPEN 10:00 A. M. TO 2:00 A. M.

AMERICAN AND ITALIAN STYLE DINNERS

- MENU -

BACON AND EGGS	90¢
HAM AND EGGS	90¢
MERCHANT'S LUNCH – Served 11 to 1:30	65¢
FISH DINNER Deluxe	$1.50 to $2.00
ORDER OF RAVIOLI	75¢
ORDER OF SPAGHETTI	60¢
½ FRIED CHICKEN	$1.75
NEW YORK CUT STEAK	$2.00
CHICKEN DINNER Deluxe	$2.25
NEW YORK CUT STEAK DINNER Deluxe	$2.50
REGULAR ITALIAN DINNERS	$1.25 to $1.50
PRIME ROAST BEEF DINNER	$1.75
BAKED VIRGINIA HAM DINNER	$2.00
VEAL CUTLETS DINNER	$2.00

HOURS – 11:00 TO 2:00 AND 5:00 TO 8:00

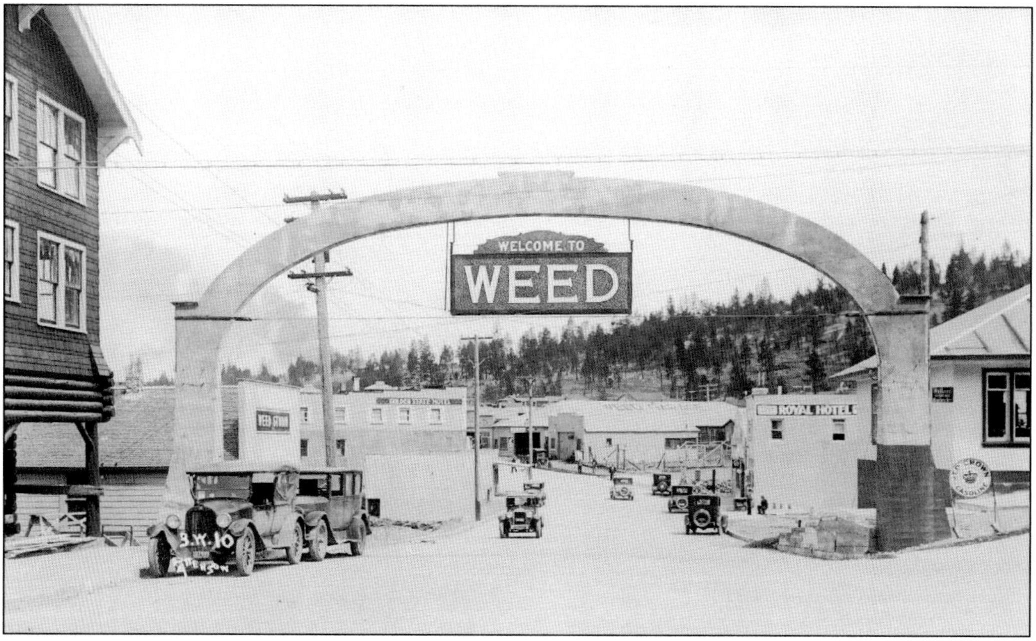

The first Weed Arch was built in 1922 by George E. Condrey. It was torn down in 1963 because it was deemed unsafe but was so sturdy it took three weeks to remove. On the left of Main Street are the Weed Studio and Golden State Hotel. On the right side are Carl Phelps Mountain Service Station, Royal Hotel, and Weed Garage. Phelps was instrumental in having the Weed Arch built.

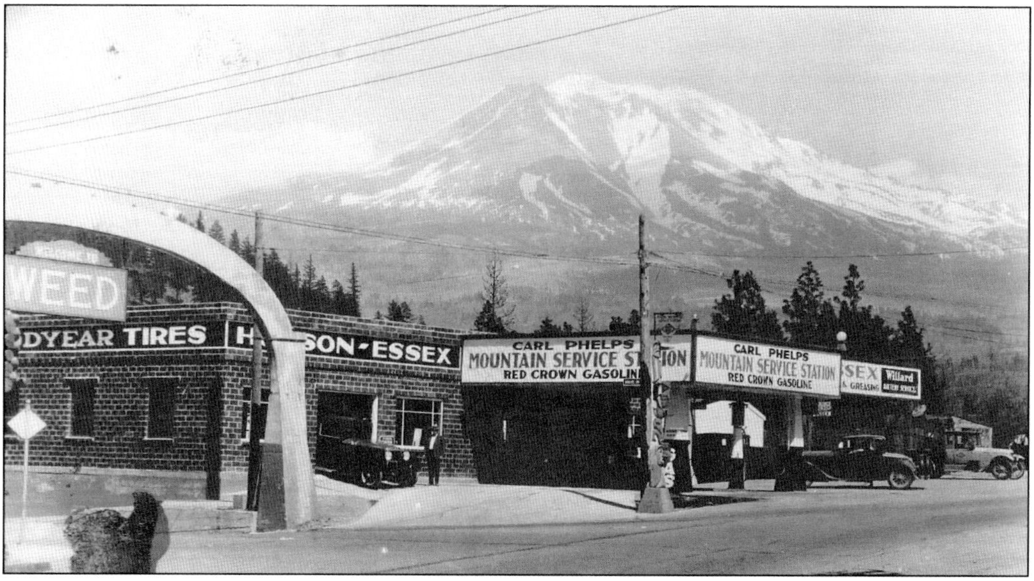

Phelps was a moving force for the improvement of Highway 97, the "Alaskan Highway," and in 1922, he installed a totem pole to attract attention. The totem pole points towards Diller Canyon, which was named by C. Hart Merriam during his biological survey of Mount Shasta in 1898 after J. S. Diller, a prominent geologist who spent many years conducting studies of Mount Shasta. (Photograph by Frank Paterson.)

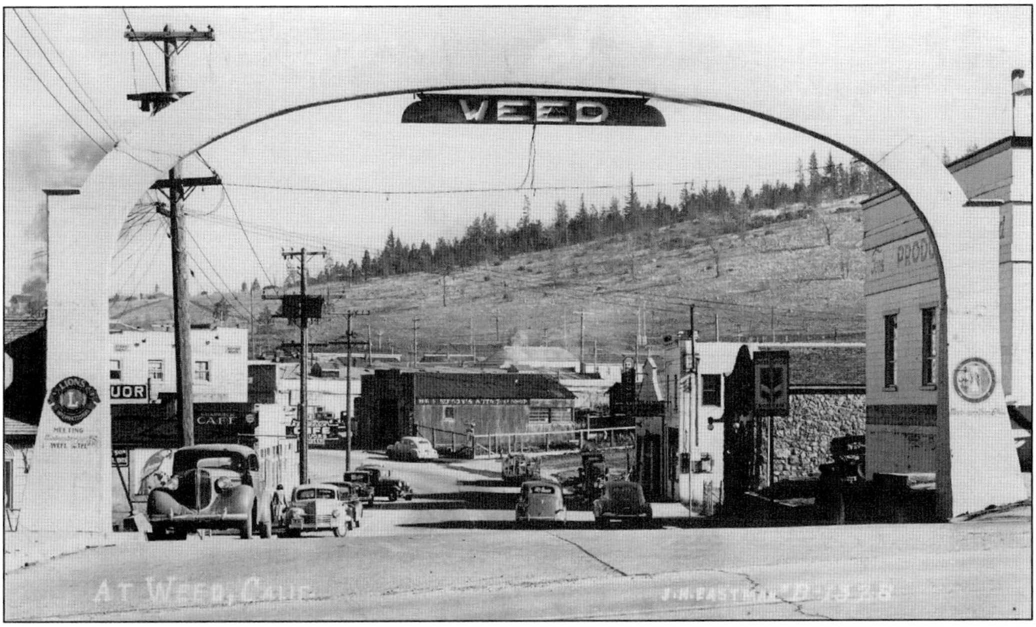

The famous Weed Arch, shown above in 1941, is at the entrance to Main Street. The Log Cabin Hotel (below) was built by Lon Wright and opened for business on December 6, 1917. He constructed it around the original Sullivan saloon, built in 1906. In his memoirs, Lawrence Sullivan said, "Ed Wright built a beautiful bar [for Thomas Sullivan] out of cedar panels, but Dad got to be his own best customer, so Mama made him sell it to Lon Wright and Johny Crane." The Log Cabin Hotel was a famous landmark until 1957 when the lower part of the building was moved to 854 South Weed Boulevard. (Above photograph by J. H. Eastman.)

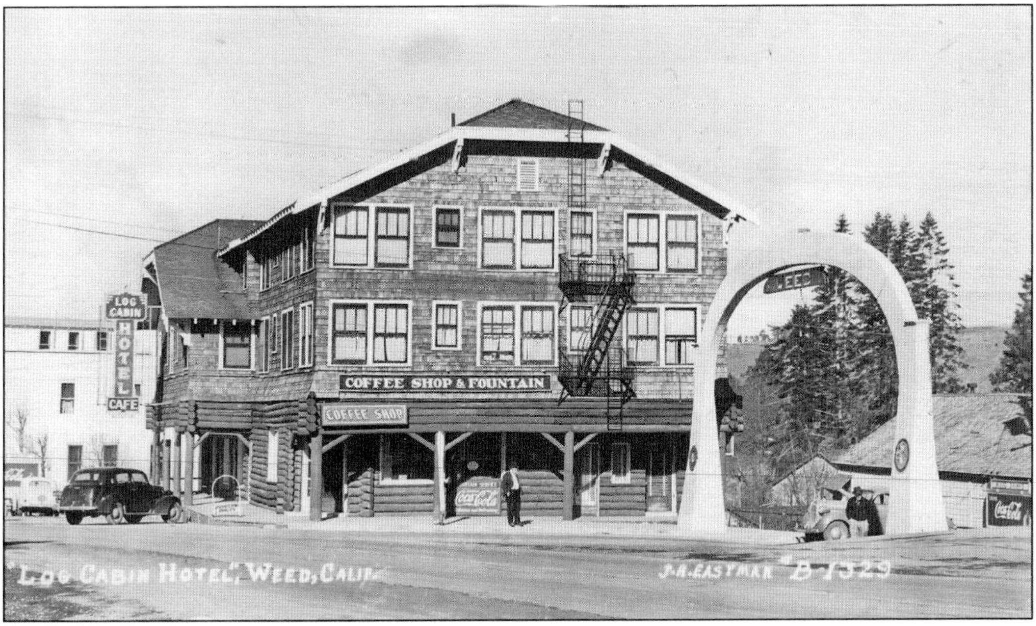

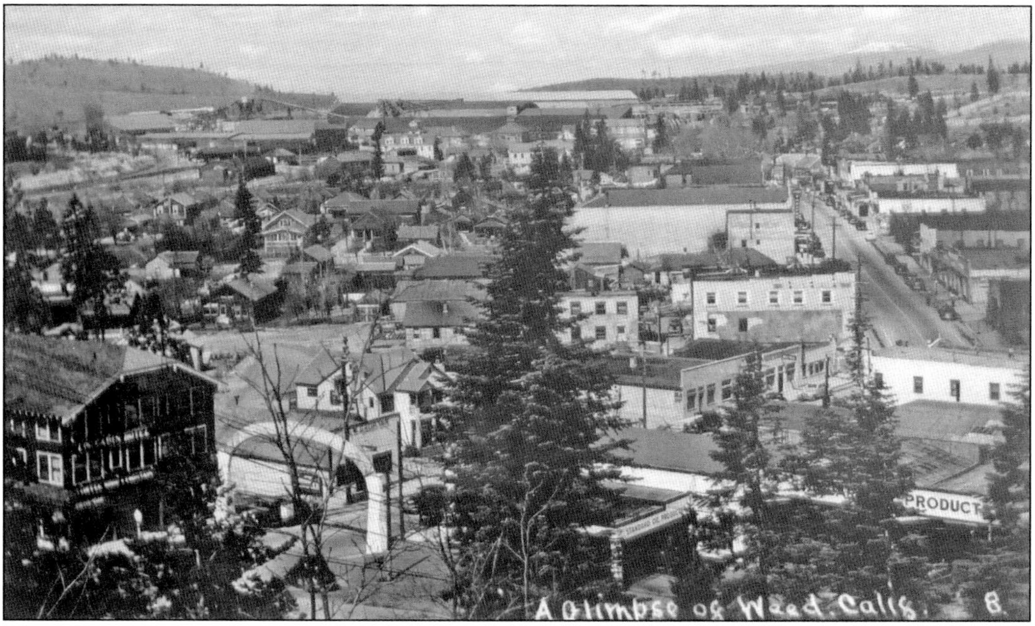

Pictured is a 1941 view of the Log Cabin Hotel, Weed Arch, and the famous "jog" on Main Street. Louie's Tires is the white building this side of the bend (right center). Opposite Louie's Tires is the Medo-Bel Dairy, Weed Press, Rizzo's Barbershop (originally the Kinnicut Saloon, still standing at 92 Main Street), Golden State Hotel, and Weed Theater. The Dew Drop Inn can be seen through the arch. (Photograph by J. H. Eastman.)

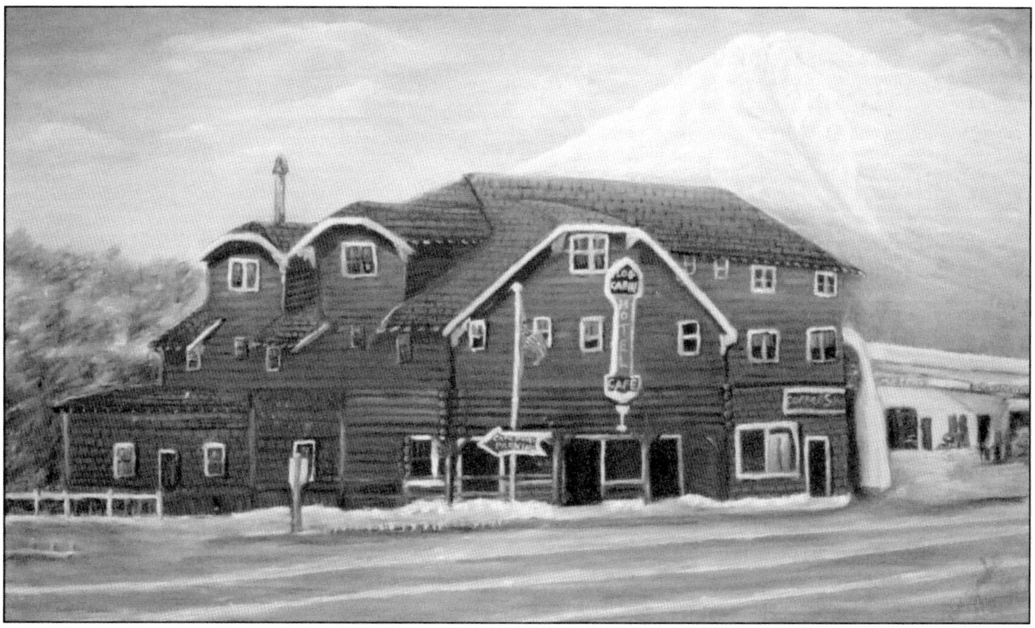

Opal Yandell painted pictures of the Log Cabin Hotel in oils, a hobby she dearly loved. She won several ribbons for her paintings at the Siskiyou County Fair. The artist and her husband, Spike Yandell, moved to Weed from Oklahoma around 1937 when she was 19 years old. Her husband worked at Long-Bell Lumber Company, loading logs onto the deck with a 45-ton Wagner tractor. (Courtesy Opal Yandell.)

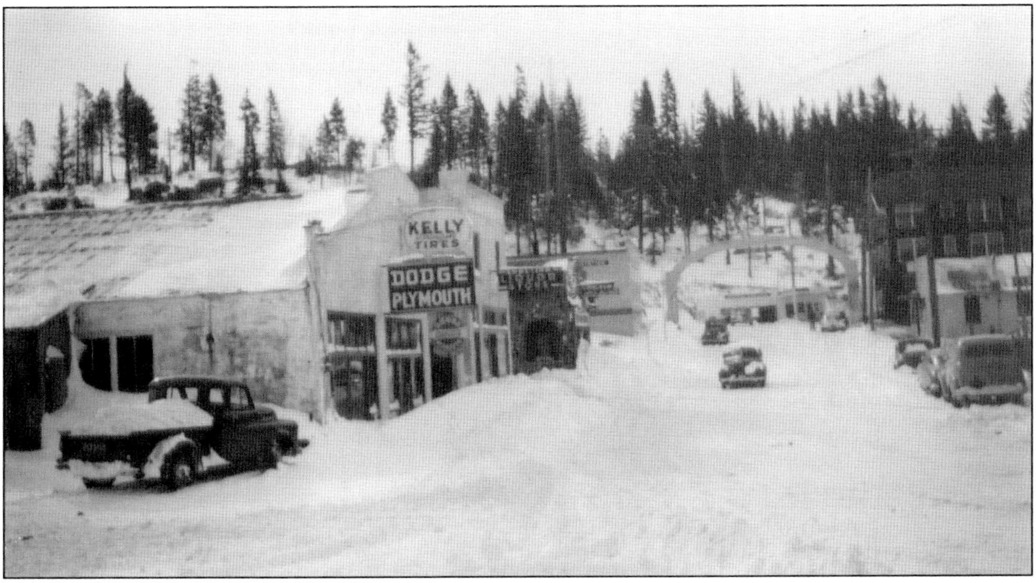

Main Street is shown here after a snowstorm in January 1952. The building on the left, with the Kelly Tires and Dodge Plymouth signs, is Louie's Tire Shop, owned by Louie Paroletti. It was formerly the Ben Carson Garage. The Log Cabin Hotel is to the right of the arch, and the Dew Drop Inn is the white building next door. (Photograph by Cy Rippon; courtesy Eleanor Rippon Wilmarth.)

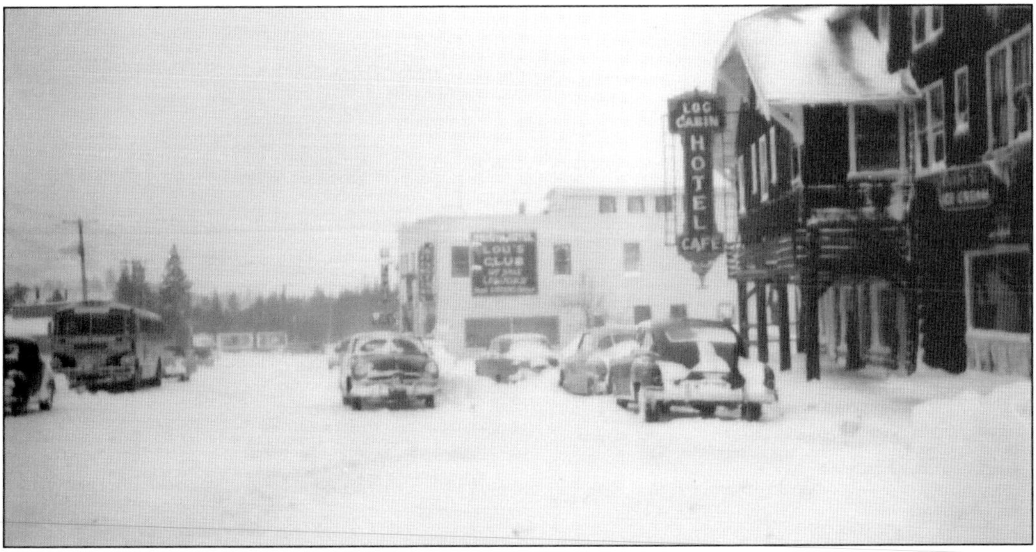

This picture is looking north on Weed Boulevard in January 1952 with a view of the Log Cabin and Genova Hotels. Antonio Sbarbaro and his kin built the Genova Hotel in 1924. In 1939, their son Louie Sbarbaro added Lou's Club lounge. The Genova Hotel is still standing today. Just beyond the Genova Hotel is Highway 97 at "the beginning of the Alaskan Highway." (Photograph by Cy Rippon; courtesy Eleanor Rippon Wilmarth.)

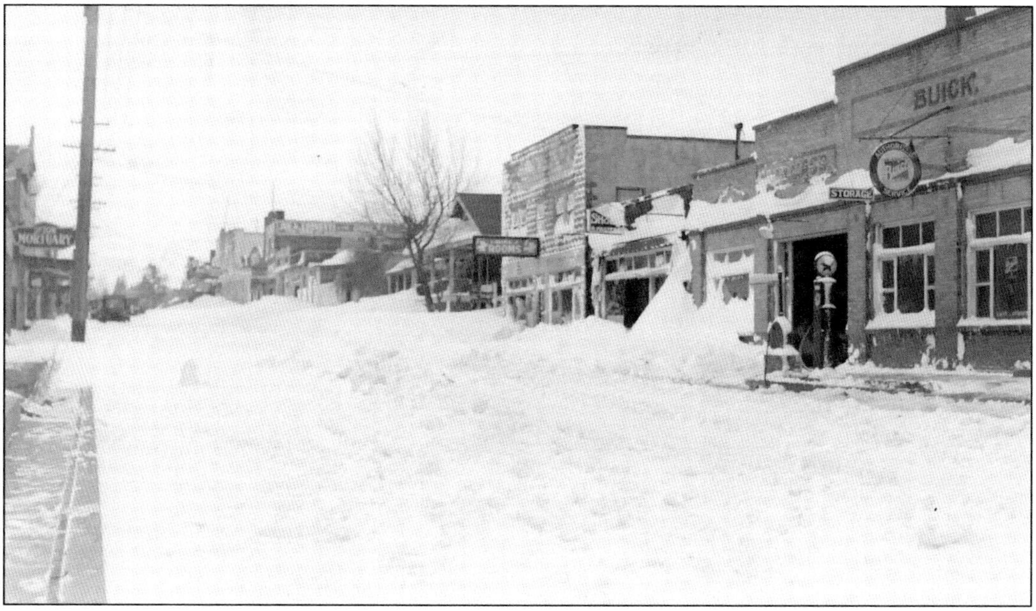

DeBon's Garage, R. Pastega Shoe Store, Dial Rooms, and the Joe A. Leonetti Quality Store are on the right side of Main Street, looking north, in this March 1938 photograph. In the mid-1920s to early 1930s, Darrell Papst managed the Copco electric store in the Dial building. On the left is the Upton Mortuary, established in 1925 and still standing today. Muriel C. Upton became the Siskiyou County coroner in 1930.

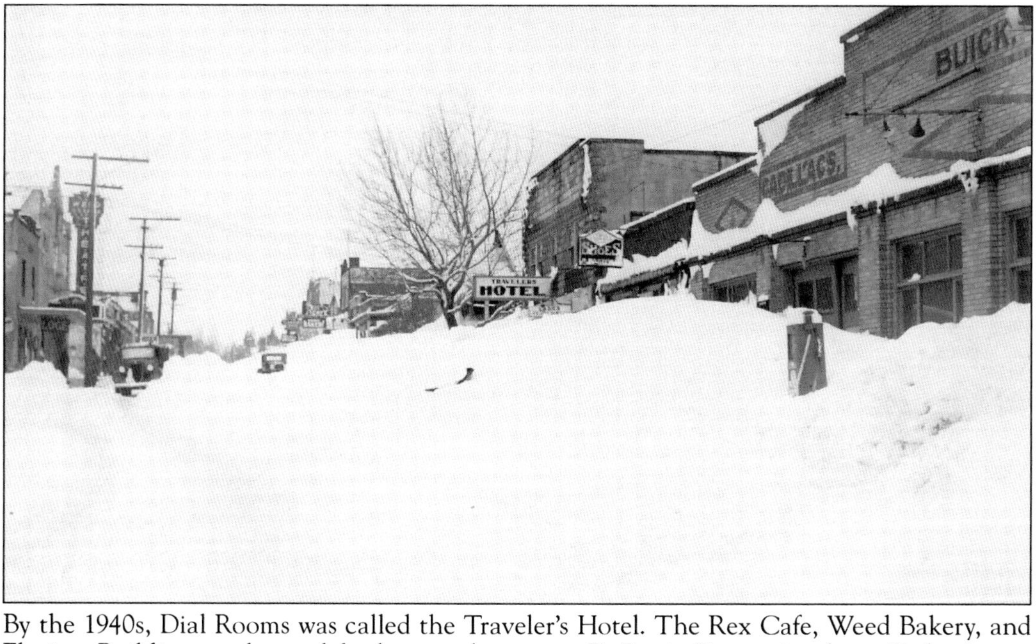

By the 1940s, Dial Rooms was called the Traveler's Hotel. The Rex Cafe, Weed Bakery, and Florista Building are located farther up the street. DeBon's Garage is where Cedar Lanes Bowling is now located. The brick facade is still in place. On the opposite side of the street is the Weed Theater.

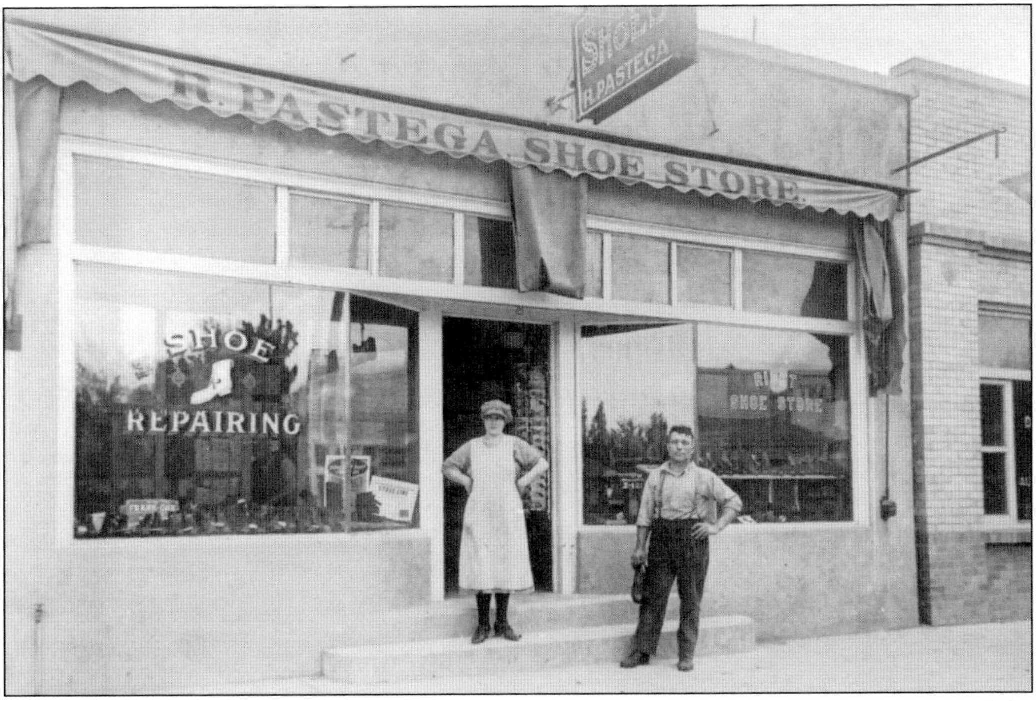

Giuseppina "Josephine" (Cunial) Pastega (above, left) and Romano Pastega stand in front of the R. Pastega Shoe Store on Main Street in 1923. Romano and Josephine came to America from Italy in 1907 and 1912, respectively, and were married at St. Joseph's Catholic Church in Yreka on April 10, 1912. Romano was apprenticed as a shoemaker in Italy. After he moved to Weed, he worked for Long-Bell Lumber Company and then established his own shoe business in 1923. Although Josephine and Romano had six children, only Mario (below, second from right) and Bianca survived. Romano's assistant Vittorio Pastega (below, left), Romano, Mario, and Josephine are shown inside their shoe store around 1927. In 1920, Vittorio was a filer at the box factory and, in 1930, was a tallyman in the mill. (Both courtesy Dr. Scott Durbin.)

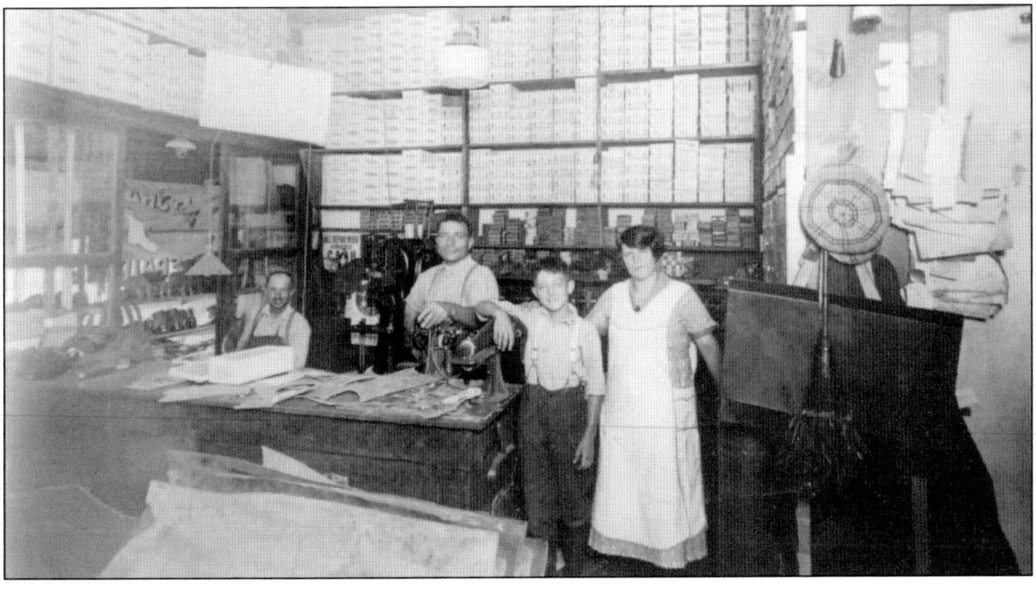

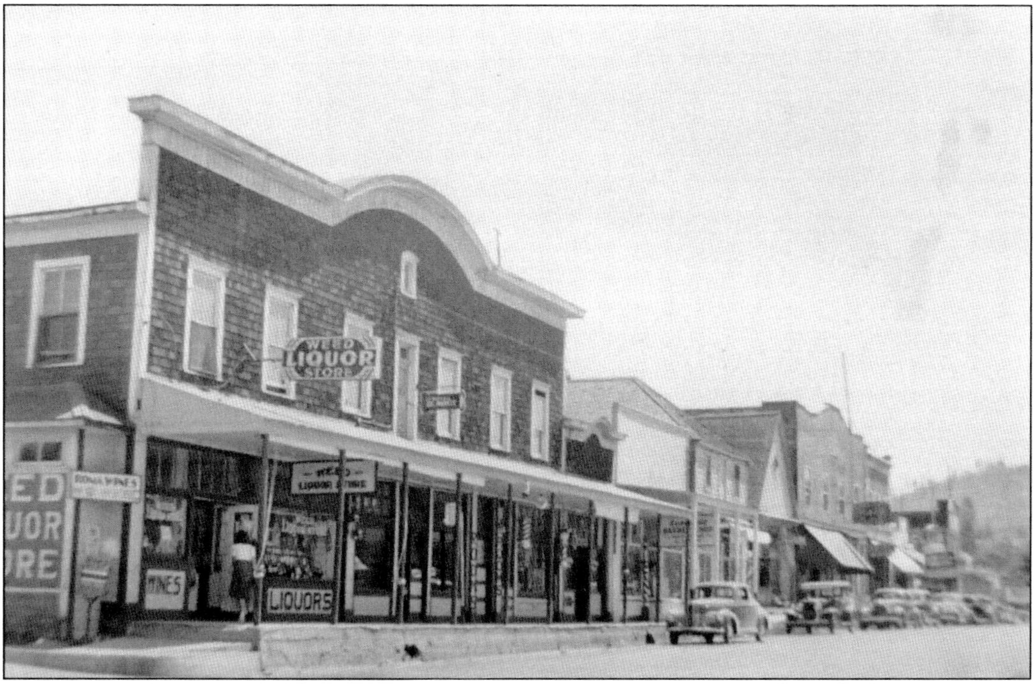

The 1938 photograph above shows the Weed Liquor Store, along with a barbershop, housed in the El Monte Hotel (left). To its right is another barbershop, run by Henry C. Kirk; Jim and Frances (Belcastro) Deluca's shoe shop; and Mike Paletta's Shoe Shop, previously Frank Borgnis' shoe store. The building with the steep roof is the Pastime Saloon, originally the Mazzini Brothers Saloon. These five buildings escaped the 1917 Shastina fire because Ed DeBon had started construction on the Black Butte Saloon (right of the Pastime), and the foundation stopped the fire. The photograph below shows the same buildings during a January 1952 snowstorm: the El Monte, Kirk's barbershop, the Deluca's, Mike Paletta's Shoe Shop, the Pastime Saloon, and the corner of the Black Butte Saloon, completed in 1917. (Below photograph by Cy Rippon; courtesy Eleanor Rippon Wilmarth.)

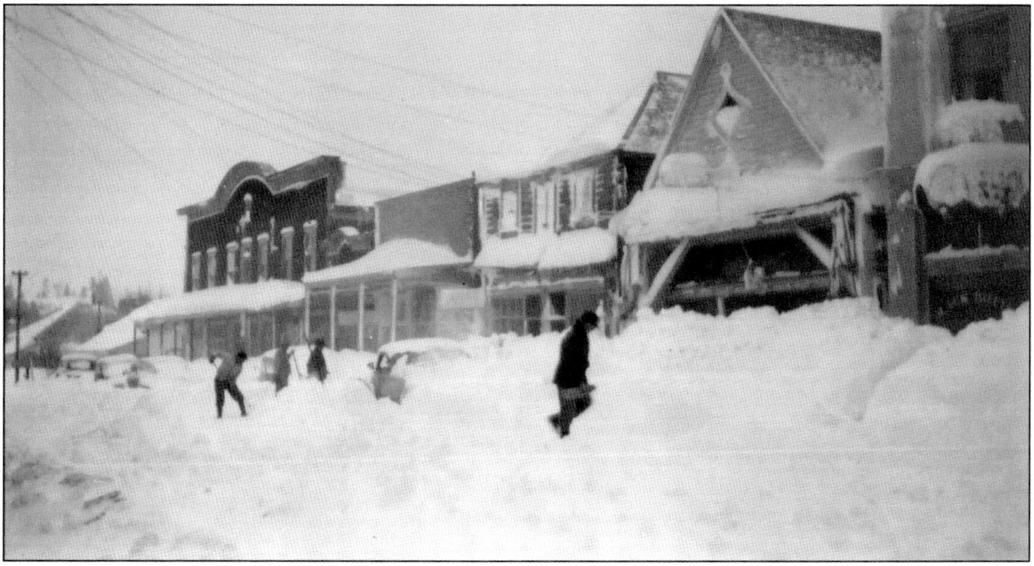

Nellie and Sherman Ferguson, with one of their six children, Harold, stand in front of a Weed's Quality Bakery truck. They came to Weed from Kentucky and ended up in Tennant in the 1920s. Sherman was a train engineer for Long-Bell Lumber Company out of Tennant. The Weed Bakery in Shastina is the oldest business in Weed that is still in operation today. (Courtesy Donna Steffenson Sartor.)

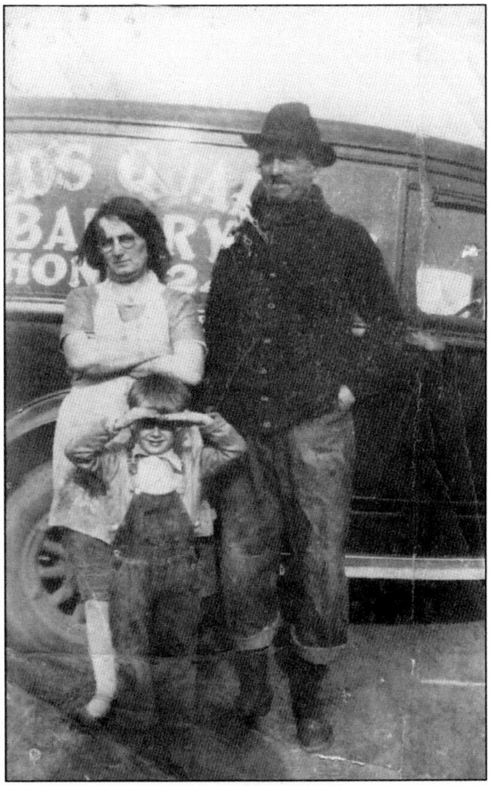

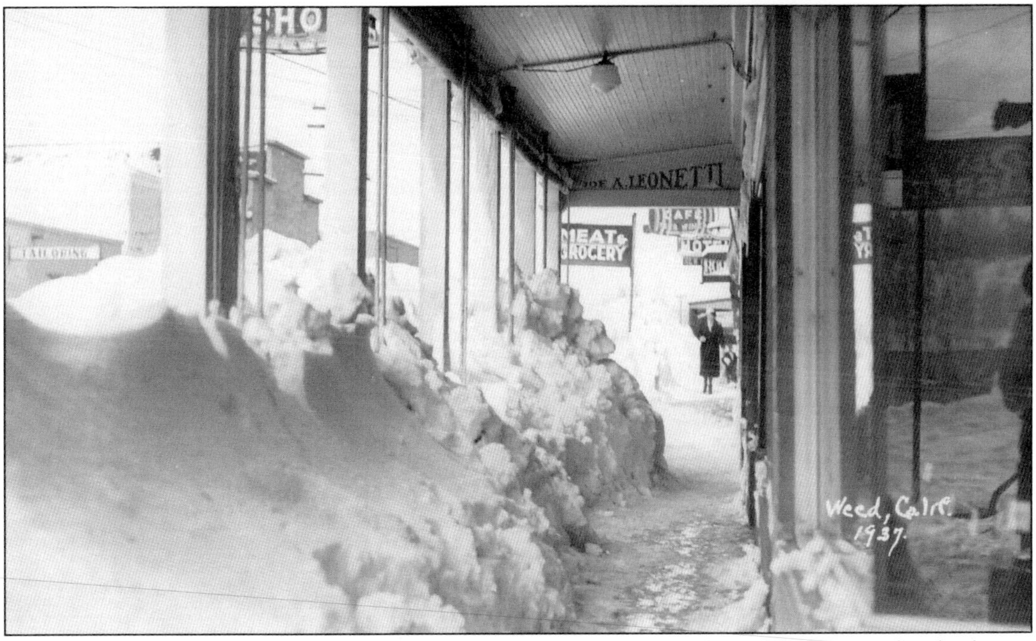

Here is Joe A. Leonetti's Quality Store in a 1937 snowstorm. In the summertime, the shades on the open wall to the left were pulled down to protect the goods in the store from the sun. Another familiar feature of the Leonetti store, not visible in this photograph, is the wrought-iron gate with the owner's initials, JAL. Over the years, Weed children have played "jail" behind these bars.

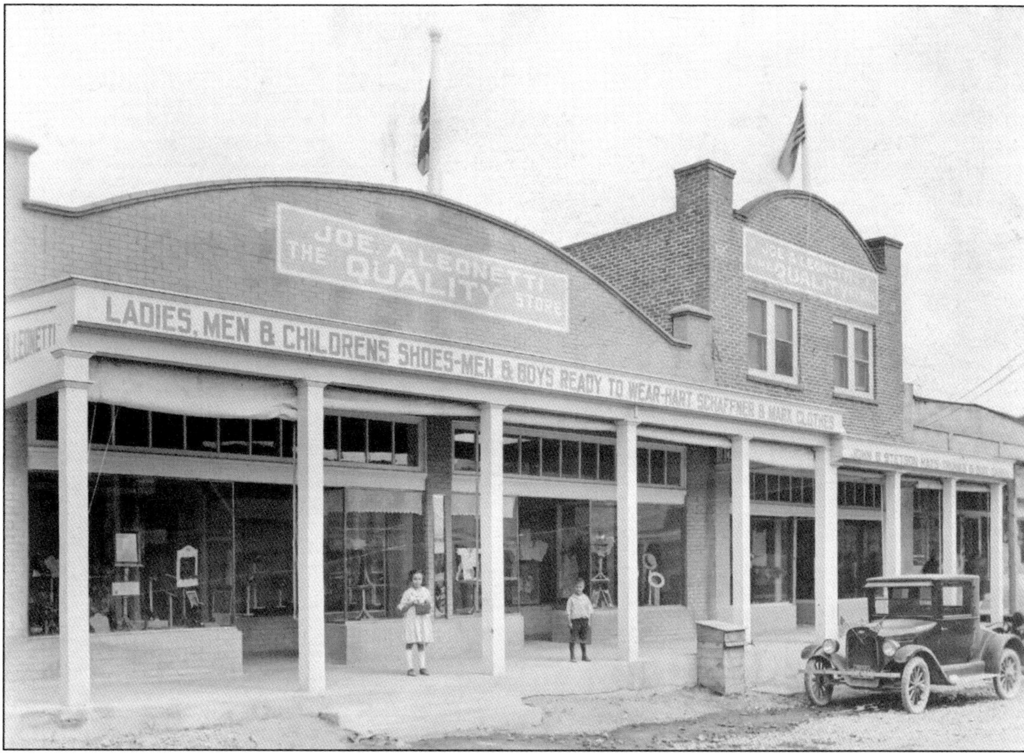

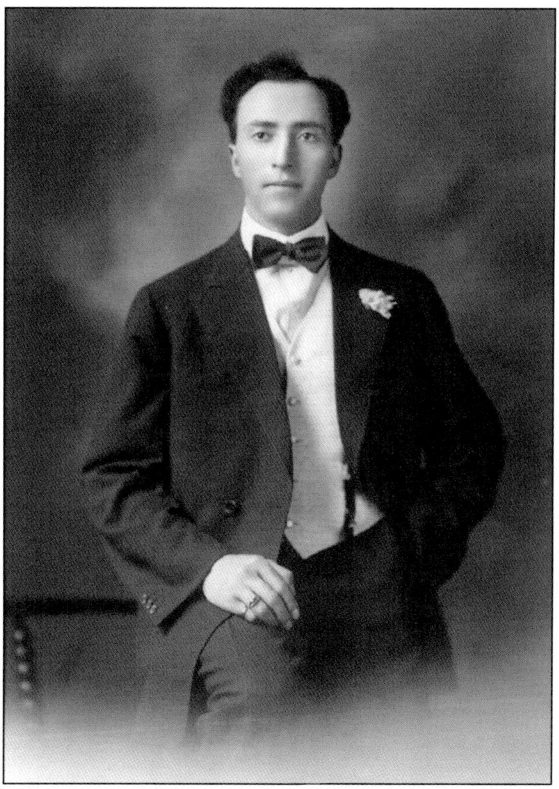

Giuseppe Antonio "Joe" Leonetti (at left) came to America from Casino, Italy, in 1902. He worked in McCloud, San Francisco, and Fort Bragg before settling in Weed. He began work at the Weed Mercantile store in the men's department. The Leonetti's Quality Store (above) around 1924, was built in two stages. After buying three lots in Shastina in 1919, he built the south half of the store in 1920–1921 and the north half two years later. The window displays were modeled after the Emporium in San Francisco. They sold shoes, luggage, blankets, and clothing. The family lived upstairs from 1921 to 1951. Rose Marie (above, left) and Frank Fred Leonetti are standing in front of the family's store. The Chevrolet parked out front belonged to Frank Girimonte, who was a clerk in the store. (Both courtesy Rose Leonetti Speer and Lisa Leonetti Whitmer.)

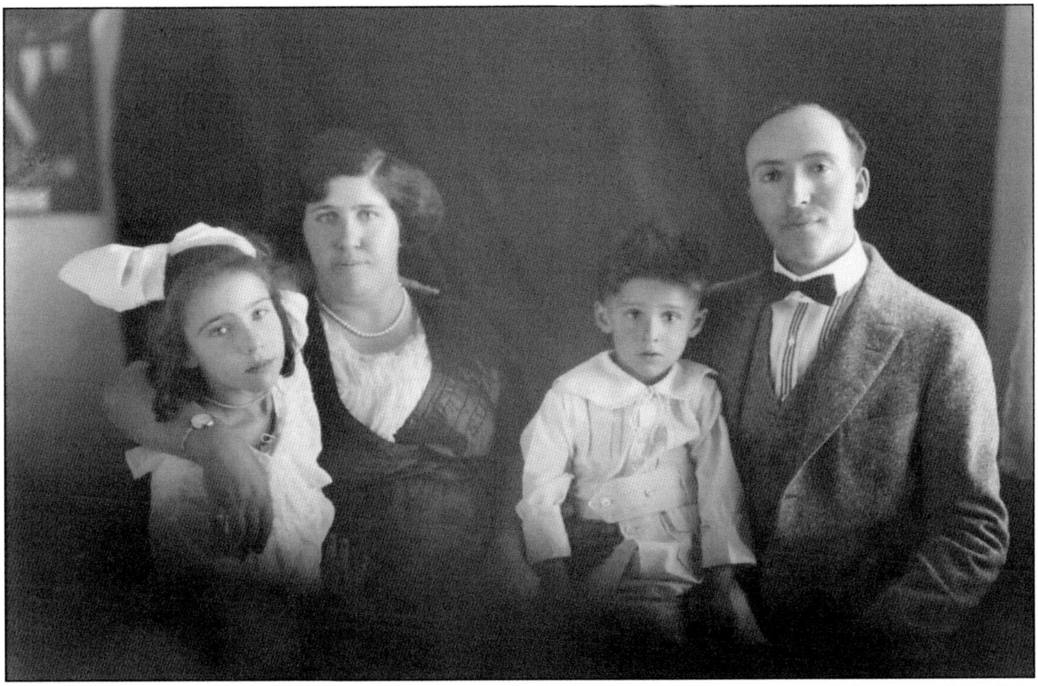

The Leonetti family is shown in the picture above in 1922. Joe Leonetti (right) married Sophia Scalise, the daughter of Frederick and Domenica Scalise of Italy, and they had two children, Rose Marie and Frank Fred. Joe worked at Weed Mercantile for eight years, so he could learn the business before opening his own store. Rose taught at Weed High School in the 1930s and 1940; Frank worked with his father and also sold real estate. Another photograph (below), taken in 1924, shows the Leonetti family in the store's office. The arch behind them connects the two buildings that make up Joe A. Leonetti's Quality Store. (Both courtesy Lisa Leonetti Whitmer.)

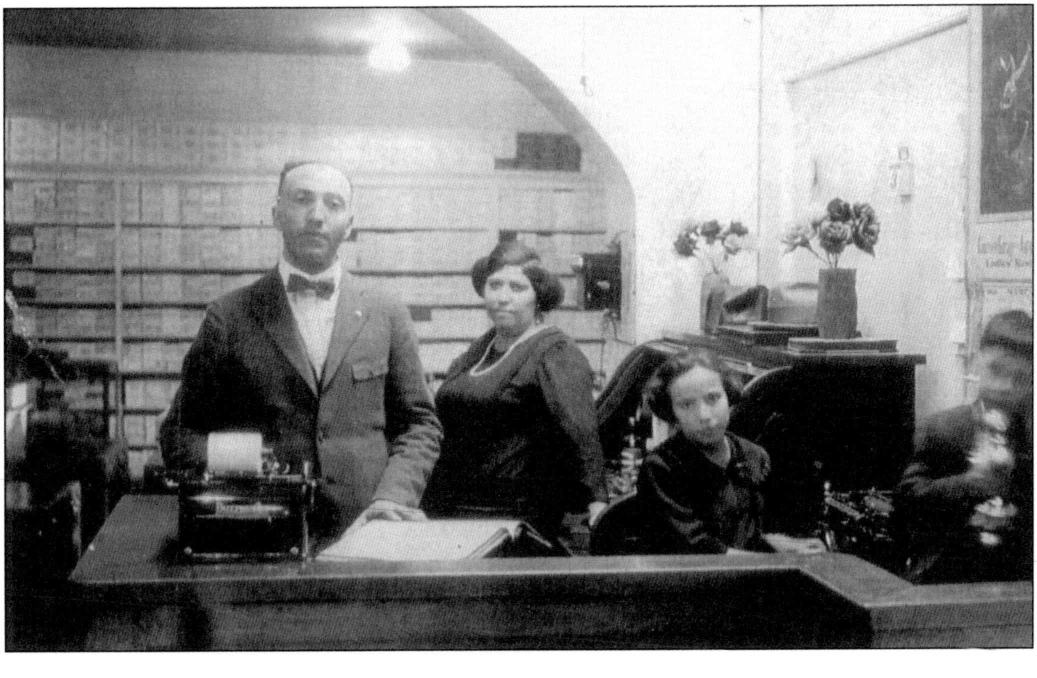

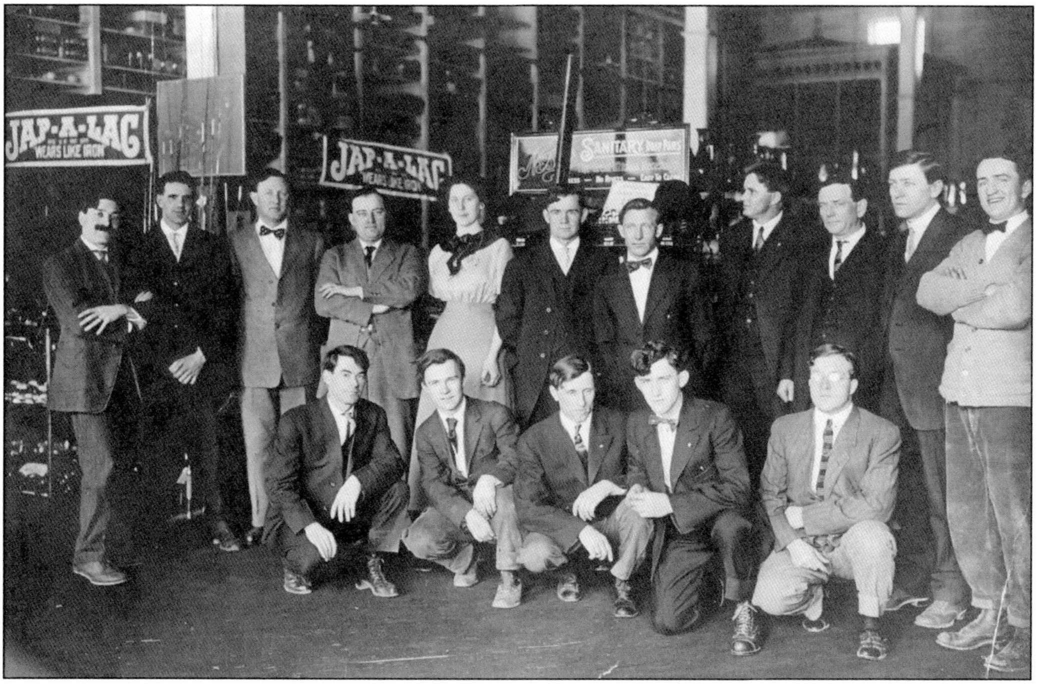

A. J. "Joe" Girimonte Sr. (above, far left) worked for the company store in the early 1920s. Around 1927, he bought *La Concordia*, the leading Italian newspaper in Northern California, serving 2,500 subscribers. E. Rosa came to America from Italy in 1897 and moved to Weed in 1912. Rosa and Antonio Sbarbaro, with the help of Antonio's relatives, built the Savoy Hotel in 1906. In 1921, E. Rosa married the widow Rosa Santucci, mother of three children. In 1922, Rosa and Antonio Sbarbaro established the People's Store (below), the largest store at the time with 8,000 square feet plus a basement. (Above photograph by Paul Quirk.)

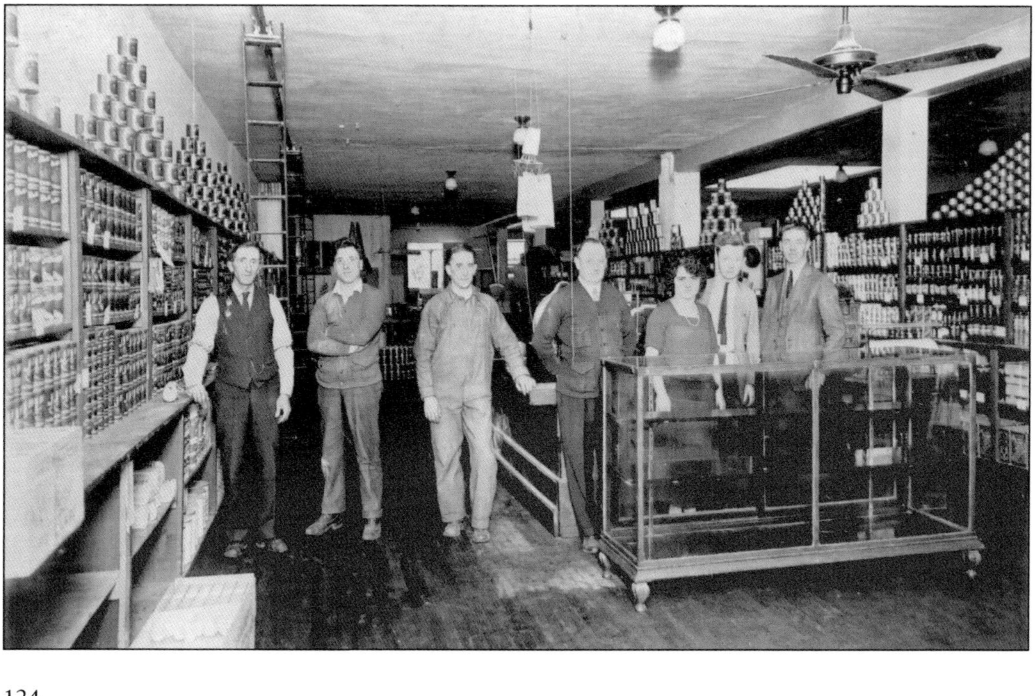

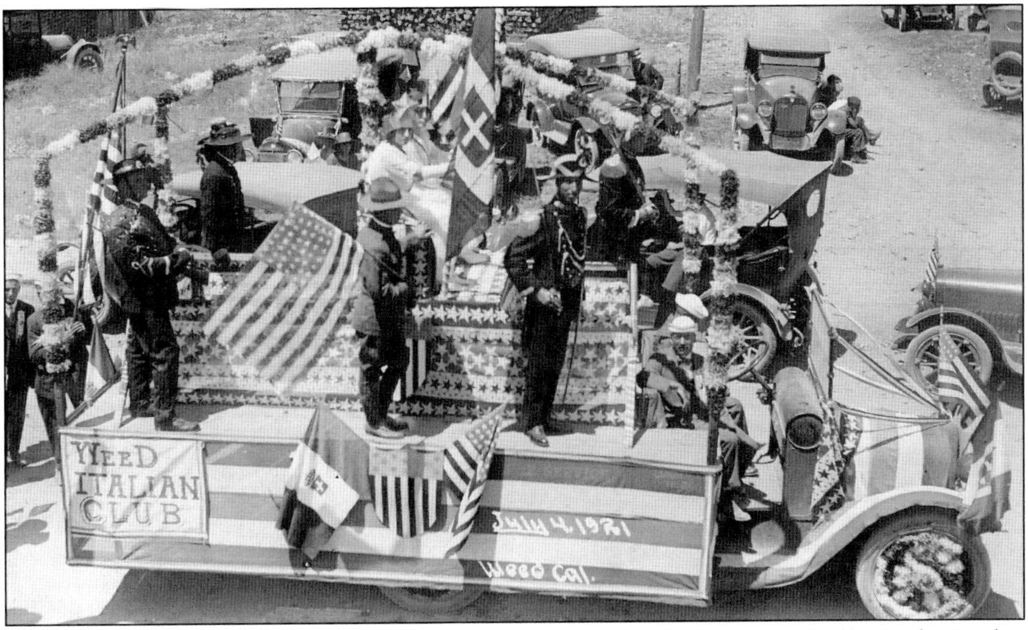

The Weed Italian Club float was one of many entries in the 1921 Fourth of July parade. By this time, many Italians had become American citizens. A March 9, 1916, newspaper article stated that 80 Italians from Weed and an estimated 300 from Siskiyou County would become citizens at the next naturalization day.

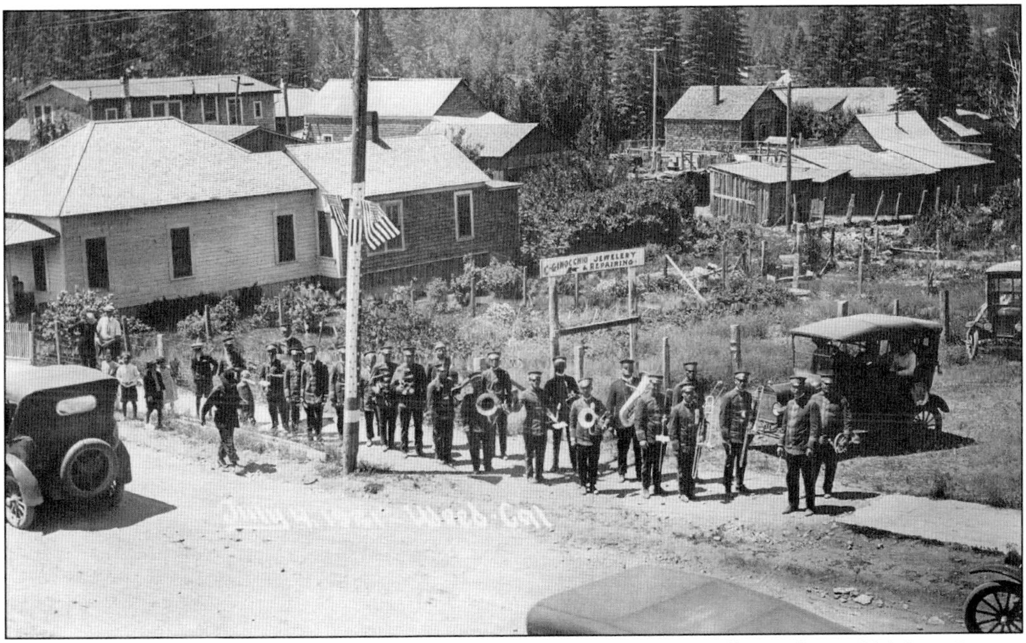

The house with an extension (left) is the Upton Mortuary, which still stands at 150 Main Street. Muriel C. La Cunnae, a professional nurse from Pennsylvania born in 1884, became a licensed mortuary operator under E. B. Hughes. She moved to Yreka in 1925 and married Albert Dustin Upton. They founded the Upton Mortuary in Weed in 1925. In 1930, she was appointed the deputy coroner of Siskiyou County. Muriel Upton's son Fielding Russ took over the family business.

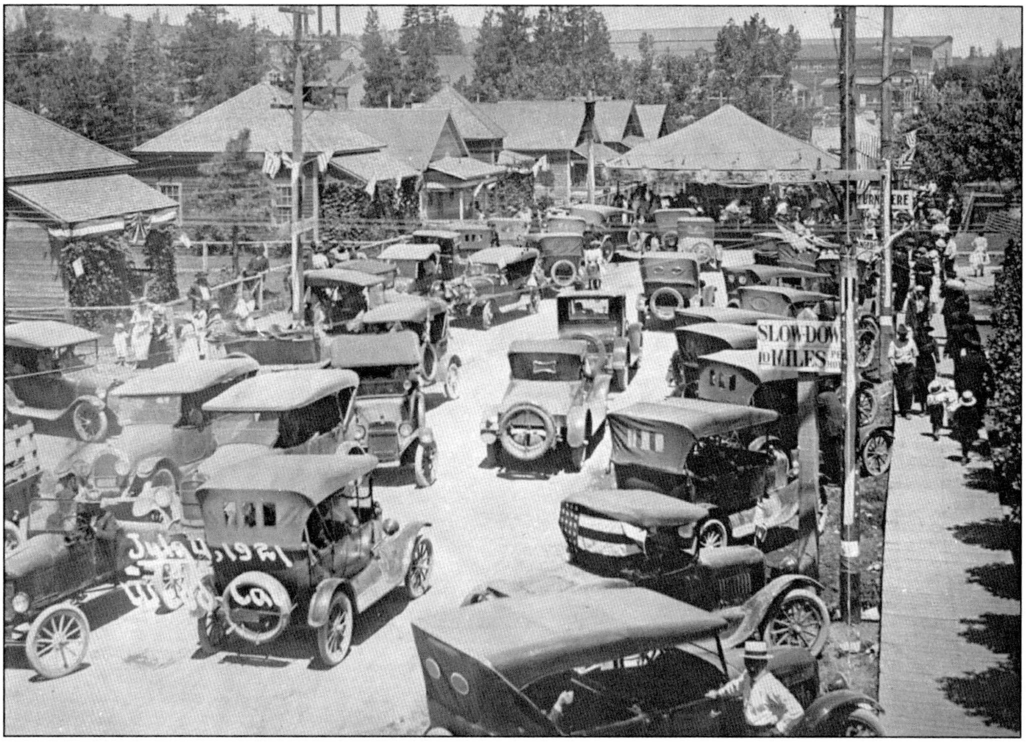

Ford Model Ts crowd the streets during the 1921 Fourth of July parade on Main Street. A merry-go-round is set up in the middle of the street for the children's enjoyment. The Weed Mercantile can be seen at the north end of Main Street. The wooden sidewalks were a trademark of Weed, but they were removed in the 1960s.

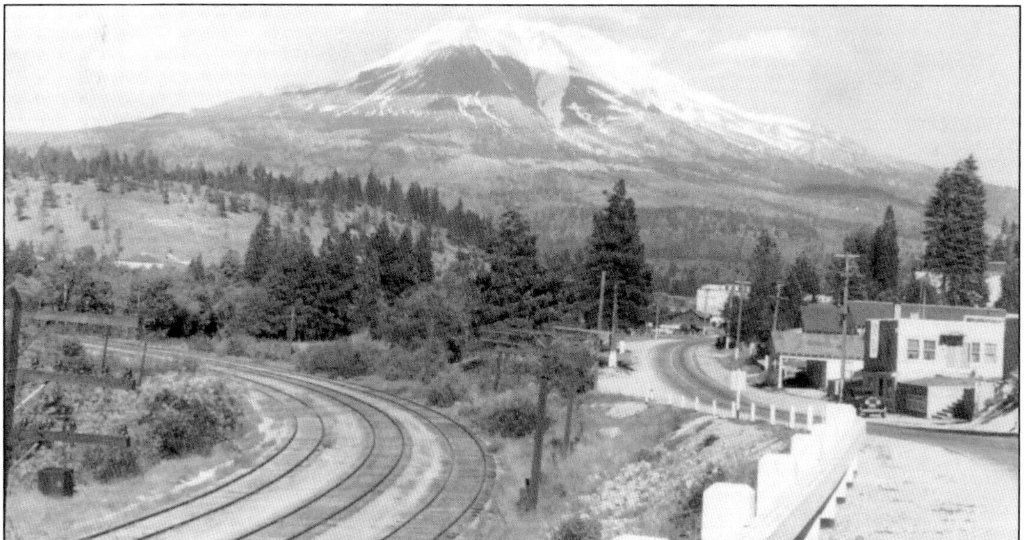

This image depicts entering Weed from the north on Highway 99. The buildings on the near right include Mallory's Garage and the Pine Tree Saloon. The large building farther down the road is the Genova Hotel. Mount Shasta looms in the distance. Schoolhouse Hill (left center) is at the base of Mount Shasta. (Courtesy College of the Siskiyous Mount Shasta Collection.)

Bibliography

Adams, Kramer. *Logging Railroads of the West*. Seattle, WA: Superior Publishing Company, 1961.

Jones, J. Roy. *Saddle Bags in Siskiyou County*. Happy Camp, CA: Naturegraph Publishers, 1953.

Langford, James Anthony. *The Black Minority of Weed—Its History, Institutions, and Politics*. Thesis. CSU Chico, summer 1984.

Lewis, Frank, ed. *The Siskiyou Pioneer and Yearbook* 3.10: Weed Edition. Yreka, CA: News-Journal Litho, 1967.

Linville, Alford, ed. *The Siskiyou Pioneer and Yearbook* 7.3: Weed Edition. Klamath Falls, OR: Graphic Press, 2000.

Rippon, Cy and Sally Rippon. *Mott. Once Booming Siskiyou Lumber and Sawmill Town*. Weed, CA: Cy and Sally Rippon, summer 1988.

Rock, James T. and Michael Hendryx, eds. *The Siskiyou Pioneer and Yearbook* 5.10: *Logging in N. E. Siskiyou County 1900–1956*. Happy Camp, CA: Naturegraph Publishers, 1987.

Roy, William N., ed. *Timberbeast: The Journal of Logging Archaeology* 7.1, 7.2, and 8. Eugene, OR: Timberbeast, spring 1989.

Shoup, Laurence H. *Speed Power, Production, and Profit: Railroad Logging in Northeastern Siskiyou County, 1900–1956*. Yreka, CA: Siskiyou County Historical Society, 1987.

Signor, John R. *Southern Pacific's Shasta Division*. Wilton, CA: Signature Press, 2000.

Silva, E. Mary Salanti. *Siskiyou County Italians, Cultural and Economic Contributions: A Collection of Biographies, Documents, Data and Recollections*. Self-published: 2007.

Stone, T. Leland, ed. "Weed . . . The Way It Was." Weed Committee of the American Revolution Bicentennial, 1776–1976. Dunsmuir, CA: Dunsmuir Printing Company, 1976.

Weed, Abner Edward Jr. *Weed: The Evolution of a Company Town*. Thesis. CSU Chico, fall 1974.

Wells, Harry L. *History of Siskiyou County, California*. Oakland, CA: D.J. Stewart and Company, 1881.

Wooldridge, Jesse Walton. *History of the Sacramento Valley, California*. Chicago, IL: The Pioneer Publishing Company, 1931.